lonely planet

Honolulu, Waikīkī & O'ahu

Ryan Ver Berkmoes, Sarah Etinas

Makapu'u Beach Park (p139)

CONTENTS

Plan Your Trip

Mokoli'i Island (p162)

The Guide

Toolkit

Storybook

Land Acknowledgement

Lonely Planet acknowledges that the state of Hawai'i rests on the unceded lands of the Kānaka Maoli (Native Hawaiians). We honor their sovereignty and connection to their lands and waters, as well as their enduring commitment to a sustainable future for Hawai'i. Lonely Planet encourages you to learn more about the history of the Kānaka Maoli, and support their continued efforts to preserve the state's fragile ecosystems for future generations by being a mindful visitor. We also encourage you to consider volunteering and connecting with a local organization during your stay. For more information, see gohawaii.com/malama.

Honu (green sea turtle; p174)

DADEROT VIA WIKIMEDIA COMMONS

Lyon Arboretum (p109), Mānoa Valley

HONOLULU, WAIKĪKĪ & O'AHU

THE JOURNEY BEGINS HERE

It sounds hokey, but for me O'ahu means smiles. This goes back to my first visit with my family, where we stayed in a huge Waikīkī resort and every day brought the joys of breakfast buffets and frolicking in the perfect temps of the ocean. My tastes have changed over the decades: now I want hikes in impossibly green *pali* (cliffs) and strolls in Chinatown, Kaimukī and the miles of paths along the beaches and parks. I've also come to appreciate the Hawaiian royalty and understand all that was lost when they were immorally overthrown by colonists.

And I continue my warm embrace. Starting when I land at the airport and feel that first embrace of trade-wind-moderated air. My smiles grow with my first plate lunch, get larger yet watching hula, and peak when I enjoy, yes, a beachfront mai tai.

Ryan Ver Berkmoes

@ryanverberkmoes

Ryan has written over a dozen books on Hawai'i and over 170 books for Lonely Planet. He wrote the Honolulu & Waikīkī chapter.

My favorite experience
The Mānoa Valley is framed by emerald *pali* and has hikes, gardens and an ancient heiau (stone temple), plus the perfect tropical cafe, **Waioli Kitchen** (p109).

WHO GOES WHERE

Our writers and experts choose the places which, for them, define Honolulu, Waikīkī & O'ahu.

WIRESTOCK CREATORS/SHUTTERSTOCK

Nestled on the Leeward side, the **Mā'ili Pillbox Trail** (p132; also called Pu'u O Hulu or the Pink Pillbox Hike) is a special spot. The bits and pieces of history – from the WWII observation pillbox to the cancer survivor names inscribed within – are just the beginning. It's really the unmatched sweeping Leeward views – and the minimal effort it takes to see them – that put this hike on the map.

Sarah Etinas

sarahetinas.com

Sarah is an O'ahu local, travel writer and author of the Hawai'i travel website, Borders & Bucket Lists. She wrote the Leeward Coast, Windward Coast and North Shore chapters.

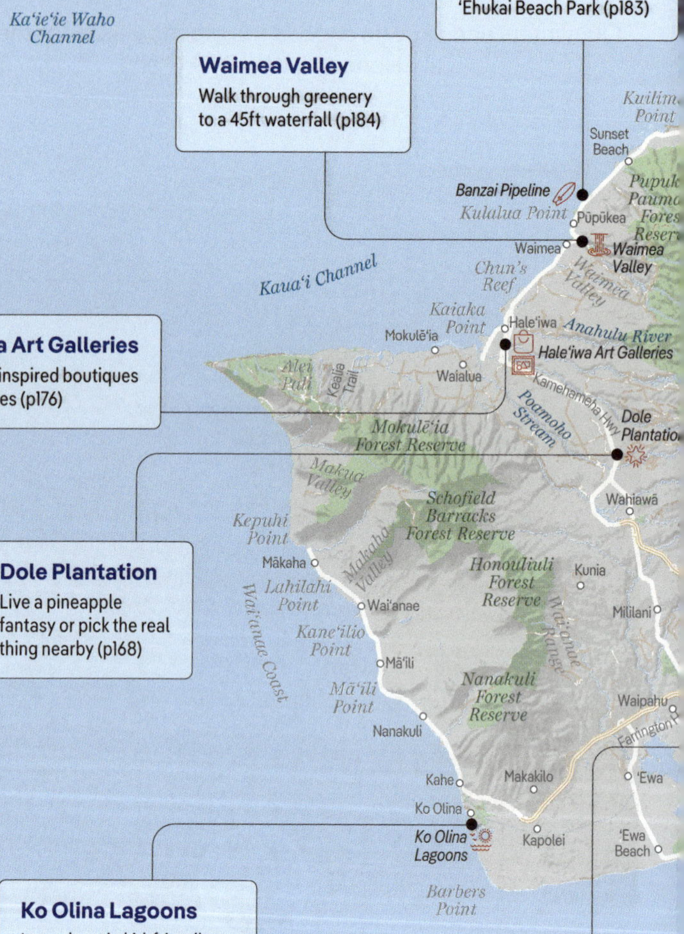

Banzai Pipeline
Watch surfers tackle massive 20ft swells at 'Ehukai Beach Park (p183)

Waimea Valley
Walk through greenery to a 45ft waterfall (p184)

Hale'iwa Art Galleries
Shop surf-inspired boutiques and galleries (p176)

Dole Plantation
Live a pineapple fantasy or pick the real thing nearby (p168)

Ko Olina Lagoons
Laze about in kid-friendly, human-made lagoons (p124)

Pearl Harbor National Memorial
Recall the attack of December 7, 1941 (p112)

0 10 km
0 5 miles
Polynesian Cultural Center
Learn about multiple Polynesian island cultures (p190)
Ho‘omaluhia Botanical Garden
Admire tropical flowers and the mountain backdrop (p159)
Kailua Beach Park
Swim at this award-winning beach (p146)
Kuli‘ou‘ou Ridge Trail
Trek to Kuli‘ou‘ou Summit for epic views (p144)
Hanauma Bay
Snorkel for a peek at O‘ahu's marine life (p138)
Chinatown
Explore Honolulu's most intriguing neighborhood (p66)
Waikīkī Beach
Enjoy sunsets, mai tais and lots of fun (p81)
Kaimukī
Stroll a great neighborhood for eating and drinking (p97)
PACIFIC OCEAN
Makahoa Point
Moku‘auia (Goat Island)
Lā‘ie
Polynesian Cultural Center
Hau‘ula
Windward Coast
Punalu‘u
Kahana Bay
Hau‘ula Forest Reserve
Kahana
Ka‘a‘awa
Ahupua‘a o Kahana State Park
Kualoa
Kāne‘ohe Bay
Waiāhole Forest Reserve
Waikāne
Waiāhole
Kipapa Stream
Kahalu‘u
Ahu o Laka Island
Mokumanu State Seabird Sanctuary
Moku o Lo‘e (Coconut Island)
‘Āhuimanu
He‘eia
‘Ewa Forest Reserve
Waimano Trail
Kalauao Stream
Popoi‘a Island (Flat Island)
Pearl City
Kāne‘ohe
Kailua
Kailua Beach Park
John A Burns Fwy
Moanalua Stream
Olomana
Lanikai
Pearl Harbor
‘Aiea
Ho‘omaluhia Botanical Garden
Wailea Point
Maunawili
Pearl Harbor National Memorial
Likelike Hwy
Pali Hwy
Maunawili Trail
Mānoa Stream
Ko‘olau Range
Manana Island (Rabbit Island)
Waimānalo
Daniel K Inouye International Airport
Kaohikaipu Island
Chinatown
Honolulu
Kuli‘ou‘ou Ridge Trail
Koko Crater
Māmala Bay
Waikīkī
Kaimukī
Kahala
Waikīkī Beach
Hawai‘i Kai
Hanauma Bay
Lāwa‘i Bay
Black Point (Kupikipiki‘o)
Ka‘iwi Channel

SUN & SAND

Most visitors to O'ahu come for the beaches and there are some fabulous ones right around this Pacific island paradise. If you're staying in Waikīkī, they're virtually right outside your door, but if you're willing to get adventurous and head further afield, it's not hard to find that perfect stretch of sand with decidedly fewer sun-worshippers. You may well discover that beach of your dreams. So common are good ones, that you can just set out and browse.

Kapu!

Never cross private property to reach a beach. Watch for '*Kapu*' (No Trespassing) signs but also simply respect non-public spaces. It is illegal to trespass in Hawai'i.

Beach Accessibility

The Department of Parks & Recreation provides free all-terrain beach mats and wheelchairs at several beaches including Kūhiō, Hanauma Bay (pictured above), Kaimana, Kailua and Kualoa.

Beach Practicalities

Do not leave valuables on the beach – even remote ones – while you swim; slippers (flip-flops) and towels are usually left alone. Drinking alcohol on the beach is illegal.

FROM LEFT: MICHAEL BARAJAS/SHUTTERSTOCK, POWEROFFOREVER/GETTY IMAGES, MATT MUNRO/LONELY PLANET

Waikīkī Beach (p81)

BEST BEACH EXPERIENCES

Escape the city at ❶ **Magic Island** (p75) in Ala Moana Regional Park. Surrounded by water, this rock-shielded cove feels more rural than urban.

Find your favorite patch of sand on fabled ❷ **Waikīkī Beach** (p81): choose Queen's Surf Beach for family-friendly fun; Kahaloa and Ulukou for people-watching; and Fort DeRussy for relaxation.

Try to leave ❸ **Kailua Beach** (p146). The calm waters, sunny skies and cooling trade winds make this strand fantastic year-round.

Choose your activity at ❹ **Waimea Bay** (p180). In summer it's great for swimming; in winter, surfers rule.

Lounge on the golden shores or snorkel with *honu* (Hawaiian green sea turtles) at ❺ **Mākaha Beach** (p130).

CHIARA SALVADORI/GETTY IMAGES

Hoʻomaluhia Botanical Garden (p159)

INCREDIBLE BEAUTY

Oʻahu's natural beauty will take your breath away. The blue Pacific crashes ashore on blindingly white ribbons of sand. Rising above it are the sharply textured *pali* (cliffs), which are draped in green and soar into the clouds. And that's from afar – up close the island also beguiles with lush plants and flowers on land and delights underwater.

Lovely Lei

Fragrant and fleeting, lei exemplify the beauty of Oʻahu's nature and the embrace of *ʻohana* (extended family and friends). When offered to visitors, a lei means 'welcome!'

Volcanic Origins

Oʻahu originates from two shield volcanoes that arose about two million years ago and formed two mountain ranges: Waiʻanae in the northwest and Koʻolau in the southeast.

BEST NATURAL BEAUTY EXPERIENCES

Pause at ❶ **Puʻu ʻUalakaʻa State Wayside Park** (p100), taking in all of Honolulu's magnificence from high above the city.

See all of Oʻahu's extraordinary flora in one curated collection at ❷ **Foster Botanical Garden** (p71).

Steady your jaw at ❸ **Kāneʻohe Bay** (p156); the turquoise waters and five dotted islands look as if plucked off a screen.

Revel in flower-filled ❹ **Hoʻomaluhia Botanical Garden** (p159), though it's really the lush Koʻolau mountains that make it a stunning site.

Cruise the ❺ **Windward Coast** (p160), a seaside jaunt filled with quiet shorelines and hidden beach swings.

HIT THE TRAILS

First-timers are often surprised at O'ahu's mountainous nature, offering a plethora of hiking opportunities. Surprisingly close to sandy beaches are verdant valleys, towering cliffs and forested mountains. Climb up high for sensational views of volcanic cones or central peaks, stick to the valleys for lush beauty, or navigate the rugged coastline.

FROM LEFT: MATT ANDERSON/GETTY IMAGES, RUGLIG/GETTY IMAGES

Sandy Jaunts

Long beaches line O'ahu's coasts. Who needs a formal trail when you can set out right along the waves for an extended stroll that combines beauty, nature and pleasure.

Happily Prepared

O'ahu's trails are easily enjoyed. You just need to remember a few items to have a magical outing: bug spray, sunscreen, a rain-proof top and sturdy footwear.

Inland Weather

Keep in mind that it can be raining in the inland mountains while it's sunny on the beaches – rainbow imagery didn't become ubiquitous here for no reason! Tracks can get both muddy and slippery.

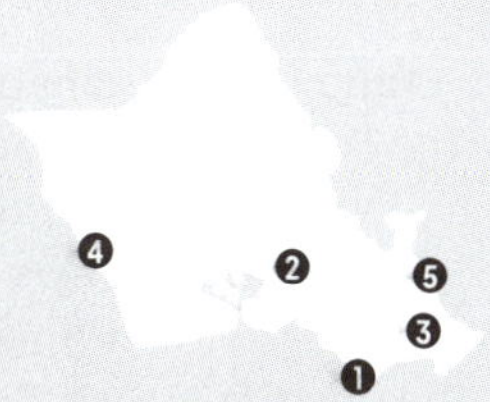

BEST HIKING EXPERIENCES

Scramble up ❶ **Diamond Head** (p99), a two-hour adventure of vistas, history, volcanic beauty, tunnels and windy outlooks.

Take in the island's lush beauty on the ❷ **'Aiea Loop Trail** (p117), with innumerable types of flowering trees along the emerald ridge.

Tackle challenging ❸ **Kuli'ou'ou Ridge** (p144; pictured right) through forests to the summit and its views of southeast O'ahu.

Set out on the ❹ **Mā'ili Pillbox Trail** (p132) in Wai'anae, an easy hike with unparalleled views of the Leeward Coast.

Climb the ❺ **Lanikai Pillbox Trail** (p148; pictured left) to marvel at views of Kailua, the Mokulua Islands and the never-ending Pacific.

HISTORY & CULTURE

O'ahu has a fascinating history, from the arrival of the Polynesians to European colonization beginning with Captain Cook, the fall of the monarchy, immigrant laborers, Pearl Harbor, statehood and through to today. Engross yourself in WWII history, the finest Polynesian anthropological museum in the world, the only royal palace in the US and Hawaiian experiences island-wide.

FROM LEFT: ALBERTO LOYO/SHUTTERSTOCK, THEODORE TRIMMER/SHUTTERSTOCK, RANDY FARIS/GETTY IMAGES

A Mix of Backgrounds

One plantation-era legacy is Hawai'i's inclusive mixing of ethnicities; cultural differences are freely acknowledged, even carefully maintained, but they don't normally divide people.

Royal Waikīkī

When Hawai'i's monarchy was overthrown in 1893, much of Waikīkī was a royal enclave. Find statues here of Queen Kapi'olani, Prince Kūhiō (pictured above) and Princess Ka'iulani.

Speaking Hawaiian

Before its ongoing renaissance, the melodious Polynesian language, 'Ōlelo Hawai'i (Hawaiian), was suppressed during the colonial era when it was eradicated from schools and official functions.

'Iolani Palace (p58)

BEST HISTORY & CULTURE EXPERIENCES

See the USA's only royal palace at Honolulu's ❶ **'Iolani Palace** (p58). No other place evokes a more poignant sense of Hawai'i's history.

Explore Polynesian history at ❷ **Bishop Museum** (p100), a fascinating storehouse of culture for Hawai'i and wider Polynesia.

Reflect at the ❸ **Pearl Harbor National Memorial** (p112) and its evocative series of memorials and museums such as the USS *Arizona* Memorial.

Feast at ❹ **Toa Luau** (p184) in Pūpūkea. This Native Hawaiian-owned and -operated lū'au incorporates traditional Hawaiian customs throughout the festivities.

Volunteer at ❺ **Kāko'o 'Ōiwi** (p158) in Kane'ohe, a nonprofit that teaches traditional Hawaiian farming practices with *kalo* (taro) in *lo'i* (wetland taro fields).

EATING LOCAL

'Ono grinds (good eats) can be found across O'ahu. Think tropical fruit such as mango and papaya, tasty seafood and multiethnic offerings introduced by waves of immigrant laborers from a swath of countries. A 'plate lunch' typically features a scoop or two of sticky rice with fried mahimahi, Korean-style *kalbi* short ribs, Filipino pork adobo or Japanese-style chicken katsu (deep-fried fillets). O'ahu has an 'eat homegrown' movement, and extraordinary and diverse local produce.

FROM LEFT: ERIC BRODER VAN DYKE/SHUTTERSTOCK, BLUESTORK/SHUTTERSTOCK, KANEOHE WINDWARD MALL

Wild Bounty

Luscious specimens of O'ahu's natural bounty are at your fingertips during hikes in the mountains. Wild fruit trees bear tiny strawberry guava, *liliko'i* (passion fruit) and mangoes (pictured above).

Now Starring: Poke

Join the love for poke, bite-sized seasoned raw fish. It's available everywhere – in addition to **Tamura's** (p97), seek out **Tanioka's** (p170) or **Ono Seafood Poke Bowl Patrol** (p141).

Farmers Markets

All over the island, farmers bring produce to town, offering the freshest fruit and veg. **Kaka'ako** (p80) and **Kailua** (p147) are extravaganzas.

Waiahole Poi Factory (p159)

BEST LOCAL EATING EXPERIENCES

Choose from a changing selection of trad faves at multi-generational, dine-in ❶ **Hamada General Store** (p79), once a grocery store with plate lunches.

Join the line for ❷ **Helena's Hawaiian Food** (p105). Family-run since 1946, it excels at even the smallest of details on classic plate lunches.

Feast on Honolulu's best poke at ❸ **Tamura's Fine Wine & Liquors** (p97) in Kaimukī. The array of choices taste as good as they look.

Taste ancient flavors at ❹ **Waiahole Poi Factory** (p159), known for its dishes of *kūlolo* (taro dessert) and poi (mashed taro), plus other traditional Hawaiian favorites.

Honor the land at ❺ **Kahuku Farms** (p194), where farm-to-table cuisine includes fruit-and-veggie-laden plates and smoothies.

LAID-BACK O'AHU

Great swaths of Honolulu are downright bustling. So where's that famous laid-back, mellow vibe for which Hawai'i (and O'ahu) are so famous? Well, you don't have to go far to lose the hustle and find a funkier, mellower mood. Neighborhoods and towns across the island still retain the island's fabled slow pace and offbeat charms.

BEST LAID-BACK EXPERIENCES

Wander the charming blocks of ❶ **Kaimukī** (p97), a Honolulu neighborhood that mixes offbeat shops with mellow cafes and bars.

Pause in the shadows of *pali* in the ❷ **Mānoa Valley** (p105), a place where rain squalls dampen excess energy and relaxation abounds.

Prowl the sidewalks of ❸ **Hale'iwa** (p172; pictured right), with its Western-esque buildings, surf-focused boutiques and plant-based eateries.

Get lazy in laid-back ❹ **Kāne'ohe** (p156; pictured left), where you can lounge around the bay or gardens, or just call it a day.

Pop into ❺ **Waialua** (p177), the oft-forgotten North Shore town with deep roots in Hawai'i's old sugar industry and a new wave of local shops.

FROM LEFT: PHILLIP B. ESPINASSE/SHUTTERSTOCK, CHRISTIAN MUELLER/SHUTTERSTOCK

Hawaiian Time

The stereotype that everyone and everything in the islands moves more slowly than on the mainland – 'Hawaiian time' – may be a bit of a joke, but also a proud local lifestyle.

Keeping it Country

North Shore residents love their simple life and steadfastly resist proposals for resorts and condos that they believe would make the region an extension of Honolulu.

Resident Status

A *kama'āina* is a person who is native to a particular place. Commonly, '*kama'āina* discounts' apply to any island resident (ie anyone with a state driver's license).

Hanauma Bay (p138)

BEST UNDERWATER EXPERIENCES

Stroll to the Diamond Head edge of Waikīkī and ❶ **Kaimana Beach** (p82) to snorkel right offshore. There's a great shallow reef.

Dive in to popular and protected ❷ **Hanauma Bay** (p138), an ideal place to look at O'ahu's underwater world.

Go on a submarine scooter tour in ❸ **Maunalua Bay** (p142) – your head stays dry while you watch turtles and tropical fish.

See the Leeward Coast from the open ocean on a boat tour in ❹ **Ko Olina** (p126) for a whole different side of O'ahu.

Explore the lovely blue waters of ❺ **Kāne'ohe Bay** (p156), where tour operators will take you out to see underwater wonders.

TAKE THE PLUNGE

The water is warm and full of wonderful sights. Expect O'ahu ocean temperatures of around 80°F (27°C) in the peak month of September and 75°F (24°C) in the coldest month of February. There's lots to look at in the water: coral, fish of all colors and sizes as well as mammals like dolphins, turtles and whales.

A Taste of Scuba

Most of O'ahu's dive operators offer some variation on a 'discovery dive,' which gets newbies in full gear underwater with close supervision. Like it? Take lessons!

Don't Head Out...

...without your snorkeling gear. Almost every O'ahu beach has at least something to see underwater (often a lot to see!) so you don't want to bemoan your lack of a mask.

SHOPPING LOCAL

While you can shop till you drop in Waikīkī and at the boutiques and malls of Ala Moana and Kaka'ako, you can also pick up unique Hawaiiana and souvenirs at locally owned stores and galleries all over O'ahu – everything from handcrafted 'ukuleles to koa wood carvings, tropical fashion items and flip-flops. More artistically, many shops carry the works of O'ahu designers, painters, printmakers, photographers and graphic and textile artists who draw inspiration from Hawai'i's cultural heritage.

Not Just Food

It's not just edibles at O'ahu's farmers markets. All also feature artists, designers and skilled crafters selling their wares. See tomorrow's famous brands today.

A Collection of Designers

The **South Shore Market** (p78; pictured above) celebrates Hawaiian brands. The shops are small but the owners/designers have huge talents. Look for clothing, accessories and aloha wear.

Aloha Wear

Bailey's Antiques & Aloha Shirts (p89) boasts the finest collection of aloha shirts in the islands. Peruse over 15,000 shirts split among new, used and vintage.

Bailey's Antiques & Aloha Shirts (p89)

BEST LOCAL SHOPPING EXPERIENCES

Discover beautiful silk-screened fabrics, local crafts and hula supplies at ❶ **Nā Mea Hawai'i** (p79) in Ala Moana. The Hawaiiana is unmatched.

Prowl the shelves at ❷ **Tin Can Mailman** (p108), a small vintage collectibles shop in Chinatown selling highly curated tiki wares, Hawaiiana books and more.

Browse ❸ **No'eau Designers** (p128) in Kapolei, a Hawaiian-owned boutique filled with locally made goodies that make great gifts.

Admire the works at ❹ **Lauren Roth Art** (p149) in Kailua. The boutique features works from 15 local artists, as well as 'souvenir-friendly' pieces.

Check out ❺ **Roger** (p176), in Hale'iwa, a North Shore–inspired boutique filled with clothing that's contemporary, minimalistic and artistic.

SURF'S UP!

O'ahu is the stuff of dreams for those into surfing. The waves are legendary, especially during late fall and winter on the North Shore, one of the world's foundational surfing centers. Modern-day surfing began on O'ahu and surfers worldwide dream of hitting the waves on the epic North Shore. There are plenty of surf spots all over though – including right outside Waikīkī's resorts – as well as plenty of rental boards, gear vendors and surf schools.

Beat the Winter Rush

Get an early start on the 'winter' big-wave surfing season on the North Shore in November, as the heaving sets start rolling in shortly after October bows out.

Big Waves = Big Competition

Waves have to reach 20ft+ for the **Eddie Aikau Big Wave Invitational** (p189; pictured above) to occur on the North Shore. From December to March, everyone waits for the right moment.

More Surfing Coverage

Where to surf, how to find out if waves are breaking and how to get on with the residents on the water are detailed on p40.

Banzai Pipeline, ʻEhukai Beach Park (p183)

BEST SURFING EXPERIENCES

Find your inner Duke Kahanamoku and flex your skills or learn to ride in ❶ **Waikīkī** (p83) – where surfing was invented.

Join residents who love the string of breaks near the shoreline at ❷ **Ala Moana Regional Park** (p74). The choices here are many.

Survive Banzai Pipeline at ❸ **ʻEhukai Beach Park** (p183). Most of the year, these North Shore waters are for professional surfers only, just one reason for its fame.

Witness the ❹ **Vans Pipe Masters** (p188). Held at the famed Pipeline, the tournament is one of the only surf competitions that rewards surfers for aerials.

Learn to ride the waves at ❺ **North Shore Oʻahu Surf School** (p184). Take to the waves yourself with the help of the pros.

REGIONS & CITIES

Find the places that tick all your boxes.

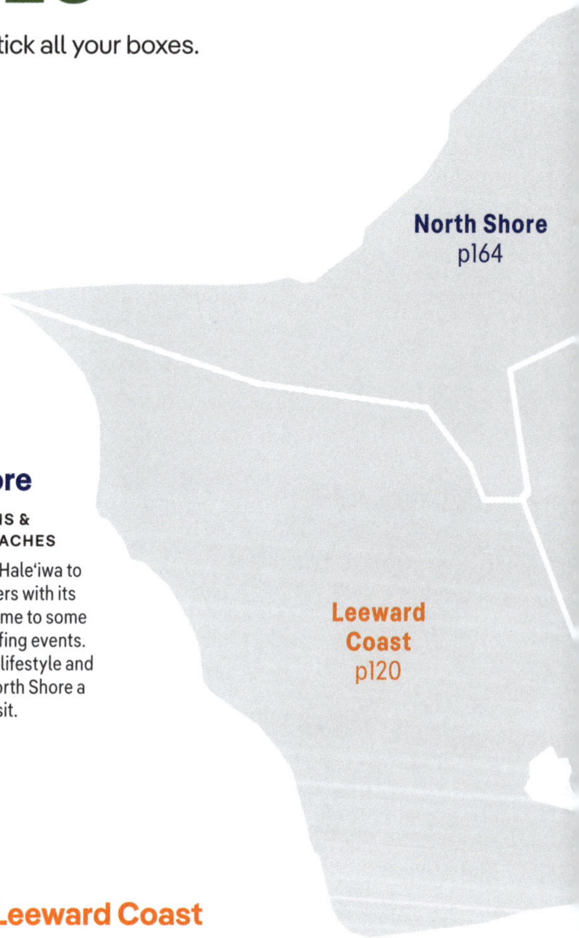

North Shore

HISTORIC TOWNS & SURFER-FILLED BEACHES

The stretch of sand from Hale'iwa to Sunset Beach lures surfers with its monster waves and it's home to some of the world's premier surfing events. Locals love their laid-back lifestyle and this attitude makes the North Shore a great place to visit.

Leeward Coast

SUNSHINE-FILLED BEACH DAYS ARE CALLING

Leeward O'ahu sees fewer visitors than the rest of the island, mainly because the road up the coast culminates in a dead end. There are lovely beaches, and while the region isn't tourist-focused, you'll find plenty of interest. Some come to the southwest tip of O'ahu to bunker down at Ko Olina's family-friendly resorts.

Windward Coast

FRAMED BY THE MOUNTAINS & THE SEA

The name Windward Coast implies wind, and that includes plenty of rainfall on O'ahu's most verdant coast. Circle O'ahu by car – the coastal highway is a highlight. There are craggy cliffs, massive mountains, beaches of all types and the cool town of Kailua. Snorkeling and diving at Hanauma Bay is a must.

Honolulu & Waikīkī

BEACHES, CULTURE, DINING & NATURE

Honolulu lets you take the pulse of multiracial O'ahu. Hit the city's historical district, Chinatown or Pearl Harbor; hike in the lush hills; and enjoy myriad great places to eat. Meanwhile, gorgeous sand and warm waters virtually on your hotel doorstep make Waikīkī an alluring place.

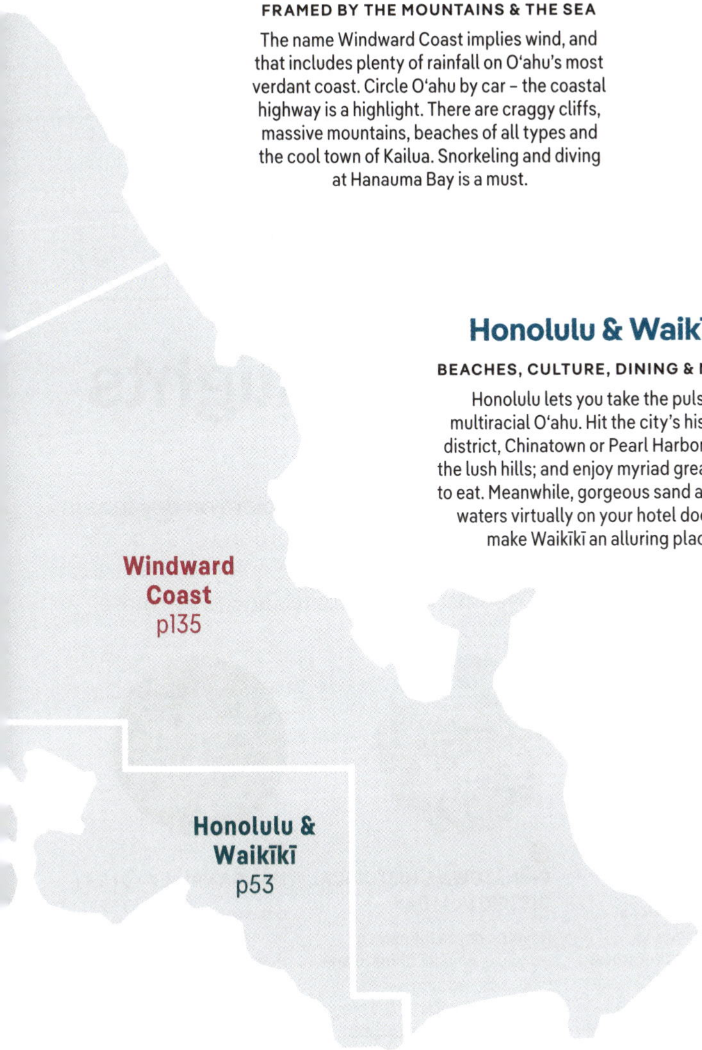

DAWNPATROL85/SHUTTERSTOCK

Magic Island (p75)

ITINERARIES

Honolulu's Highlights

Allow: 6 days **Distance:** 60 miles

This itinerary covers the many places you can explore on day trips in and around Honolulu. You can mix and match portions of these six fun days from your hotel or condo in Waikīkī. See quiet beaches, lush mountain trails, superb museums, historical sites and much more.

1 PEARL HARBOR 1 DAY

The **Pearl Harbor National Memorial** (p112; pictured above) is one of the USA's most significant WWII sites. It explains the Pearl Harbor attack and commemorates the dead. Visit the USS *Arizona* Memorial, the Battleship *Missouri* Memorial, the Pacific Fleet Submarine Museum and the Pearl Harbor Aviation Museum. After, stop at the **Sand Island State Recreation Area** (p103), which has a beautiful, quiet beach for contemplation.

2 CHINATOWN & HISTORICAL DISTRICT 1 DAY

Devote a day to the heart of Honolulu. Wander **Chinatown** (p66; pictured above) in the morning when it is at its vibrant best. Check out the markets and the idiosyncratic shops and galleries. After lunch, walk to the Historical District. Visit **'Iolani Palace** (p58), then the **Hawai'i State Capitol** (p60) with its striking, mid-century design. Don't miss the **Hawaiian Mission Houses Historic Site** (p60).

3 MĀNOA VALLEY 1 DAY

Get an early start and head inland past the University of Hawai'i and into the Mānoa Valley for a fun, short hike up to **Mānoa Falls** (p108; pictured above). Remember, it could be raining here, even if the sun's shining in Waikīkī. The soaring *pali* (cliffs) provide jagged walls of vivid green as you leave the ocean behind.

Detour: *Stop in captivating* ***Kaimukī*** *(p97) for browsing, eating and drinking. 1–2 hours*

FROM LEFT: GLOWIMAGES/GETTY IMAGES, THEODORE TRIMMER/SHUTTERSTOCK, NANI WELCH KELI'IHO'OMALU FOR LONELY PLANET

4

ALA MOANA & KAKA'AKO ⏱1 DAY

Walk along the beaches into the busy neighborhoods of **Kaka'ako** and **Ala Moana** (p74). Skip the huge mall for the local shops – many run by young Honolulu designers. **South Shore Market** (p78) and **Salt at Our Kaka'ako** (p74) are good starting points. Head to **Ala Moana Regional Park** (p74; pictured above) and **Magic Island** (p75) for sublime beach time.

5

BISHOP MUSEUM ⏱1 DAY

Visit the **Bishop Museum** (p100; pictured above), the world's top Polynesian anthropological museum and Hawai'i's version of the Smithsonian Institute.

***Detour:** Drive to the **National Memorial Cemetery of the Pacific** (p104), better known as Punchbowl. Honolulu views from the rim are great. For more views and hiking in lush nature, drive the Punchbowl, Pu'uohi'a & Round Top Drive scenic route (p106).*
⏱ 1 hour

6

WAIKĪKĪ ⏱1 DAY

Although you can spend many more days just here, make sure you have a full day set aside to savor the beaches, parks, old royal heritage and cutting-edge culture of **Waikīkī** (p81; pictured above). Turn everything off and turn on to, well, as little as possible. Take a beach walk (p90) with frequent stops to reflect, relax and enjoy a mai tai.

JIE ZHAN/GETTY IMAGES, PHILLIP B. ESPINASSE/SHUTTERSTOCK, PETER UNGER/GETTY IMAGES

YIDO KUM/GETTY IMAGES

Hanauma Bay (p138)

ITINERARIES

Wonders of the Southeast

Allow: 1–3 days **Distance:** 40 miles

A fabulous hike hidden within an icon, a woman's vision of architectural beauty and forays into O'ahu's beauty above, below and on the waves make the island's southeast unmissable. You can do it all in one long day, but you'll enjoy it far more by breaking your joy into two – or better – three days.

1

DIAMOND HEAD ⏱ ½ DAY

Get an early start and have breakfast at one of the cheerful – and creative – cafes along Monsarrat Ave. Then take the tunnel into the backdrop for untold zillions of Waikīkī selfies: **Diamond Head** (p99; pictured above). You're here early as it gets hot in the ancient volcanic crater in the middle of the day. Spectacular views from the top make the adventurous (but family-friendly) climb worthwhile.

2

SHANGRI LA ⏱ ½ DAY

You'll have to detour toward Downtown Honolulu for a tour unlike anything else on the islands. You have to start at the superb-in-its-own-right **Honolulu Museum of Art** (p75) to enjoy what may be the biggest surprise of your trip to O'ahu: **Shangri La** (p96; pictured above), Doris Duke's oceanfront hideaway at Black Point and her extraordinary paeon to Islamic art and architecture. Book your tour as far in advance as possible.

3

HANAUMA BAY ⏱ ½ DAY

With its yacht-filled marina and breezy canals surrounded by mountains, bays and beach parks, the suburb of **Hawai'i Kai** (p138; pictured above) is a great base for all manner of delights. Tops is spectacular **Hanauma Bay** (p138) with its perfect beach cove and idyllic snorkeling. Don't leave without spotting Hawai'i's state fish, the *humuhumunukunukuāpua'a*. Be sure to get a mandatory reservation in advance.

FROM LEFT: JAMISON LOGAN/SHUTTERSTOCK, PHILLIP B. ESPINASSE/SHUTTERSTOCK, ISLANDLEIGH/GETTY IMAGES

4

COASTAL DRIVE & SANDY BEACH PARK ⏱ ½ DAY

Take your time between Hanauma Bay and Makapu'u Point for an awesome scenic drive. Plus, there are some fun stops along the way like the **Lāna'i Lookout** (p141), **Hālona Blowhole Lookout** and **Sandy Beach Park** (p141; pictured above), just to start. You'll need confidence to bodyboard here, as the waves crash right onto the beach, but the thrills vastly outweigh the chills.

5

MAKAPU'U POINT ⏱ ½ DAY

Makapu'u Point (p139; pictured above) and its namesake Lighthouse Trail are highlights that are barely a 30-minute drive from Waikīkī. The views reveal **Makapu'u Beach Park** (p139). Further off are Mānana Island (Rabbit Island) and Kāohikaipu Islet Seabird Sanctuary. Toward the horizon are Lāna'i and Moloka'i. In winter you may also see whales across the whitecaps. Afterward, stop at the beach for a dip.

6

WAIMĀNALO BAY ⏱ ½ DAY

For sublime beach action, turn the corner of southeast O'ahu and make the short jaunt to the shallow crescent of **Waimānalo Bay** (p154; pictured above). With a spine-tingling backdrop of magnificent *pali*, Waimānalo Bay Beach Park is the place to pull out that bodyboard. Or just settle back in the shade of a palm tree and absorb the tropical-fantasy views while the fronds gently rustle overhead.

PHILLIP B. ESPINASSE/SHUTTERSTOCK, SUSANNE POMMER/SHUTTERSTOCK, TORNMAPS/GETTY IMAGES

SHAUN JEFFERS/SHUTTERSTOCK

Kualoa Regional Park (p160)

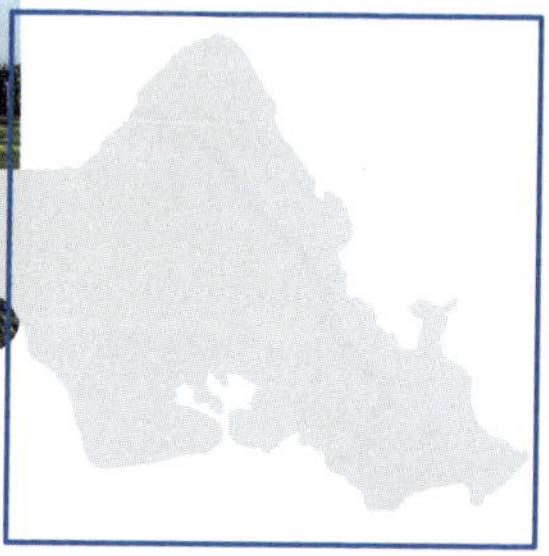

ITINERARIES

The Classic O'ahu Loop

Allow: 1–6 days **Distance:** 100 miles

The classic circumnavigation of O'ahu can be done in a day or six – try for the latter. Given the island's size, you shouldn't be surprised that this grand tour of sights covers less than 100 miles of driving, which is good as it leaves more time for enjoying the stops.

1 WINDWARD COAST ½ DAY

From Waikīkī, cross to the **Windward Coast** (p135) on the Pali Hwy, stopping at the **Nu'uanu Pali State Wayside** (p160; pictured above) at the pass on your way to check out the beguiling town of Kailua.

Note: you can start this trip via the Wonders of the Southeast itinerary (p26). This will take longer than a day, but if you stay in Kailua, you can enjoy a multi-day epic.

2 KAILUA ½ DAY

Kailua (p146) is such a charmer that the area deserves extra time – that's if you can escape the lures of **Kailua Beach Park** (p146; pictured above) and **Lanikai Beach** (p146). Rent a kayak and paddle to **Mokulua Islands** (p152). Or head up the hill for the **Lanikai Pillbox Trail** (p148) and its challenging route and rewarding views. Prowl compact Kailua for galleries and offbeat cafes.

3 KĀNE'OHE BAY ½ DAY

It's a short hop north to **Kāne'ohe Bay** (p156; pictured above) and its namesake town. Start by counting the shades of turquoise in the bay waters. Then head down for some snorkeling surprises. Consider a tour, which will take you to hidden sites ideally matched to the day's weather and tide conditions. Save hunger for the **Waiahole Poi Factory** (p159) and treats made with local ingredients.

FROM LEFT: PHILLIP B. ESPINASSE/SHUTTERSTOCK, MALACHI JACOBS/SHUTTERSTOCK, WARREN ISHII/500PX

4

KUALOA ½ DAY

Head north to **Kualoa Regional Park** (p160) to check out Mokoli'i Island and the magnificent Kualoa mountains. Paddle a kayak or SUP out to the picture-perfect islet. **Kualoa Ranch** (p162; pictured above) beckons with activities that can fill a day. It's a magical, emerald landscape where you can learn royal history, dig into legends, taste Hawaiian foods and see famous film sites.

5

PŪPŪKEA ½ DAY

Loop around Kahuku Point and ready yourself for the fabled North Shore. Stop for garlic shrimp at the **food trucks** (p193) in Kahuku. **Pūpūkea** (p180) is the name for the series of beaches that define the shore – the home of world-famous surf events. Start beach-hopping at **Sunset Beach Park** (p183; pictured above) and **'Ehukai Beach Park** (p183), home to the famous Banzai Pipeline.

6

HALE'IWA ½ DAY

Hale'iwa (p172; pictured above) dates back to sugar plantation times and feels a bit like the mainland's Old West. Today the frontier meets luxe with boutiques, surf shops and galleries, plus characterful cafes, lunch trucks and restaurants. Surfing dominates life in the winter surf season. Other times there's fabulous snorkeling and just plain lounging at Hale'iwa Ali'i Beach Park.

ALEXANDRE.ROSA/SHUTTERSTOCK

Dole Plantation (p168)

ITINERARIES

Westward via the Center

Allow: 1–3 days **Distance:** 115 miles

Start in the island's heart, where memories of long-gone pineapple plantations are everywhere. Head west to the Ko Olina resorts and turn north along the Leeward Coast, which feels like forgotten O'ahu. There are magnificent white-sand beaches, Native Hawaiian pride is alive and well, and there are good spots to hike.

1

WAHIAWĀ ⏱ ½ DAY

Buzz north to the town of **Wahiawā** (p168), a humble residential center once the domain of workers at the now-closed plantations. Experience a gaudy vestige of this era at the **Dole Plantation** (p168), where pineapples get small-time theme-park treatment. For more authenticity, tour the nearby working **Dole pineapple factory** (p169). Afterwards, savor the lush beauty at **Wahiawā Botanical Garden** (p170; pictured above).

2

'AIEA ⏱ ½ DAY

Point yourself Leeward, stopping in **'Aiea** (p110) for Hawaiian culture, great food and hiking. Heading up into the green hills you'll discover the **Keaīwa Heiau State Recreation Area** (p116; pictured above). Here, the namesake heiau is a beautifully preserved example of a temple once used for medicinal purposes. It's also a good time to grab an early lunch or picnic at the dozens of fine – and popularly priced – storefront Asian eateries.

3

KO OLINA ⏱ ½ DAY

From the freeway, spot the expanding Skyline, the mostly elevated Honolulu rapid-transit project. At the end of the H-1 Fwy, visit the upscale **Ko Olina** (p124; pictured above) resorts and golf course, which feel a bit out of place here in western O'ahu. Four Waikīkī-style resorts are built around the same number of artificial lagoons that are fed by the Pacific. Have lunch at the tasty **Monkeypod Kitchen** (p125).

FROM LEFT: MICHAEL JONES/GETTY IMAGES, MAKANA CHAI VIA WIKIMEDIA COMMONS, TRIGGERPHOTO/GETTY IMAGES

4 WAI'ANAE ½ DAY

Following the coast north, drive to **Wai'anae** (p129; pictured above). A workaday town, it also lends the most commonly used local names for the Leeward Coast: 'Wai'anae Coast' or 'Wai'anae Side.' This region has a high percentage of Native Hawaiians – look for the green, yellow and red colors of the Kingdom of Hawai'i flags that seem to adorn every other pick-up.

5 LEEWARD BEACHES ½ DAY

Beaches of many personalities are in and around Wai'anae. **Mākaha Beach Park** (p130) is a good place in summer to see *honu* while snorkeling. Sheltered **Pōka'ī Bay Beach** (p131) is best-suited for swimming. Don't miss the remains of an old Hawaiian **Kū'ilioloa Heiau** (p131). At the north end, **Keawa'ula Beach** (p131; pictured above; aka Yokohama Bay) is a secluded surfing hot spot.

6 KA'ENA POINT ½ DAY

You don't have to be well versed in Hawaiian legends to know that something mystical occurs at the dramatic convergence of land and sea in the northwestern corner of the island at **Ka'ena Point** (p131; pictured above). An abandoned railroad makes for an excellent 2.5-mile hike from Keawa'ula Beach to the point, which then continues another 2.5 miles around the point to the North Shore trailhead.

STEVE HEAP/SHUTTERSTOCK, PIKAPPA/GETTY IMAGES, LANACANADA/GETTY IMAGES

WHEN TO GO

Year-round balmy weather is a Hawai'i trademark, as are the pleasant trade winds. There's no bad time to visit O'ahu.

O'ahu is a great place to visit any time of the year. The busy winter tourist season has more to do with weather elsewhere, as many visitors escape cold winters back home. The weather in Hawai'i is enjoyable year-round. It's a bit rainier in winter and a bit hotter in summer, but there are no extremes, thanks to cooling trade winds that modify the heat throughout the year. Some activities do have seasons; the best waves for surfing curl offshore in winter.

Saving Money

To save money, avoid the busy period surrounding Christmas and New Year's Day when prices and crowds peak. The rest of the year should pose few problems, although any US holiday period such as Thanksgiving will see flocks of people from the West Coast hopping flights for a break. At any time, book your accommodations as early as possible as last-minute bargains are uncommon.

I LIVE HERE

WINTER FESTIVALS

Ryan Field lives in East Honolulu and revels in seldom needing to bother with checking the weather.

'My favorite season would have to be our "winter" season. It does get rainy sometimes and it's slightly cooler. I love the holiday season here, going to community parades and seeing the colorful lights. I loved this as a kid and now I can experience it all again with my kids. But, really, it's tough to choose a favorite season when I can golf year-round.'

Waikīkī Beach (p81)

NOT A KONA WIND!

Hawai'i's famous trade winds with their cooling temperatures blow from the ocean to the northeast up to 270 days a year. In contrast, few residents enjoy the hot and humid kona winds, which blow from the south or southwest when storms change the weather patterns.

Weather Through the Year: Honolulu

JANUARY	FEBRUARY	MARCH	APRIL	MAY	JUNE
Avg. daytime max: **80°F**	Avg. daytime max: **80°F**	Avg. daytime max: **81°F**	Avg. daytime max: **83°F**	Avg. daytime max: **85°F**	Avg. daytime max: **87°F**
Days of rainfall: **14**	Days of rainfall: **11**	Days of rainfall: **13**	Days of rainfall: **12**	Days of rainfall: **11**	Days of rainfall: **12**

PEAK SEASON?

Certain activities have peak seasons. Winter is the best time for surfing, though beginners can learn any time. The flipside, summer, is true for windsurfing when winds blow their best. But one advantage with O'ahu is that just about everything can be enjoyed year-round.

Major Events

King Kamehameha Day Celebrations The state holiday features a ceremony at the king's statue in **Honolulu** (p63), followed by a parade and street party. Later in the month, a hula festival is held in the king's honor. **June 11**

Duke Kahanamoku Ocean Festival *(dukekahanamokuoceanfestival.org)* Outrigger-canoe and surfing competitions, island-style food, traditional Hawaiian games, art and crafts, and entertainment for a week at Kahanamoku Beach in Waikīkī. **August**

Honolulu Pride *(honolulupride.com)* Hawai'i's largest LGBTIQ+ event. A huge parade begins on **Magic Island** (p75) in Ala Moana Regional Park and follows Kalākaua Ave to **Kapi'olani Regional Park** (p94), where there's music and a festival. **October**

Sunset Pro (p188) World-class surfing competition held in late November at Sunset Beach Park, which is known for its powerful and challenging waves at this time of year. The schedule depends on the surf. **November**

Celebrating the Arts

Honolulu Festival *(honolulufestival.com)* Three days of music, dance and drama in Honolulu and Waikīkī. The cultural festival features an arts-and-crafts fair and a grand parade followed by fireworks. **March**

Pan-Pacific Festival *(panpacificfestival.org)* Expect outdoor hula shows and *taiko* drumming as part of an Asian and Polynesian performing-arts showcase in Honolulu and Waikīkī. Don't miss the huge *ho'olaule'a* (celebration) block party and parade. **June**

Aloha Festivals *(alohafestivals.com)* Begun in 1946, this month-long festival is the state's premier cultural festival. The signature events are Waikīkī's royal court procession, block party and floral parade. **September**

Hawai'i International Film Festival *(hiff.org)* Screenings of Pacific Rim, Asian, mainland American, European and Hawai'i-related films at venues in Honolulu and Waikīkī. It's popular; book ahead. **October**

I LIVE HERE

SUMMER'S A BEACH

Jeremy Lawi was born and raised on O'ahu. Picking a favorite time of year is tough for him, as he can enjoy so much of life on the island year-round, but summer nudges out other times.

'Summer is my favorite, because of the perfect beach weather. I love getting acai bowls with fresh fruit and heading out onto the sand. The King Kamehameha Parade and Prince Lot Hula Festival are great to check out, for locals and visitors alike. They are such fun scenes.'

King Kamehameha Day Parade

WHY MAY & SEPTEMBER?

May and September are the two months of the year when visitor numbers abate a bit and you can enjoy O'ahu with the highest percentage of residents. Both months straddle the busier summer season and don't include school or major holidays.

JULY	AUGUST	SEPTEMBER	OCTOBER	NOVEMBER	DECEMBER
Avg. daytime max: **88°F**	Avg. daytime max: **89°F**	Avg. daytime max: **89°F**	Avg. daytime max: **87°F**	Avg. daytime max: **84°F**	Avg. daytime max: **81°F**
Days of rainfall: **14**	Days of rainfall: **13**	Days of rainfall: **13**	Days of rainfall: **13**	Days of rainfall: **13**	Days of rainfall: **15**

FROM LEFT: JEWHYTE/GETTY IMAGES, MAXIMUM FILM/ALAMY

Hiking, Diamond Head (p99)

GET PREPARED FOR HONOLULU, WAIKĪKĪ & O'AHU

Useful things to load in your bag, your ears and your brain.

Clothes

Casual, comfortable clothes This is the central island of the state where aloha shorts are worn by CEOs to important meetings. Cotton and comfy should be your mantra when packing. If you plan top-end dining, you might check for dress codes, but these are rare. However, singlets, shorts and flip-flops (thongs) won't cut it at fancier places at night.

Light, waterproof jacket For tropical windward showers and wind-whipped, cloud-shrouded *pali* (cliffs or mountains).

Shoes with traction When trails get muddy, flip-flops just don't cut it.

Sunglasses Essential for the glare of all those days of sunshine.

Manners

Two words you'll hear a lot are *aloha* (hello and goodbye) and *mahalo* (thank you). Use them sincerely.

If you're given a lei, wear it with gratitude. Never take it off in the presence of the person who gave it to you.

Hawai'i is a US state; refer to the 48 states across the Pacific as 'the Mainland,' *not* the US or the States.

Dive certification Bring your card and logbooks if you're going to take the plunge. Snorkel sets are easily rented or borrowed.

Aloha spirit This is the islands. Slow down and hang loose.

READ

Song of the Exile (Kiana Davenport; 1999) Honolulu-born Davenport writes of two fictional families from WWII through US statehood.

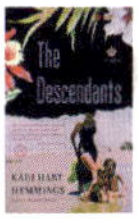

The Descendants (Kaui Hart Hemmings; 2007) O'ahu-born Hemmings made a splash when her first novel was made into a popular movie.

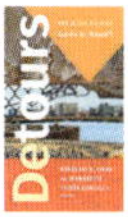

Detours (Multiple authors; 2019) Compelling essays about what a modern Hawai'i would look like in a post-colonial world.

Saturday Night at the Pahala Theatre (Lois-Ann Yamanaka; 1993) Award-winning anthology; its author is known for gritty depictions of local life.

Words

Common Hawaiian Words

Aloha Love, hello, welcome, goodbye.

Heiau Religious temple.

Kane Man.

Kapu Taboo, restricted.

Mahalo Thank you.

Makai Toward the sea.

Mauka Toward the mountains.

'Ono Delicious, tasty.

Wahine Woman.

Common Slang

Brah Shortened form of *bradah* (brother); also used as 'hey you.'

Buggahs Guys, as in '*da buggahs* went to [blank] without me!'

Kay den 'Ok then,' as in '*kay den*, we go beach.'

Laydahs I'll see you later, as in, '*kay den, laydahs.*'

Talk story Casual conversation.

WATCH

The Descendants (Alexander Payne; 2011; pictured above) George Clooney in an Academy Award winner about generational loss and drama.

Blue Hawaii (Norman Taurog; 1961) Elvis Presley sings in Waikīkī and gives the then-new Hilton Hawaiian Village a star turn.

The Haumana (Keo Woolford; 2013) The director of a schlocky Waikīkī tourist show rediscovers Hawaiian art and culture.

Endless Summer (Bruce Brown; 1966) The original life-in-search-of-the-wave surfing epic. Early paeon to the North Shore.

TV shows, such as **Chief of War**, **Hawaii Five-0** and **Lost**.

FOLLOW

Honolulu Civil Beat (*civilbeat.org*) is an excellent source of independent news.

Honolulu magazine (*honolulumagazine.com*) is a great source for food, drink, shopping and culture news.

Learn the latest about O'ahu's heritage at **Historic Hawai'i Foundation** (*historichawaii.org*).

Follow current conditions at **O'ahu's State Parks** (*dlnr.hawaii.gov/dsp/parks/oahu*).

Get your questions answered on a helpful **Reddit forum** (*reddit.com/r/VisitingHawaii*).

@ainamomona Socially aware, with a focus on tourism's price.

@ehoopilimai Clever takes on the Hawaiian language.

@adamkeawe Clear-eyed takes on indigenous and cultural issues.

@fetia.fetia 'Crime-fighting foodie' prowls Honolulu seeking good eats.

LISTEN

KINE Radio (105.1 FM) Classic and contemporary Hawaiian music 24/7 with a few musician interviews; from Honolulu.

What School You Went? PBS Hawai'i podcast. Host Ron Mizutani plays off the slang name for the show to interview guests on local topics.

KHPR Radio (88.1 FM) NPR news, commentary and features, with Hawai'i content. Also online at hawaiipublicradio.org.

Manu Minute Podcast from Hawai'i Public Radio that takes a brief and engaging look at a bird species in each episode.

JOSHUA RAINEY PHOTOGRAPHY/SHUTTERSTOCK

Poke bowl

THE FOOD SCENE

Eating in Hawai'i is a festival of flavors. Hawaiian food and cuisines from around the Pacific are creatively combined in delicious ways.

'Dis is seriously broke da mout!' That's the ultimate local compliment: the food's so delicious that it breaks the mouth. Honolulu, Waikīkī, Waimānalo, Kahuku and the North Shore are just some of the places you'll find exceptional – often creative – fare. So eat everything in sight – it's all *'ono grinds* (good eats).

Cheap, tasty and filling, local *grinds* (food) is the stuff of cravings and comfort. There's no better example than the classic plate lunch, a fixed-plate meal of 'two scoop' rice, macaroni ('mac') or potato salad and a meat dish reflecting Hawai'i's polyglot food heritage, such as fried mahimahi, teriyaki chicken, Korean-style *kalbi* short ribs, Filipino pork adobo or Japanese-style katsu pork or chicken.

Since the 1990s, Hawai'i Regional Cuisine (HRC) has become a common and beloved cuisine. This style incorporates fresh island ingredients from local farmers, ranchers and fishers; borrows liberally from Hawai'i's ethnic groups; and is marked by creative fusion combinations such as Peking duck in ginger-*liliko'i* (passion fruit) sauce.

Native Hawaiian Food

In general, Native Hawaiian cuisine is very filling, if not the most flavorful – there's a lot of emphasis on starch and meat. With its earthy flavors and Polynesian ingredients, Native Hawaiian cooking is a distinct culinary genre. *Kālua* pig is traditionally roasted whole underground in an *imu*, a

Best Hawai'i Regional Cuisine

LŪ'AU
Outside of tourist spectacles, lū'au are celebratory Hawaiian banquets.

POKE
Raw marinated seafood; chefs proudly invent their signature variations.

SPAM MUSUBI
Rice cakes with a savory slice of canned meat; far better than it sounds.

SHAVE ICE
Snowy shavings packed into a cup and drenched with sweet syrups and flavors.

pit of red-hot stones layered with *ti* and banana leaves. Cooked this way, the pork is smoky, salty and succulent.

Poi – a purplish paste made of pounded taro root, often steamed and fermented – was sacred to ancient Hawaiians. Tasting bland to mildly tart or even sour, poi is usually not eaten by itself but as a starchy side dish.

A popular main dish is *laulau*, a bundle of pork or chicken and salted butterfish wrapped in taro or *ti* leaves and steamed until it has a soft, spinach-like texture.

Drinks

Hawai'i was the first US state to grow coffee. The finest coffee beans come from the Big Island, where 100% Kona coffee has worldwide cachet. But O'ahu is also in on the action.

Given that fruit trees thrive on O'ahu, it's a shame that most supermarket cartons contain imported purees or sugary 'juice drinks' such as POG (passion fruit, orange and guava, which are more flavorings than actual juice). Look for real, freshly squeezed and blended juices at island cafes, health-food stores, farmers markets and roadside fruit stands.

Several microbreweries are now firmly established on O'ahu. A hallmark of local craft beers is the addition of a hint of tropical flavors, such as Kona coffee, coconut or *liliko'i*.

Market, Chinatown (p66)

Shave ice

TOP FESTIVALS & MARKETS

Hawai'i Food & Wine Festival *(hawaiifoodandwinefestival.com)* O'ahu's one main food and drink festival is held in Honolulu in late October. Star chefs, sustainable farmers and food lovers come together for wine tastings, cooking demonstrations and dining events. Otherwise, O'ahu's markets serve as year-round festivals of the island's bounty.

Chinatown's daily markets (p66) Loaded with treats plus scrumptious ready meals.

Kaka'ako Farmers Market (p80) One of Hawai'i's best weekly markets. Every Saturday morning food lovers browse the goods on offer from over 110 vendors.

Wai'anae Farmers Market (p131) On the Leeward Coast; this is small but a real find.

Kailua Town Farmers Market and **Lōkahi Kailua Market** (p147) Two good Sunday choices in Kailua, on the Windward Coast.

PUPU	PLATE LUNCH	CRACK SEED	GARLIC SHRIMP	LOCO MOCO
Snacks or appetizers that are served with drinks and come in myriad variations.	The iconic quick meal at noon or other times; comes in endless versions.	Popular packaged snack; can be sweet, sour, salty, spicy or some combination.	Food-truck staple sold island-wide; it stars in plate lunches.	Breakfast of champions: rice, fried eggs and a hamburger patty doused in gravy.

Local Specialties

Often eaten with disposable chopsticks on disposable plates, plate lunch meals pack a flavor (and caloric) punch: fried, salty and meaty. Healthier plates come with options for brown rice and salad greens.

Sticky white rice is more than a side dish in Hawai'i. It's a culinary building block, an integral partner in everyday meals. Without it, the *loco moco* would be nothing more than an egg-and-gravy-covered hamburger patty. Just so you know, sticky white rice means exactly that. Not fluffy rice. Not wild rice. And definitely not instant rice.

Hawai'i is the only US state where you can eat Hormel's iconic canned meat Spam with pride. Residents consume around seven million cans per year. The most popular preparation is Spam *musubi*: a block of rice with a slice of cooked Spam on top (or in the middle) and wrapped with nori (Japanese dried seaweed).

One must-try is poke (poh-keh), a savory dish of bite-size raw fish (typically 'ahi – yellowfin tuna), seasoned with *shōyu* (soy sauce), sesame oil, green onion, chili-pepper flakes, sea salt, *ogo* (crunchy seaweed) and *'inamona* (a condiment made of roasted, ground *kukui* – candlenut tree – nuts).

Spam *musubi*

Another favorite local food is saimin, a soup of chewy Chinese egg noodles swimming in Japanese broth, garnished with green onion, nori, *kamaboko* (steamed fish cake) and *char siu* (Chinese barbecued pork).

On a hot day, nothing beats a mound of snowy shave ice packed into a cup and drenched with sweet syrups in an eye-popping rainbow of hues. Purists stick with just ice, but for added decadence, ask for sweet azuki beans, *mochi* (sticky, sweet Japanese pounded-rice cakes) or ice cream underneath.

MEALS OF A LIFETIME

Honolulu's Chinatown has two superb places to eat among many good choices: Fête and Senia. **Fête** (p68) is renowned for ever-changing seasonal menus while **Senia** (p68) is a creative and enticing top-end dining.

Sushi Sasabune (p80) Sublime Japanese restaurants are many in Honolulu. Try the *omakase* (chef's tasting menu) sushi.

Roy's Waikiki (p84) Chef Roy Yamaguchi's island-born chain is perfect for celebrating the good life. The **Original Roy's** (p140) in Hawai'i Kai is convenient for the Windward Coast.

'Ono Seafood (p95) Get a taste of true, local poke in Honolulu. Between the fresh fish and impeccable seasoning, it makes a sublime picnic.

THE YEAR IN FOOD

SPRING

Tropical fruits such as mango, papaya and pineapple hit their prime. Look for festivals celebrating food all over the island. Farmers markets burst with fresh and flavorful fare.

SUMMER

What isn't in season during the dry, temperate days of O'ahu's summer? It's a time of enormous bounty. You should be able to book a top table anywhere as the tourist season slows down.

FALL

Autumn enjoys the same mild, tropical weather that graces O'ahu and the islands year-round. This ensures that it's always a good time to eat in Honolulu and the rest of the island.

WINTER

Peak tourist season means that you will want to book ahead for top restaurants in Honolulu (especially Chinatown) and Waikīkī. Crowd-pleasing avocados, tangerines and strawberries are ripe.

JEWHYTE/GETTY IMAGES

Royal Hawaiian Hotel (p84)

HOW TO... Choose a Waikīkī Resort

Waikīkī has a dizzying array of lodging choices, from fancy beachfront resorts to tidy budget hotels on backstreets. Trying to decide where to stay can be bewildering. The main beachfront strip, along Kalākaua Ave, is lined with hotels and sprawling resorts. Some of them are true beauties with historic or boutique atmospheres. Further from the sand, look for inviting, smaller places. And don't forget the hundreds of condos, timeshares and apartments offered as short-term and holiday rentals.

Prioritize Your Amenities

How much of the cliched Blue Pacific you see from your room directly affects your rate. So too does proximity to the shore – but note, you're never far from the sand anywhere in Waikīkī. Is there a balcony? And, what's the level of service? Do you want to brew your own coffee, or can you request a silver-pot-full? And, are the furnishings functional or memorable?

Practical Considerations

Budget When comparing rates, it's essential to determine the final nightly cost. To the base rates, add resort fees, taxes and parking.

Hidden fees Vacation rentals can be a minefield of hidden fees. The low nightly rate can balloon once large cleaning fees, parking and other surcharges are added.

Parking Parking can be expensive: $50 a night or more (thus 'free parking' deals are worthwhile). Consider only getting a rental car for the days you'll need it.

Taxes Tax for Honolulu (including Waikīkī) hotel stays is almost 15%. Some hotels levy a 'taxes and fees' charge that's over 15%, which is just an 'added profit' fee.

Dreaded Resort Fee

Waikīkī is ground zero for the resort fee scam. Never optional, the fees are simply a way for hotels to make their base rates seem smaller than they really are. Resorts will defend those fees and say that they include 'free' wi-fi, maybe a welcome drink, a small bottle of water and/or meaningless discounts for affiliated businesses such as 15% off in the hotel's overpriced restaurant.
And just like airlines and baggage fees, hotels have found resort fees (or 'convenience fees' or 'hospitality fees') a great way to sneakily increase their profits. The fees keep increasing; $50 a night is common.

RESORT TYPES

Famous & fancy Exemplified by the Royal Hawaiian, these resorts are the stuff of legend and line the sandy shores. High-priced.

Huge Join the masses at vast corporate properties where amenities are many but service is functional.

Condo Often short-term rental units; expect a balcony, kitchen, sturdy furnishings and, in many cases, good value.

Backstreet Away from the beach, dozens of smaller, older hotels range from restored, retro gems to beloved veterans with a loyal following and low rates.

Hostels Waikīkī has a surprising number of budget hotels, many clustered around well-located Lemon Rd at the south end.

Banzai Pipeline, 'Ehukai Beach Park (p183)

TRIP PLANNER

SURFING ON O'AHU

Modern surfing began on O'ahu and was exported to the world. This ancient Hawaiian sport continues to thrive. Go to Waikīkī to rent a board and learn to ride a wave; head to the North Shore to become a star. It's why so many vacations here have become permanent.

HONOLULU & WAIKĪKĪ

Duke Kahanamoku grew up on the sands of Waikīkī where, along with a handful of others, he swam, fished, dove and rode the reefs on traditional boards (which were all that remained of a traditional Hawaiian sport that had largely died out). Their derring-do caught the attention of outsiders near the beginning of the 20th century. In the succeeding years, Kahanamoku spread the gospel of surfing, traveling the world to demonstrate the Hawaiian 'Sport of Kings.'

Over 100 years later, surfing is alive and well where Duke saved it from extinction – it's the very heart of tourism on O'ahu and the entire state. The breaks are tightly packed along the shores of Honolulu and **Waikīkī** (p81; pictured top right). Scores of surf schools and board-rental places dot the streets. Many of the people living in and around Waikīkī live here so they can surf every day.

NORTH SHORE

When it comes to surf, nowhere on the planet gets as much attention as O'ahu's North Shore. While the south shore of O'ahu goes quiet in winter, the North Shore roars to life. During this time, powerful storms in the Gulf of Alaska send intense northwest swells in the general direction of the 'Seven-Mile Miracle,' the stretch of waves and sand from **Hale'iwa** (p172) to **Sunset Beach** (p183), where occasionally the surf can top 30ft on the outer reefs.

LEEWARD COAST

Before there was a North Shore (in terms of surfing!) there was O'ahu's Leeward Coast. The northern stretch known as the

GAUGING SURF CONDITIONS

Knowing how big the next swell is and when it's coming are essential. This is where streaming webcams, surf reports and forecasts come in. For O'ahu, the following sources are useful; and don't forget common sense – if conditions look intimidating, stay on shore.

Hawaii News Now Surf Report *(hawaiinewsnow.com/page/surf-report)* A quick and easy graphical summary of conditions.

Live Surf Camz Hawaii *(livesurfcamhawaii.com)* An index to scores of live surf cams on O'ahu and across the state.

National Weather Service *(weather.gov/hfo/srf)* The official wave conditions and surf report for O'ahu.

Surfline *(surfline.com)* Great omnibus site with massive amounts of information.

Wai'anae Coast is where big-wave surfing got its start, specifically at **Mākaha** (p130). Beginning after WWII, locals learned how to deal with the winter waves, which reach 15ft. Today the break still attracts experts, but it's not the same glossy scene you'll find on the North Shore. Innovative changes to surfboards in the 1960s, particularly the move from heavy redwood boards to lighter balsa-wood boards and the addition of a surfboard fin, made tackling the North Shore's giant waves more feasible, so the scene shifted there.

WINDWARD COAST

For all its beauty and other attributes, O'ahu's Windward Coast is not prime surfing territory. The 'wind' in the name offers the clue: water sports dependent on wind power are in their prime here, especially on **Kailua Bay** (p146). But the island shelters the ocean, and breaks are modest at best.

FOMINAYAPHOTO/SHUTTERSTOCK

Waikīkī (p81)

O'AHU SURF ETIQUETTE

- When it comes to dealing with the resident surfing populace, remember one word: respect.
- As a visitor on O'ahu, there are some places you go, and some places you don't. Residents are usually willing to share surf spots that have become popular tourist destinations but they reserve the right to protect other 'secret' surf grounds. As a newbie in the lineup, don't expect to get every wave that comes your way. There's a definite pecking order and, frankly, tourists are at the bottom. That being said, usually if you give a wave, you'll get a wave in return. Be generous in the water, understand your place and enjoy yourself.
- The situation is more intense at famous breaks where surfers can be ferociously territorial. At breaks such as the Banzai Pipeline at **'Ehukai Beach Park** (p183), definitely ask a local for an introduction.
- The gist is don't be a wave hog and don't get in the way of other people while they're riding. If you're taking lessons, ask your instructor to explain the etiquette to you. Or if you're fending for yourself, don't be afraid to ask somebody in the water – they'll probably be happy to help and could end up giving you some local insight.
- Basically, be humble, be kind, share and always surf with a smile.

Kuli'ou'ou Ridge Trail (p144)

TRIP PLANNER

HIKING ON O'AHU

Even though O'ahu is Hawai'i's most populous island, nature sits right behind Waikīkī and Honolulu. That jagged green wall of *pali* (cliffs) is laced with trails. Across the island, you'll find walks and hikes suited for every level of difficulty and distance. About 25% of the island is made up of protected natural areas ready for exploration on foot.

HONOLULU & WAIKĪKĪ

If you don't have a lot of time, plenty of hikes can be accessed near Waikīkī. The island's classic hike, and its most popular, is the short but steep trail to the city overlook at the crater's summit in **Diamond Head State Monument** (p99). It's easily reached from Waikīkī and ends with a panoramic city view.

In Honolulu, the **Mānoa Falls Trail** (p108) is a rewarding – albeit incredibly popular – excursion. Many more trails can be reached via the circuitous Round Top Drive (p106).

Just west of Honolulu in the Pearl Harbor area, the **'Aiea Loop Trail** (p117) is popular with hikers and mountain bikers. It's contained within the **Keaīwa Heiau State Recreation Area** (p116), where you can also visit an ancient temple.

NORTH SHORE

On the North Shore, the **'Ehukai Pillbox Trail** (p185) is a short walk with the sort of views you'd expect from an old military lookout. Elsewhere, the mixed sand-and-rock coastline at **Turtle Bay** (p192) makes for beautiful hikes and walks. With miles of oceanfront, Lā'ie and Kahuku offer cliffside walks, strolls along the beach and views of the many offshore islets.

LEEWARD COAST

Far from anywhere else, one of the most stunning of the island's hikes is the **Ka'ena Point Trail** (p131) at the northwest edge of

TOP HIKING INFO SOURCES

Hawaiian Trail & Mountain Corp *(htmc1910.org)* Volunteer-run hiking club that arranges intermediate to challenging group hikes all over the island. Trail descriptions and safety tips available online.

Nā Ala Hele Trail & Access Program *(hawaiitrails.hawaii.gov/trails)* This official state government website for trails is an excellent source for printable topo maps and announcements of recently developed or reopened paths. Search the dozens of trails listed across O'ahu, and the other islands as well.

Sierra Club O'ahu Group *(sierracluboahu.org)* The Hawai'i chapter of the nonprofit national organization leads weekend hikes and other outings around O'ahu, including volunteer opportunities to rebuild trails and combat invasive plants.

Leeward O'ahu. The trail hugs the dramatic coastline. A good short trail is the **Mā'ili Pillbox Trail** (p132). Views are great as it's one of many abandoned military observation towers dotted around O'ahu.

WINDWARD COAST

On the Windward Coast, the **Maunawili Demonstration Trail** (p149) near Kailua provides a varied walk that covers a lot of different territory. For an excellent beach stroll, take to the sands outlining Kailua Bay. The area has other stunning trails. The most popular is the **Lanikai Pillbox Trail** (p148). Officially known as Ka'iwa Ridge, this short, 30-minute hike looks intimidating but it's doable for most visitors. **Kuli'ou'ou Ridge Trail** (p144) is an easy-to-access adventure. More adventuresome, there's a thrilling short hike on the offshore islet of **Moko'li'i** (p162).

In O'ahu's southeast corner is another of the island's premier hikes, the **Koko Crater Trail** (p141; pictured top right).

Mānoa Falls Trail (p108)

BARRY WINIKER/GETTY IMAGES

HIKING SAFETY

O'ahu is a very safe place to hike, but there are a few things to keep in mind.

Hike with at least one other person At the very least, tell someone where you are going and when you expect to be back.

Take along plenty of liquids Allow 4 pints (2L) of water for a full-day hike.

Wear a hat and sunscreen and start early It can get very hot in the middle of the day.

Don't get bugged The damp mountains are thick with biting insects.

Wear sturdy footwear Good traction is vital; it's often muddy.

Weather changes quickly Even when the sun is shining in Waikīkī, it can be pouring with rain only a few miles inland, so be prepared.

Ridges can be exposed to strong winds Take an extra layer of clothing for ridge hikes.

Flash floods Streams can rise quickly during thunderstorms, so use common sense in heavy rain.

Leptospirosis This is a bacterial disease found in freshwater ponds and streams that have been contaminated with animal urine. Never drink stream water; avoid getting cuts by wearing long trousers; and don't go swimming in ponds.

Nightfall Darkness falls fast once the sun sets, and ridgetop trails are no place to be caught unprepared at night. Always carry a flashlight just in case.

LEFT: AARONEJBULL87/SHUTTERSTOCK; TOP RIGHT: BENNY MARTY/SHUTTERSTOCK

Honu **(green sea turtle; p174)**

TRIP PLANNER

DIVING & SNORKELING ON O'AHU

Of the 700 fish species that live in Hawai'i's waters, nearly a third are found nowhere else. Divers and snorkelers can also often see spinner dolphins, green sea turtles and manta rays. The waters hold corals, unusual sponges and much more. Then there's the plethora of beautiful tropical fish. You may not want to come up for air.

DIVING

Whether you're an old pro or a beginner, O'ahu has plenty to offer under the sea: lessons, boat dives, shore dives, night dives, reef dives, cave dives and wreck dives. The water temperatures are perfect for diving, with yearly averages ranging between 72°F (22°C) and 80°F (27°C). Even better than the bathwater temperatures is the visibility, which is usually perfect for seeing the abundance of fish, coral and other sea creatures. Because of its volcanic origins, the island also has some cool underwater caves and caverns.

You'll find many dive shops in Honolulu and Waikīkī. You can arrange trips that cover all the dive spots around the island as well as rent anything you might need. Shops can also be found on the north coast in **Hale'iwa** (p172), and southeast in **Hawai'i Kai** (p138). Numerous spots along the south coast are good for winter diving. The best is **Hanauma Bay** (p138), which, while known for snorkeling, is also a spectacular site for diving.

SNORKELING

There's no excuse not to go snorkeling on O'ahu. The water is warm, the currents are generally gentle and the underwater visibility is awesome. Shallow reefs and nearshore waters are awash with fish and

UNDERWATER INFO

Good sources of info include:

Franko's Maps *(frankosmaps.com)* Produces an illustrated O'ahu dive map that's widely sold around the island and lists dive sites and descriptions. It also offers a handy laminated fish card.

DAN (Divers Alert Network; *diversalertnetwork.org*) Provides advice on diving insurance, emergencies and decompression services

To-Hawaii *(to-hawaii.com/underwaterworld.php)* Has a detailed and illustrated online guide to local fish. Also, sharks, sea turtles and a jellyfish calendar.

Hanauma Bay Fish Identification Card (*honolulu.gov*; search for 'Fish ID Card') Produced by the University of Hawai'i, this is a free download and provides pictures and descriptions of the fish you'll likely see around O'ahu.

colorful corals. As activities go, this is about as cheap as it gets, with mask and snorkel rentals available nearly everywhere. Some resorts offer gear for free.

If you're staying in Waikīkī you needn't go far to explore O'ahu underwater as you can don a mask at any of the beaches and spot some coral and fish (plus, gear-rental stands are everywhere). **Kaimana Beach** (p82) features a shallow reef close to shore and a breakwater that make for wave-free, protected waters.

On the North Shore, Hale'iwa is a top spot, as is **Pūpūkea** (p182). On the Leeward coast, **Mākaha Beach Park** (p130) is excellent for snorkeling while **Ko Olina** (p124) is family-friendly.

Over Windward, **Hanauma Bay** (p138; pictured top right) in Southeast O'ahu is hugely popular. **Kāne'ohe Bay** (p156) offers many opportunities. If you're lucky, a Hawaiian green sea turtle will paddle by.

Seabed, Shark's Cove (p182)

BENNY MARTY/SHUTTERSTOCK

RESPONSIBLE DIVING & SNORKELING

The popularity of underwater exploration is placing immense pressure on many dive sites. Follow the following tips when diving and snorkeling.

Don't touch the turtles Minimize your disturbance of marine animals. It is illegal to approach endangered marine species too closely; these include whales, dolphins, sea turtles and the Hawaiian monk seal.

Don't feed the fish Doing so disturbs their normal eating habits and can encourage aggressive behavior.

Be conscious of the coral Don't touch coral with your body (never stand on it) or drag equipment across the reef. If you must hold on, only touch exposed rock. Be conscious of your fins; even without contact, the surge from heavy strokes near the reef can damage delicate organisms. Don't kick up organism-choking clouds of sand when treading water.

Take only pictures Resist the temptation to collect coral or shells from the seabed. Get an underwater case for your phone and take pictures instead.

Pack it out Ensure that you remove all your trash and any other litter you may find. Plastics are a serious threat to marine life.

Practice proper buoyancy Major damage can be done by divers descending too fast and colliding with the reef. Make sure you are correctly weighted and that your weight belt is positioned so you stay horizontal.

LEFT: DOUGLAS PEEBLES PHOTOGRAPHY/ALAMY; BELOW: SANDRA FOYT/SHUTTERSTOCK

Kayaking, Mokulua Islands (p152)

THE OUTDOORS

It's not just surfing, hiking and underwater adventures – O'ahu offers excitement in many forms that are far greater than the island's size.

If you want to get wet, O'ahu is the place for you. Surfing is the obvious option, but there are many other ways you can explore above and below the surface. You'll find plenty of thrills in a huge range of water sports.

Think of Hawai'i and it's natural to think of sun, sand and waves, but there are lots of things to do on land, too. O'ahu is mountainous and green and residents are fit and active, enjoying life on their mid-Pacific island paradise.

Swimming & Bodysurfing

O'ahu has distinct coastal areas, each with its own seasonal water conditions. As a rule, the best places to swim in winter are in the south, and in summer, the north.

A warning: around 10 days after a full moon, box jellyfish swim into the shallow waters, especially around Waikīkī, and stay for a day or two. The **Waikīkī Aquarium** (p87) has an online calendar of when the jellyfish peak; see waikikiaquarium.org/interact/box-jellyfish-calendar.

Bodysurfing is a great way to catch some waves, sans equipment. There's a bit of a knack to it, but once you've found the groove, it's good times ahead. The ideal locations are sandy shore breaks where the inevitable wipeouts aren't that painful.

Bodysurfing and bodyboarding have myriad choices. The island's most popular bodyboarding site is **Kapahulu Groin** (p82) in Waikīkī's Kuhio Beach Park. **Kaka'ako**

More Outdoor Action

SKYDIVING
Jump out of a plane over the **Dillingham Kawaihapai Air Field** (p179), the best place to go skydiving on O'ahu.

UNDERWATER RIDE
Go for an underwater ride on a 'submarine scooter' tour (p143) in **Hawai'i Kai**, which lets you cruise about spotting fish.

BIRD-WATCHING
Spot many of Hawai'i's dozens of species on a bird-watching tour at the **James Campbell National Wildlife Refuge** (p194).

FAMILY ADVENTURES

Enjoy activities in Waikīkī – especially those on or near the beach and water (p81), as almost all are family-friendly. People of all ages can spend days here in relaxed and fun pursuits.

Take the jaunt along the **Mānoa Falls Trail** (p108) and the **'Aiea Loop Trail** (p117) near Pearl Harbor. They are enjoyable for all ages.

Say hello to *honu* (Hawaiian green sea turtles) lounging on the golden shores of **Laniākea Beach** (p175) in Pūpūkea. But, remember, everybody needs to keep their distance.

Take a peek below the surface in the calm waters of **Hanauma Bay** (p138), where *honu*, tropical fish and dolphins await.

Have fun at the pineapple theme park that is the **Dole Plantation** (p168) in Wahiawā – don't leave without trying the original Dole Whip.

Waterfront Park (p74) is another good spot in Honolulu. On the Leeward Coast, **Keawa'ula Beach** (p131; Yokohama Bay) has good breaks. If you're just getting started, **Waimānalo Bay Beach Park** (p154) in Windward O'ahu has a gentle shore break.

Kayaking

The top kayaking destinations are along the Windward Coast. **Kailua Beach Park** (p146) has the three uninhabited Mokulua Islands within the reef that are made for exploring via kayak. Landings are allowed on two: Moku Nui, which has a beautiful beach good for sunbathing and snorkeling; and Popoi'a Island (Flat Island), with its inviting walking trails. Kayaking to the little island of **Mokoli'i** (p162) is another memorable and popular experience.

In Waikīkī and nearby Honolulu beach parks, you'll see kayaks for rent. You can enjoy relaxed shore paddles in areas with reef or breakwater protection.

Outrigger canoeing (p84), Waikīkī

Cycling & Mountain Biking

A lot of people use pedal power on O'ahu, both for transportation and for fun. **Biki** (*gobiki.org*) is Honolulu's bike-share system, with stations all over town. The **Bike Shop**, with locations in Honolulu, 'Aiea and Kailua, is a good place to get a bike.

The state and Honolulu are busily adding bike lanes across the island, although usage is spotty and they are still often blocked by parked vehicles. Waikīkī's beachfront walks are excellent for cycling.

Mountain biking is popular, which is no surprise given all the trails. In Honolulu, the myriad trails off **Round Top Drive** (p106) offer a lot of challenging rides up and down and around the lush mountains. Near Pearl Harbor, there's the lofty **'Aiea Loop Trail** (p117).

Surfing, Hiking & Diving

O'ahu is a superb destination for surfing (p40), hiking (p42), and diving and snorkeling (p44). There are a huge number of opportunities around the entire island's coast and across its lush interior.

HORSEBACK RIDING
Go for a horseback ride on the beach on the North Shore with **Hawaii Polo Trail Rides** (p179).

OUTRIGGER CANOEING
Paddle furiously to ride the surf to shore in **Waikīkī** (p84) – although the pros do 90% of the work.

WHALE-WATCHING
Watch for migrating whales off the shores of O'ahu from December to May. **Diamond Head** (p94) is a good place for spotting.

GOLF
Tee off at the award-winning **Ko Olina Golf Club** (p127), a landscaped oasis of green – it's one of 40 courses on O'ahu.

ACTION AREAS

Where to find Honolulu, Waikīkī & O'ahu's best outdoor activities.

Hiking

1. Makapu'u Point Lighthouse (p139)
2. Pu'u 'Ohi'a (p105)
3. Ka'ena Point (p131)
4. Mānoa Falls (p108)
5. Diamond Head (p99)

Surfing

1. Hale'iwa Ali'i Beach Park (p172)
2. Pūpūkea (p180)
3. Waikīkī (p81)
4. Ala Moana Regional Park (p74)
5. Kaka'ako Waterfront Park (p74)

Beaches

1. Queen's Surf Beach (p82)
2. Kailua Beach Park (p146)
3. Lanikai Beach (p146)
4. Kahaloa & Ulukou Beaches (p90)
5. Magic Island (p75)

0 10 km
0 5 miles
Kayaking
1 Kāne'ohe Bay (p156)
2 Mokulua Islands (p152)
3 Mokoli'i Island (p162)
PACIFIC OCEAN
Snorkeling & Diving
1 Hanauma Bay (p138)
2 Kaimana Beach (p82)
3 Diamond Head Beach Park (p94)
4 Kāne'ohe Bay (p156)
5 Mākaha Beach Park (p130)
Makahoa Point
Moku'auia (Goat Island)
Lā'ie
Kaipapa'u Valley
Hau'ula
Windward Coast
Punalu'u
Kahana Bay
Hau'ula Forest Reserve
Kahana
Ka'a'awa
Ahupua'a o Kahana State Park
Kualoa
Waiāhole Forest Reserve
Waikāne
Kāne'ohe Bay
Ahu o Laka Island
Mokumanu State Seabird Sanctuary
Kipapa Stream
Waiāhole
Kahalu'u
Moku o Lo'e (Coconut Island)
'Āhuimanu
Ewa Forest Reserve
He'eia
Waimano Trail
Kalauao Stream
Popoi'a Island (Flat Island)
Pearl City
Kāne'ohe
John A Burns Fwy
Kailua
Moanalua Stream
Olomana
Lanikai
'Aiea
Ho'omaluhia Botanical Garden
Wailea Point
Pearl Harbor
Maunawili
Mānana Island (Rabbit Island)
Maunawili Trail
Likelike Hwy
Pali Hwy
Waimānalo
Kaohikaipu Island
Daniel K Inouye International Airport
Honolulu
Mānoa Stream
Koko Crater
Mākua Bay
Waikīkī
Kaimukī
Kahala
Hawai'i Kai
Lāwa'i Bay
Black Point (Kupikipiki'o)
Ka'iwi Channel

HONOLULU, WAIKĪKĪ & O'AHU

THE GUIDE

Chapters in this section are organized by hubs and their surrounding areas. We see the hub as your base in the destination, where you'll find unique experiences, local insights, insider tips and expert recommendations. It's also your gateway to the surrounding area, where you'll see what and how much you can do from there.

Hanauma Bay (p138)

SAN HOYANO/SHUTTERSTOCK

MATT MUNRO/LONELY PLANET

For places to stay in Honolulu & Waikīkī, see p118

Above: Waikīkī Beach (p81); Right: Waikīkī view from Diamond Head (p99)

THE MAIN AREAS

DOWNTOWN HONOLULU
Royal heritage and colonial past. **p58**

CHINATOWN
Historic and walkable area. **p66**

KAKA'AKO & ALA MOANA
Trendy shopping, great eating options and waterfront parks. **p74**

WAIKĪKĪ
Resorts, beaches and the holiday life. **p81**

Researched by
Ryan Ver Berkmoes

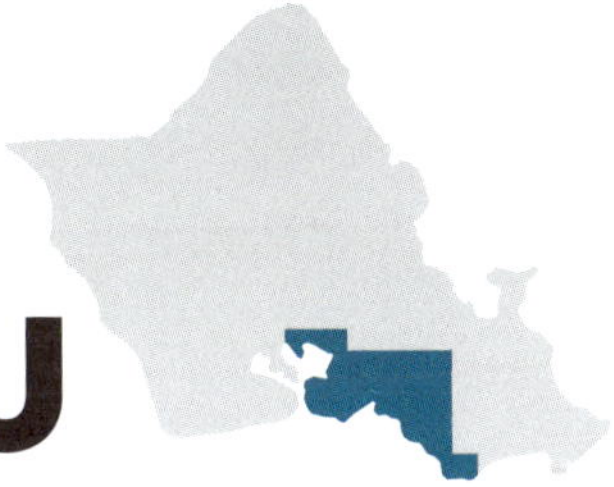

Honolulu & Waikīkī

BEACHES, CULTURE, DINING & NATURE

It's hard to imagine a trip to Hawai'i without time in the neighborhoods, beaches and mountains that define this city.

In Honolulu, you get to rub elbows with today's Hawai'i. A boisterous, vibrant Polynesian capital, Honolulu is steeped in history and delivers an island-style mixed plate of experiences. See extraordinary royal buildings from before the monarchy was dethroned and a sovereign nation was stolen. Then plunge into the warren of Chinatown, the city's oldest neighborhood.

MARIDAV/SHUTTERSTOCK

Explore Kaka'ako and Ala Moana, with hip restaurants and shops. Or wander old Kaimukī, an appealing district of shops, cafes and pubs. On the shore, ocean breezes rustle palm trees, while in the cool, mist-shrouded Ko'olau Range and valleys, tropical-forest hiking trails offer postcard city views.

Technically part of Honolulu, Waikīkī's name alone will have you thinking of boundless horizons, Pacific sunsets and hula dancers gently swaying to the beat of island rhythms. Once the playground of Hawaiian royalty, this remains O'ahu's quintessential ribbon of sand.

Waikīkī captures the popular imagination as an idyllic tropical island vacation complete with flower lei, aloha shirts and romance. Hawai'i's most-visited beach offers more than mass tourism, with stylish resort hotels, backstreet hangouts and welcoming restaurants. Take a surfing lesson, sip a mai tai as the sun sets, listen to lilting 'ukuleles and just enjoy life.

Honolulu is bookended by iconic sights. To the east, Diamond Head is the backdrop to Waikīkī photos. And it offers a superb short hike to a view of the city, the green mountains and the blue Pacific. To the west, Pearl Harbor is a destination for most visitors. The USS *Arizona* Memorial and other sights and museums explain the events of December 7, 1941, and a war that still resonates today.

DIAMOND HEAD & KAIMUKĪ
Thrilling nature and neighborhood delights. **p94**

GREATER HONOLULU
Mountain hikes, museums and plate lunches. **p100**

PEARL HARBOR & 'AIEA
Memories of world-changing events. **p110**

FROM THE AIRPORT

Most visitors arriving at Honolulu's airport will head to Waikīkī. Many rent cars, only to discover pricey and limited parking in the resort enclave. Depending on traffic, a car, taxi or rideshare can take 20 to 45 minutes. Buses are slow.

CAR

Having a car in Honolulu is a hassle. Parking is at a premium, whether in garages or along the streets, where non-wired meters gobble up quarters. Roads are often potholed or blocked by construction. Traffic is coagulated.

RIDESHARE & TAXI

Grabbing a taxi at a resort or summoning a ride with an app is easy. Distances are short, which helps keep charges down. Still, given the city's sprawl, the number of rides you take can quickly add up. Within Waikīkī, you can get around on foot.

PUBLIC TRANSIT

Honolulu's bus system, **TheBus** *(thebus.org)*, covers much of the city, if you have the time. Service can be infrequent, and with transfers, journey times can be long. The official app is essential for navigating the routes. The train system, **Skyline** *(honolulutransit.org)*, serves the airport and the west (p110).

Find Your Way

Honolulu's 68 sq miles stretch along O'ahu's southern Pacific coast. From the bustling flatlands, the city extends up valleys, surrounded by the emerald *pali* (cliffs) of the Ko'olau Range. Daytime traffic on the city's freeways and surface streets is legendary. Neighborhoods are walkable, but longer journeys require wheels for navigating the sprawl.

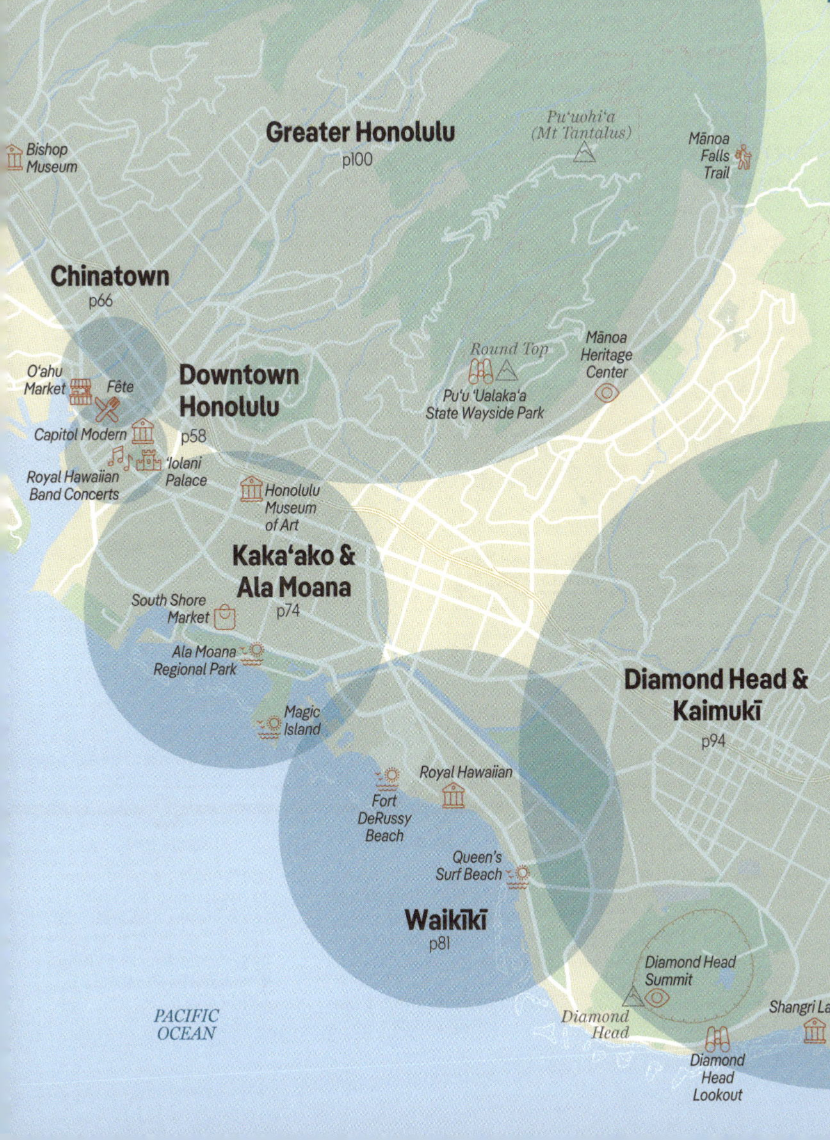

Plan Your Days

Culture or beaches? Nature or shopping? A plate lunch or a fine meal? At least your wardrobe won't matter – whatever makes you comfortable. And maintain this mantra: hang loose, stay mellow.

POMINOZ/SHUTTERSTOCK

USS *Arizona* Memorial (p113)

Day 1

Morning

- Walk **Waikīkī's beach** (p90). Take your time and ponder the **statues** (p87) of royalty and surfers. Soak up the views.

Afternoon

- Have **lunch beachside** (p83). Reflect on your walk and choose a beach. There's the perfect swimming at **Queen's Surf Beach** (p82), the buzzy people-watching of **Kahaloa & Ulukou Beaches** (p81), or the uncrowded expanse of **Fort DeRussy Beach** (p81).

Evening

- Choose from Waikīkī's many fine restaurants for **dinner** (p84). Afterward, revel in the wealth of live music on offer. Start at the **House Without a Key** (p87) and then follow your ears from venue to venue.

HIGH SEASON

SHOULDER SEASON (LOW SEASON: MAY)

JAN & FEB

The high season runs past New Year's. Then, the holiday rush tapers off as crowds return to the mainland. Meanwhile, **Chinese New Year** adds color throughout town, most explosively in Chinatown with a lion dance parade.

MAR

Coinciding with a bump in visitors thanks to Spring Break, **Honolulu Festival** is the city's largest cultural event. A celebration of Asian, Pacific and Hawaiian cultures, it features artists and performers, plus a huge parade.

APR–JUN

Late spring is a wonderful time to visit Honolulu and Waikīkī. Crowds are few, days are longer and the weather is great (as always!). Watch for May's **King Kamehameha Floral Parade**, which honors the royal heritage.

Day 2

Morning

- Tour **Chinatown** (p72) on foot. Prowl the **markets** (p66) and buy treats at a **bakery** (p70). Buy a **lei** (p69) and a **book** (p71) and enjoy unusual drinks in vintage settings, possibly amid faux-tiki surrounds. Consider a **tattoo** (p69).

Afternoon

- After lunch, walk to Honolulu's historic core. Tour **'Iolani Palace** (p58), tip your sunhat to the **Kamehameha the Great Statue** (p63). Reflect on colonial history at the **Hawaiian Mission Houses Historic Site** (p60). Learn about the islands as a state at the **State Capitol** (p60).

Evening

- Return to Chinatown for dinner at its unmatched selection of **restaurants** (p68).

Day 3

Morning

- Understand the attack on **Pearl Harbor** (p112) with a visit to the **USS *Arizona* Memorial** (p113), having reserved a spot weeks before. Walk the decks of the **USS *Missouri*** (p114) and learn about WWII at the **Pearl Harbor Aviation Museum** (p114).

Afternoon

- Have a cheap and cheerful lunch in **'Aiea** (p111) or **Kalihi** (p104). Consider a spot of shopping in **Kaka'ako** and **Ala Moana** (p78). Then venture up the green Mānoa Valley for the popular hike to **Mānoa Falls** (p108).

Evening

- Stroll the inviting streets of old **Kaimukī** (p97) and pick a place for dinner. Return to Waikīkī and finish with more **live music** (p87).

HIGH SEASON | SHOULDER SEASON (LOW SEASON: SEP) | HIGH SEASON

JUL–SEP

Late summer brings two unmissable cultural events. July's **Prince Lot Hula Festival** celebrates hula and traditional culture. September's **Aloha Festivals** is Hawai'i's greatest cultural event, drawing more than 100,000 people for local music and dance.

OCT & NOV

The state's food fame is celebrated in late October with the **Hawai'i Food & Wine Festival**, when Honolulu is the center of the Hawaiian food universe. Visitors flood in for the Thanksgiving holiday.

DEC

Early December is relatively quiet after the mad rush of Thanksgiving, but excitement and crowds build as Christmas nears. Honolulu takes the holiday seriously, with decorations, lights, parades and festivals in profusion.

Downtown Honolulu

ROYAL HERITAGE AND COLONIAL HISTORY

GETTING AROUND

Downtown Honolulu is easily walked. It's a park once and forget about the car kind of place (and you'll find street parking and plenty of pay lots). If coming from Waikīkī, do yourself a favor and don't drive at all. Make a day of it by walking the under 2 miles via Ala Moana Regional Park and the waterfront and Kaka'ako. Or take one of the many buses. Chinatown is immediately west.

Downtown Honolulu was center stage for the political intrigue and social upheavals that ripped apart the fabric of Hawai'i during the 19th century. You can take in a lot of Hawai'i history on a short stroll that takes you past significant Hawaiian royal sites, including the unmissable 'Iolani Palace. Churches and early homes of the colonists and missionaries can also be visited. More importantly, the State Capitol is here with the courts, legislature and governor's office.

Down by the water, you can view it all from the iconic Aloha Tower, even if you might have to dodge crowds of strolling visitors from huge, hulking cruise ships. Busy during the workday, Downtown is much quieter at night.

Elegant 'Iolani Palace

Evocative home of lost royalty

No other place evokes a more poignant sense of Hawai'i's history than the **'Iolani Palace** *(iolanipalace.org; adult/child $28/13)*. It was built under King David Kalākaua in 1882, and the kingdom was overthrown by powerful US-connected business interests (for more, see p219) just over a decade later.

In 1895 the former queen, Lili'uokalani, who had succeeded her brother David to the throne, was convicted of treason and spent nine months imprisoned in her former home. Later, the palace served as the capitol of the republic, then the territory and later the state of Hawai'i. In 1969 the government finally moved into the current State Capitol. Fans of the original *Hawaii Five-0* TV series will recognize the palace as McGarrett's headquarters.

Take a docent-led or self-guided **tour** (buy tickets in advance online) to see 'Iolani's restored interior. If you're short on time, you can browse the exhibits in the basement, including royal regalia, historical photographs and a reconstructed kitchen.

Highlights of the expansive palace grounds include the former barracks of the Royal Household Guards. Nearby, the domed **Keli'iponi Hale** pavilion dates to 1883. Escape the sun in **Banyan Tree Terrace**, an ancient grove on the north side.

TOP TIP

Downtown Honolulu has few accommodations. The vast majority of rooms are in Waikīkī, which is not far to the east. Weekday cafes and fast-food joints for office workers and students abound. Choices are limited at night and on weekends, but many great options in Chinatown and Kaka'ako are nearby.

DOWNTOWN HONOLULU

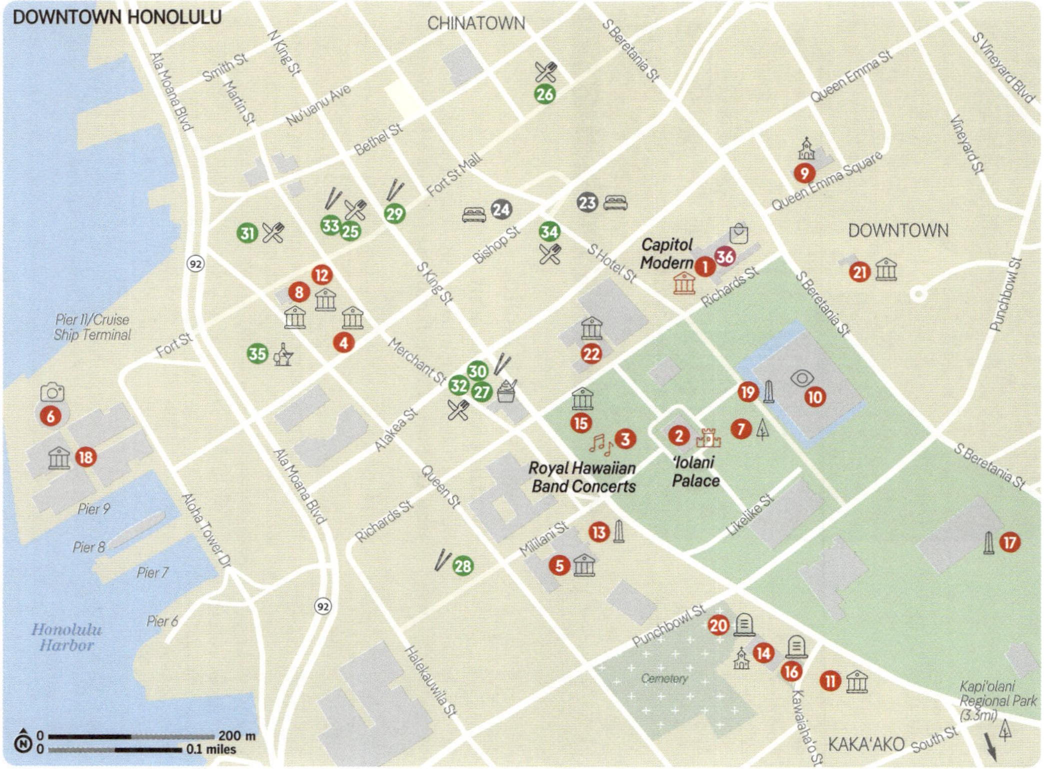

HIGHLIGHTS
1 Capitol Modern
2 'Iolani Palace
3 Royal Hawaiian Band Concerts

SIGHTS
4 Alexander & Baldwin Building
5 Ali'iōlani Hale
6 Aloha Tower
7 Banyan Tree Terrace
8 C Brewer & Co Building
9 Cathedral of St Andrew
10 Hawai'i State Capitol
11 Hawaiian Mission Houses Historic Site
12 Judd Building
13 Kamehameha the Great Statue
14 Kawaiaha'o Church
15 Keli'iponi Hale
16 Mission Cemetery
17 Nagasaki Peace Bell
18 Pacific Islands Ocean Exploration Center
19 Queen Lili'uokalani Statue
20 Tomb of King Lunalilo
21 Washington Place
22 YWCA Laniākea Building

SLEEPING
23 AC Hotel Honolulu
24 Aston at the Executive Centre Hotel

EATING
see 22 Cafe Julia
25 Downtown Coffee
26 Drip Studio
27 Honolulu Rose Cake Shop
28 Irifune Restaurant
29 Marugame Udon
30 Onigiri Onibe
31 PAI Honolulu
32 Podmore Casual
33 Tonkatsu Sangi
34 'Umeke

DRINKING & NIGHTLIFE
35 Bar Leather Apron

SHOPPING
36 Mori by Art+Flea

THE ROYAL HAWAIIAN BAND

Founded in 1836 by King Kamehameha III, the beloved **Royal Hawaiian Band** *(rhb-music.com)* is the only band in the US with a royal legacy. And it's the only full-time municipal band, as it's part of the Honolulu government. Primarily a brass band, it has over 40 musicians and specializes in Hawaiian songs, especially those written by the royal family as well as 19th-century classics and big band and whimsical new works.

The band performs across O'ahu, but you can find them most Fridays at noon on the grounds at 'Iolani Palace. These free concerts are popular and the seats go fast, but there's always room on the vast lawn.

You can also catch them in Waikīkī's Kapi'olani Regional Park (p94) on Sundays.

JOHN SEATON CALLAHANR/GETTY IMAGES

Aloha Tower

Hawai'i's State Capitol

The state's democratic heart

Built during the architecturally cliche-busting 1960s, the **Hawai'i State Capitol building** *(free)* is a poster child of conceptual postmodernism: two cone-shaped legislative chambers have sloping walls to represent volcanoes; the supporting columns shaped like coconut palms symbolize the archipelago's eight main islands; and a large encircling pool represents the Pacific Ocean. Visitors can walk through the open-air rotunda and peer into the legislative chambers. All the exposed wood is *Acacia koa*, which only grows in Hawai'i.

Pick up a self-guiding tour brochure from the governor's office, Room 415. Interesting guides and digital resources are available online at governor.hawaii.gov/contact-us/hawai'i-state-capitol-tours. Some elements may be hidden by construction barriers as the state tries to deal with decades of deferred maintenance, such as the leaking 'ocean.' Protestors along Beretania St demand action on issues such as post-fire recovery on Maui.

Where Colonial Hawai'i Began

Relive the 1820s

Occupying the original headquarters of the Sandwich Islands mission that forever changed the course of Hawaiian history, the **Hawaiian Mission Houses Historic Site** *(missionhouses.org)* offers a fascinating look at when missionaries arrived in the islands. It's free to explore the grounds with their free-range cocks, but you'll need to take a **tour** *($20, reserve online)* to see inside the buildings.

The first missionaries packed more than their bags when they left Boston in 1819 – they brought a prefabricated wooden house – pedantically called the **Frame House** – with them around the Horn. Designed to withstand New England winter winds, the small windows instead blocked out Honolulu's cooling trade winds, which kept the two-story house hellaciously hot.

The **Mission Cemetery** across Kawaiahaʻo St offers a who's who of colonial history: early Protestant missionaries are buried alongside other important figures, including the notorious Sanford Dole, who became the first territorial governor of Hawaiʻi after Queen Liliʻuokalani was overthrown. Note how the signage would have you believe that the space is filled with 'Scottish missionaries,' when the many graves marked 'Castle,' 'Cooke' and 'Dole' indicate that this is where you'll find the early Europeans most responsible for the betrayal of the monarchy, the exploitation of the islands and the creation of the Big Five (p63).

Towering Aloha

See the sea, see the city

Built in 1926, the 10-story landmark **Aloha Tower** on Pier 9 was once Honolulu's tallest building. In the golden days when all tourists arrived by ship, this pre-WWII waterfront icon greeted every visitor. These days, Hawaiʻi Pacific University occupies the mostly defunct Aloha Tower Marketplace, which was meant to ensnare people arriving at the cruise-ship docks. Take the elevator to the top-floor **observation deck** *(check hours; free)* for fabulous 360-degree views across Honolulu.

Nearby, the **Pacific Islands Ocean Exploration Center** *(sanctuaries.noaa.gov; free)* is a simple room of displays with an impressive name and plans to grow. Run by the National Marine Sanctuaries, it highlights the wonders of the ocean reserves that stretch hundreds of miles beyond the Hawaiian Islands.

Palace of Justice

Regal quarters for Hawaiʻi's legal heritage

The monumental **Aliʻiōlani Hale** was ordered by the Hawaiian monarchy in 1874 to be a royal palace, although it was never used as such. Designed by Australian architect Thomas Rowe, the 'House of Heavenly Kings' today houses the state Supreme Court. Don't miss the **King Kamehameha V Judiciary History Center** *(jhchawaii.org; free)*, where you can browse historical displays about martial law during WWII, the overthrow of the monarchy and the reign of Kamehameha I. Fans of the recent iteration of *Hawaii Five-0* will recognize it as McGarrett's headquarters.

HONOLULU'S HISTORY

In 1793 the English *Butterworth* became the first foreign ship to sail into what is now Honolulu Harbor. In 1809 Kamehameha the Great moved his royal court from Waikīkī to Honolulu to control the burgeoning international trade. In the 1820s Hotel St was lined with bars and brothels thronged by crews of whaling ships. Newly arrived Christian missionaries were not impressed. In 1893 a small group of their descendants seized control of the kingdom from Queen Liliʻuokalani and declared an independent republic. Hawaiʻi was annexed by the USA in 1898.

Until WWII, Honolulu was the sleepy center of an island economy built on sugarcane and pineapples. Postwar, the population exploded and in the 1960s jet travel sparked the tourism boom.

EATING & DRINKING IN DOWNTOWN HONOLULU: TOP CHOICES

Cafe Julia: In the landmark Julia Morgan–designed YWCA building opposite ʻIolani Palace; superb service, cuisine and outdoor seating. *11am-2pm Mon-Fri* $$

Podmore Casual: Fine dining with a short menu offering luxe sandwiches, seafood, steak and pasta. Popular for brunch; has a fine bar. *11am-10pm Tue-Sun* $$

PAI Honolulu: Top-end dining with tasting menus of internationally accented American fare. Live vocalists some nights. *5:30-10pm Thu-Sat* $$$

Bar Leather Apron: Old-school with serious cocktails crafted by wizards. A casual yet elegant dark bar for Honolulu's best cocktails. *5pm-midnight Wed-Sat*

NAGASAKI PEACE BELL

Honolulu's ties to the Japanese city of Nagasaki are many. For one, the torpedoes that killed so many sailors and sunk so many ships at Pearl Harbor were manufactured in Nagasaki.

Later, after the war was over and Nagasaki became the second city in the world (and last to date) destroyed by a nuclear bomb, the city's people made reproductions of the bell from their destroyed Christian cathedral and sent them to Japan's wartime enemies. Honolulu received the USA's because of the Pearl Harbor connection.

Today, it's known as the Nagasaki Peace Bell and is part of a lovely sculpture that stands east of the State Capitol. Every year around December 7, the bell is rung at a ceremony that brings together people from both nations.

Coral Kawaiaha'o Church

The 'Westminster Abbey of Hawai'i'

Kawaiaha'o Church *(kawaiahao.org; free)*, O'ahu's oldest, was built on the site where the first missionaries constructed a thatch church shortly after their arrival in 1820. The original structure seated 300 Hawaiians on *lauhala* mats, woven from *hala* (screwpine) leaves. This 1842 New England Gothic-style church is made of 14,000 coral slabs, which divers chiseled out of O'ahu's underwater reefs – a weighty task that took four years.

The **Tomb of King Lunalilo** is found at the main entrance to the Kawaiaha'o Church grounds and features small fountains. Lunalilo died from tuberculosis on February 3, 1874, after a short reign of a year. He was Hawai'i's first elected monarch as King Kamehameha V died in 1872 without naming a successor.

Hawai'i's Art at Capitol Modern

Intriguing works in a beautiful building

The state's art museum, **Capitol Modern** *(capitolmodern.org; free)*, displays contemporary art from across Hawai'i.

The state mandates that 1% of the budget for taxpayer-financed construction projects be spent on public art and a rotating selection of these works are on display. Special exhibitions of paintings, sculptures, fiber art, photography and mixed media are displayed around themes, such as Hawai'i's Polynesian heritage, modern social issues or the island's natural beauty.

Special events are a delight. **First Friday** is a monthly evening of live entertainment and free events such as Pride celebrations. Celebratory **Island Pulse** takes place on the third Friday and features local tunes and reggae, plus food, drink and crafts vendors. The excellent lobby shop, **Mori by Art+-Flea** *(moribyaf.com)*, is filled with goods by local creatives.

Tidy Washington Place

A seaman's home lives on

Formerly the governor's residence, the colonial-style **Washington Place** *(washingtonplace.hawaii.gov; free)* mansion was built in 1846 by US sea captain John Dominis. The captain's son became the governor of O'ahu and married the Hawaiian princess who later became Queen Lili'uokalani. After the queen was released from house arrest inside 'Iolani Palace in 1896, she lived here until her death in 1917. Public **tours** are offered at 10am Thursdays; reserve online several weeks ahead.

EATING IN DOWNTOWN HONOLULU: LUNCH PICKS

'Umeke: Organic island produce, natural foods, and a vegetarian- and vegan-friendly take-out deli counter. Large dining area. *8am-2pm Mon-Fri* $

Onigiri Onibe: Lines form early at this shop, where you can choose from over 40 ingredients, including salmon and pork belly, for custom *musubi. 7am-2pm Mon-Sat* $

Irifune Restaurant: Popular Japanese lunch spot with the slogan: 'shut up and eat.' There are tree-shaded tables on a pedestrian plaza. *11am-2pm Mon-Fri* $

Tonkatsu Sangi: Owned by a local family, this lunch place serves some of Downtown's best Japanese fare. There are several more neighboring options. *10:30am-2pm Mon-Fri* $

THEODORE TRIMMER/SHUTTERSTOCK

Queen Lili'uokalani Statue

Stolid Cathedral of St Andrew

Echoes of Queen Victoria

King Kamehameha IV built the **Cathedral of St Andrew** *(cathedralhawaii.org; free)* and founded the Anglican Church in Hawai'i in 1861. Queen Emma, Kamehameha's wife and royal consort, had an affinity for Queen Victoria, whom she had visited in Britain, and raised the actual money to build the cathedral. The cornerstone was laid in 1867 on St Andrew's Day – hence the French Gothic building's name. Wander out back where there is a lonely **statue of Queen Emma**.

Significant Statues

Important royals

Standing before the Ali'iōlani Hale, the gilded bronze **Kamehameha the Great Statue** faces 'Iolani Palace. Note: this is the second statue; the original was lost on its way to Hawai'i from Itay. Later recovered from the ocean floor, it now stands in Kohala on Hawai'i, the Big Island, where Kamehameha I was born.

The **Queen Lili'uokalani Statue** stoically holds a copy of the Hawaiian constitution she wrote in 1893 in a futile attempt to strengthen Hawaiian rule in the face of US aggression; 'Aloha 'Oe,' a popular song she composed; and *kumulipo*, the traditional Hawaiian chant of creation.

THE BIG FIVE

The Big Five were the American corporations that effectively ran the Hawaiian Territory in the early 20th century. Through sugar plantations and trade, they controlled the local economy. Today, their architectural legacy survives in a tight cluster Downtown.

The stunning 1929 **Alexander & Baldwin Building** combines powerful authority with tropical flair. Note the height of each floor and the veranda up top that rings the zenith of the palm-fronted and imposing facade. Asian and Hawaiian details abound throughout.

Around the corner, the 1899 **Judd Building** was once home to various Big Five entities and their financiers, the Bank of Hawai'i. Next door, the 1930 **C Brewer & Co Building** is a fascinating tropical confection with wide breezeways and even hints of residential style.

EATING & DRINKING IN DOWNTOWN HONOLULU: QUICK PICKS

Drip Studio: At this locally owned cafe, choose from over 40 beans from small roasters. Good snacks and baked goods too. *7am-2pm Mon-Sat* $

Downtown Coffee: Looking nondescript in the lobby of a Fort St Mall office building, this locally owned coffee vendor does superb brews and snacks. *6am-2:30pm Mon-Sat* $

Marugame Udon: Popular chain serving noodle soups and other freshly made Japanese dishes; at the Downtown outlet your food seems ready almost as you order. *10am-7pm* $$

Honolulu Rose Cake Shop: Don't settle for a candy bar when you can have an exquisite cake from this sweet shop. Treats are made fresh daily. *9am-3pm Mon-Fri* $

WALKING TOUR

Historic Honolulu on Foot

Honolulu's historical district spans more than 200 years. It's so compact that you can take your time and still easily savor all the sights. There's a lot of intriguing history and art here, which is right next to Downtown's tall buildings and only a 10-minute walk from both Chinatown and Kaka'ako. Enjoy this tour at your leisure – it can take anywhere from one hour to most of a day.

'Iolani Palace

Start at ❶ **'Iolani Palace** (p58), the only royal palace in the US. At the back of the palace, check out the massive banyan trees, then head *mauka* (toward the mountains) to the ❷ **Queen Lili'uokalani Statue** (p63) standing between the palace and the State Capitol building. Lili'uokalani was queen at the time of the overthrow of the Kingdom of Hawai'i in 1893.

The Walk: Go towards Beretania St.

Hawai'i State Capitol

Built in the 1960s, after Hawai'i became the 50th state in 1959, the ❸ **State Capitol** (p60) building is unlike any other and takes conceptual postmodernism to a new level. Out front on Beretania St, check out the impressive stylized ❹ **Father Damien Statue**, the now-sainted priest who died of Hansen's disease with his flock on Moloka'i in 1889.

The Walk: Cross Beretania St to Washington Pl. (If you think Beretania is an unusual name for a local street, you're right. It came from the Hawaiian transliteration of the word Britannia.)

Washington Place & the Cathedral

A colonial-style vision in white from 1846, ❺ **Washington Place** (p62), formerly the governor's official residence (a newer house on the gated grounds now serves that role), is now used for ceremonial events. Admire it before carrying on northwest along

CHRISTIAN MUELLER/SHUTTERSTOCK

Hawai'i State Capitol (p60)

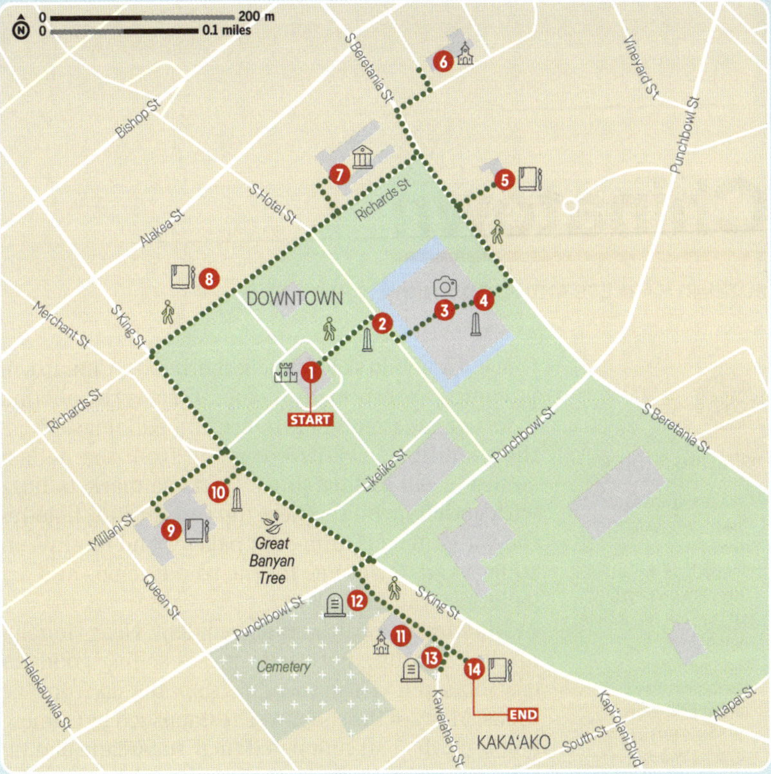

Beretania St to the 1867 6 **Cathedral of St Andrew** (p63).

The Walk: Walk southwest along Richards St.

Capitol Modern & YWCA

The grand 1928 Spanish Mission Revival-style building with two big heads out front is 7 **Capitol Modern** (p62). Further along Richards St, the 1927 8 **YWCA Laniākea Building** is the work of the great Bay Area architect Julia Morgan, whose works include Hearst Castle in California. The Beaux Arts–style facade's elegance is surpassed by the interior courtyard's mannered, tropical charm.

The Walk: Turn left on King St.

Ali'iōlani Hale

You'll know you're at 9 **Ali'iōlani Hale** (p61), now the Supreme Court of Hawai'i, when you see the magnificent gold-helmeted 10 **Kamehameha the Great Statue** (p63).

The Walk: Walk down S King St past the vast canopy of a **great banyan tree** to the nearby church.

Kawaiaha'o Church

11 **Kawaiaha'o Church** (p62) was built in 1842 in New England Gothic style and nicknamed the 'Westminster Abbey of the Pacific.' Don't miss the 12 **Tomb of King Lunalilo** (p62) out front. Behind the church off King St, the small 13 **Mission Cemetery** (p61) is a who's who of local 19th-century missionaries and robber barons.

The Walk: Just across Kawaiaha'o St is the final stop.

Hawaiian Mission Houses Historic Site

The 14 **Hawaiian Mission Houses Historic Site** (p60) is on the site of the original headquarters of the Sandwich Islands Mission, which forever changed the course of Hawaiian history.

Chinatown

BUZZING MARKETS AND FOODIE HIGHLIGHTS

GETTING AROUND

Chinatown is west of Downtown. Its mostly narrow streets are wonderfully walkable. There are parking lots, but they are expensive during the week. Numerous major bus routes run along King and Beretania Sts, many running as far as Waikīkī. Although you'll see the disruptive construction down by the water, the Skyline train running through here to Ala Moana won't open until at least 2031.

TOP TIP

The north side of Chinatown, particularly along Nu'uanu Stream and the River St Pedestrian Mall, should be avoided after dark. There are a lot of unhoused people in Chinatown, which discourages some from wandering the streets at night. Rideshares and taxis are easily summoned; street crime remains the exception.

One of Honolulu's oldest neighborhoods, Chinatown is a must-see, especially on foot. Discoveries abound in its narrow streets of 19th-century buildings, where the granite sidewalks are made from the ballast stones of old sailing ships. Daytime markets buzz with activity while endless top restaurants, hole-in-the-wall kitchens, dim-sum palaces and family-run stalls await. Save time for the trendy shops and art galleries. And buy a lei!

Chinatown's location is no accident. Near Honolulu's busy trading port, enterprises selling goods to city folks and visiting seafarers sprang up from the 1820s. Many of the shops were established by Chinese laborers who had completed their sugarcane plantation contracts. Some opened raucous bars catering to sailors. Though the most successful families have long since moved away, new arrivals, mostly from across Asia, keep Chinatown vibrant. The neighborhood's heritage is on explosive display every Chinese New Year (late January to mid-February). Festivities include a parade with flamboyant lion dances.

Chinatown's Vibrant Markets

Seafood, produce and more

Chinatown's frenetic daytime energy comes from its markets and food shops. Noodle factories, pastry shops and produce stalls line the narrow sidewalks, always crowded with cart-pulling vendors and families. In these busy warrens, you'll see the whole range of O'ahu's bounty from land and sea. Plus, you'll see all manner of textiles and other daily needs.

Like a daily farmers market, the stalls inside **Kekaulike Market** sell whole fish, dry goods, prepared foods and Hawai'i's plethora of produce. Out front, vendors hawk fruit and vegetables from displays on the pedestrianized street.

The adjoining **Maunakea Marketplace** hosts popular food stalls, including the standout **Maguro Brothers** *(magurobrothershawaii.com)*. Wind your way to this little stall in the

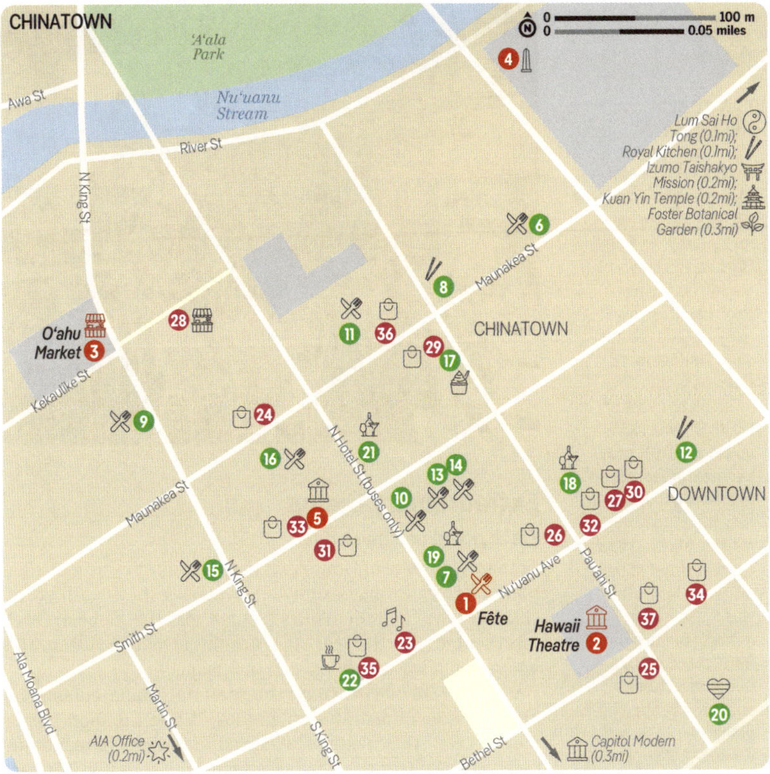

HIGHLIGHTS
1 Fête
2 Hawaii Theatre
3 O'ahu Market

SIGHTS
4 Dr Sun Yat-sen Statue
5 Hawai'i Heritage Center

EATING
6 Duc's Bistro
7 Giovedì
8 Lam's Kitchen
9 Lee's Bakery & Kitchen
10 Lucky Belly
see 28 Maguro Brothers
11 Maunakea Marketplace
12 Mei Sum
13 Mille Fête Bakery
see 22 O'Kims
14 Po'ai
15 Senia
16 Sing Cheong Yuan Bakery
17 Wing Ice Cream Parlor

DRINKING & NIGHTLIFE
18 EP Bar
19 Manifest
20 Scarlet Honolulu
21 Skull & Crown Trading Co
22 Tea at 1024

ENTERTAINMENT
23 Dragon Upstairs

SHOPPING
24 Cindy's Lei Shoppe
25 Fighting Eel
26 Hook & Hide
27 Hound & Quail
28 Kekaulike Market
29 MP Lei Shop
30 Native Books at Arts & Letters
31 Old Ironside Tattoo
32 Roberta Oaks
33 Sig on Smith
34 Skull-Face Books & Vinyl
35 Tin Can Mailman
36 Tina's Lei Shop
37 Valia Honolulu

back where everything sparkles, especially the fish. For lunch, sashimi comes in many forms atop rice bowls, or opt for the perfectly grilled garlic 'ahi (yellowfin tuna) or teriyaki salmon.

An institution since 1904, **O'ahu Market** has everything an Asian-food cook needs: ginger root, quail eggs, jasmine rice, luscious slabs of 'ahi, long beans and salted jellyfish. Amid the medley of spice smells, you'll catch a whiff of the harbor just steps away.

LAST CALL BEFORE WAR

Before WWII, Hotel St was the notorious center of shore leave for sailors from Pearl Harbor. The crews of the big battleships each had their 'own' bar – a place the men would gather for raucous nights out.

The block south of Smith St even today still looks like it could be a set for *From Here to Eternity*, the classic film about prewar military life on O'ahu. Linger in front of the old vet at No 19; this was the longtime home of Smith's Union Bar. Closed in 2026 due to structural concerns (reopening plans are ceaseless), it was bar of choice for the USS *Arizona* crew, the battleship that was sunk on December 7, 1941, with a loss of more than 1100 men (the last survivor died in 2024).

NANI WELCH KELI'IHO'OMALU FOR LONELY PLANET

Fête

Extraordinary Dining

Fresh, local and inventive

Chinatown is one of Honolulu's best and most exciting neighborhoods for dining. Casual Asian eateries, the beguiling cuisine of Hawai'i, and cuisines from across the globe are well represented. But the real stars are the inventive restaurants where you'll want to book well in advance.

At **Fête** *(fetehawaii.com)*, the seasonal island cuisine adheres to a local farm-to-table ethos. While the food menus may be short, the cocktails, wine and 'after dessert' menus are extensive. Among the bevy of awards showered on Fête are those for the creations of bartender Fabrice McCarthy, whose libations change seasonally.

The energy hits you when you enter **Senia** *(restaurantsenia.com)*, and the food is local and creative. Hot seats (reserve even further in advance) are the Chef's Counter seats, from where you look into the kitchen and see cooking techniques verging on mad science.

First Fridays in Chinatown

Monthly special events

Chinatown's atmospherically grungy and historic Nu'uanu Ave and Hotel St are the anchors for the monthly evening dose of urban art and culture, socializing and bar-hopping known

EATING IN CHINATOWN: TOP PICKS

Giovedì: One of Chinatown's hottest tables, with a fusion of Asian and Italian flavors. Enjoy flavor surprises in the romantic courtyard. *5-10pm Tue-Sun* $$

O'Kims: Superb, family-run Korean cafe with garden seating; bibimbap (bowl of mixed rice) is served in many ways using top-quality ingredients. *11am-9pm Mon-Sat* $$

Lucky Belly: This sleek bistro crafts hot and spicy Asian-fusion bites and mains, plus cocktails. Tables are packed elbows-to-shoulders. *5-10pm Mon-Sat* $$

Duc's Bistro: Swank French-Vietnamese bistro with a tiny bar; a culinary oasis for sophisticated fusion fare and excellent service. Book ahead. *4-9pm* $$

as **First Friday** *(firstfridayhawaii.com)*. From 5pm, many shops and galleries have special events and live music through 9pm. Drink specials in bars abound. A quick walk east, the art museum Capitol Modern (p62) has concerts starting at 6pm.

The Hawaii Theatre

Sumptuous entertainment

Who can resist the seductive glow of the elaborate neon signage at the **Hawaii Theatre** *(hawaiitheatre.com)*. This neoclassical landmark first opened in 1922, when silent films were played to the tunes of a pipe organ. Dubbed the 'Pride of the Pacific,' the theater ran continuous shows during WWII. After multi-million-dollar restorations in the 1990s, this nationally registered historic site is now a major venue for dance, music and theater. Performances include top Hawaiian musicians, contemporary plays, international touring acts and film festivals.

Chinatown Tours

Learn from the community

Local volunteers with family ties to the community run the **Hawai'i Heritage Center** *(hawaiiheritagecenter.org; $1)*, a crowded gallery with changing exhibitions about O'ahu's Chinese, Japanese and other ethnic communities. It runs excellent **Chinatown tours** *(per person $17-35)* Wednesday and Friday mornings. Book ahead.

Professional architects lead **AIA Chinatown Walking Tours** *(American Institute of Architects; aiahonolulu.org; $20)* on some Saturday mornings. The tours deconstruct Honolulu's most historic neighborhood, where you'll find some of Hawai'i's most significant architectural treasures. AIA also sells superb walking guides at its Downtown office and it runs tours of the Downtown area.

Get a Lei

The ultimate Hawaiian accessory

In Chinatown, a score of traditional lei makers continue a beautiful and fragrant tradition. Lei date back to the Polynesians, who wore garlands of everyday objects such as flowers and feathers for status, honor and beauty.

The tradition of giving lei to visitors to Hawai'i dates to the 19th-century ships that first brought tourists. Passengers were greeted by local vendors who would toss garlands around the

'STEWED, SCREWED & TATTOOED'

In Hawai'i, you're in the land of the tattoo. Long before ink became part of international pop culture, tattoos were an integral element of Hawaiian and Polynesian culture. The word itself, 'tattoo,' comes from the Polynesian word *tatau*, meaning 'to write.'

During WWII, 'stewed, screwed and tattooed' was the proud motto of sailors and soldiers stationed in Honolulu. Hotel St was lined with brothels, bars and tattoo parlors; the legendary guy to get your $3 tattoo from was Norman Collins, aka Sailor Jerry, who died in 1973. His memory lives on in his old shop, **Old Ironside Tattoo** *(instagram.com/oldironsidetattoo)*, and every June at the **Sailor Jerry Festival**, which features music, stand-up comedy and plenty of drinking.

EATING IN CHINATOWN: CHEAP EATS

Royal Kitchen: Line up for famous *manapua* (steamed or baked buns) with sweet and savory fillings at this humble storefront takeaway. Enjoy along the river. *6am-2pm* $

Mei Sum: It's dim sum from morning to night at this no-nonsense corner stop, cranking out little plates and Chinese mains. *9am-8pm Thu-Tue* $

Lam's Kitchen: Woks roar at lunchtime at this neighborhood stalwart; a recent spiff up has given it a fresh look. Great soups and Cantonese fare. *8am-3:30pm* $$

Wing Ice Cream Parlor: As small as a kiddie cone, this idiosyncratic shop makes superb treats with flavors that change on the whim of the sole proprietor. *3-9pm Tue-Sun* $

LEI TRADITIONS

During the golden era of steamship travel to the islands from the mainland in the mid-20th century, it was believed that if passengers threw their lei into the sea as their departing ship passed Diamond Head, and the flowers of the lei floated back toward the beach, they'd be guaranteed to return to Hawai'i someday. Given that the prevailing ocean current would drive the lei where everyone wanted it to go, it was a guaranteed dream come true.

In the 1970s, when United Airlines led the way in promoting tourism to Hawai'i, passengers could order their lei in advance, assured that a winsome local would be waiting to place it around their necks. No package-tour brochure was complete without a bullet-pointed 'Lei greeting!'

necks of *malihini* (newcomers, or foreigners). Today, there's still a signposted row of drive-up lei shops at the airport.

At the landmark **Cindy's Lei Shoppe**, you can watch aunties craft flower lei made of orchids, plumeria, twining maile, lantern *'ilima* (flowering ground cover) and ginger for all occasions (from $10). Most shops will pack a lei for you to carry back home.

Tina's Lei Shop anchors a cluster of a dozen fine choices. Nearby, **MP Lei Shop** is a chaotic collection of posies that could be works of folk art.

Edgy Nightlife

Options abound

Long the center of Honolulu's most raucous nightlife, Chinatown's edgy bar scene ranges from dive bars to stylish lounges.

Right above the low-key dive, Hank's Cafe, **Dragon Upstairs** *(instagram.com/thedragonupstairs)* is a hideaway with stylized masks on the walls and a sedate vibe. It hosts a rotating lineup of jazz, folk and karaoke. Try the specialty drink: the pineapple upside-down cake.

Skull & Crown Trading Co *(skullandcrowntrading.com)* puts a flamboyant spin on the already theatrical tiki bar motif with a dash of the occult. Eye-catching drinks and bites are served by a brilliant staff.

Ages-Old Temples

Incense-filled holy places

Founded in 1899, the **Lum Sai Ho Tong Society** *(free)* was one of more than 100 societies started by Chinese immigrants in Hawai'i to help preserve their cultural identity. The small and ornate **Tin Hau temple** on the 2nd floor is open in the morning for worship and visits. It's thick with incense and the scents of lavish fruit and floral offerings.

With its ceramic-tile roof and bright red columns, the ornate Chinese Buddhist **Kuan Yin Temple** *(free)* is Honolulu's oldest. The richly carved interior is filled with the sweet smell of burning incense. The temple is dedicated to Kuan Yin, bodhisattva of mercy, whose statue is the largest in the interior prayer hall.

Built by Japanese immigrants in 1906, **Izumo Taishakyo Mission** *(izumotaishahawaii.com; free)* is just across a serene stretch of the canal. It features the **Bell of Peace**, a gift from the people of Hiroshima. Thousands of good-luck amulets are sold here, especially on January 1, when the temple heaves with people seeking New Year's blessings.

EATING IN CHINATOWN: BAKERIES & CAFES

Lee's Bakery & Kitchen: A big range of fruit pies and snacks sold in simple surrounds. Try to eat only one silky custard tart! *6am-3pm* $

Sing Cheong Yuan Bakery: Handles big groups with aplomb. A traditional outlet for mooncakes and other Chinese treats. *7am-5pm* $

Mille Fête Bakery: An outlet of the noted restaurant serving up exquisite baked goods with tropical flavors. Try the 'banana butterscotch handpie.' *10am-6pm* $

Po'ai: Upscale cafe serving coffee drinks and superb iced tea with island flavors, plus baked goods from 'Ulu & Kalo Bakery featuring *'ulu* (breadfruit) and *kalo* (taro). *7:30am-4pm Tue-Sun* $

CHRIS-MUELLER/GETTY IMAGES

Izumo Taishakyo Mission

O'ahu's Top Bookstores

Surprising selections

Skull-Face Books & Vinyl has outlandish decor and book offerings that are deep in noir, grunge lifestyle, sci-fi, pop culture and history.

Native Books at Arts & Letters stocks an extraordinary selection of Hawaiiana books. If it's in print and it's about the islands and their culture, you'll likely find a copy here. There's an excellent section on the independence movement. If you don't know where to start, staff recommendations are superb.

Bodacious Foster Botanical Garden

Lush, historic, gorgeous

Tropical plants you've only ever read about can be spotted in all their glory at spectacular **Foster Botanical Garden** *(honolulubotanicalgardens.com; $5/1)*, which first took root in 1850. Among its rarest specimens are the Hawaiian *loulu* palm and the East African *Gigasiphon macrosiphon*, both thought to be extinct in the wild. Several of the towering trees are the largest of their kind in the USA. Don't miss the blooming orchids or the elegant – and appropriately named – royal palms. The self-guided tour is excellent and celebrates Hawai'i's plants and trees, but don't miss the free tours at 10:30am.

CHINATOWN'S BEST SHOPPING

Roberta Oaks: Namesake shop for a top Hawai'i designer known for women's wear and men's tailored shirts – aloha-print or palaka (plantation-style checkered).

Fighting Eel: One-stop made-in-Hawai'i shop for blowsy, draped dresses in modern solids, resort flowers and geometric prints.

Hound & Quail: Welcoming shop that's a top source for vintage postcards and intriguing period gift items that are easily carried home.

Sig on Smith: Chinatown outlet for famed Hawaiian shirt designer Sig Zane of Hilo, Hawai'i. Not your polyester knock-offs.

Hook & Hide: Get a new custom wallet, belt, bag and more made at this stylish store and workshop. Some items made from fish leather.

Valia Honolulu: Top local clothing and designer brands at decent prices. Large store also has decor and household items.

DRINKING IN CHINATOWN: OUR PICKS

Tea at 1024: Retro teahouse serving cutesy sandwiches, scones and cakes in the afternoon. A big choice of tea. *11am-2pm Wed-Mon*

Manifest: Lofty space with provocative decor. A serene coffee shop by day and cocktail bar by night. *10am-midnight Mon-Sat*

EP Bar: Dark, intimate bar that mixes good drinks and good tunes courtesy of the huge vinyl collection. *5-11pm Mon-Sat*

Scarlet Honolulu: Popular LGBTIQ+ bar and nightclub with regular drag shows. *8pm-2am Fri & Sat*

WALKING TOUR

Chinatown on Foot

Steeped in history, Chinatown is Honolulu's most walkable neighborhood. The scent of incense wafts through buzzing markets, dragons spiral up building columns and steaming dim sum awakens even the sleepiest of appetites. Explore in the morning (many shops catering to residents close by 2pm), when you can expect to see elders doing tai chi by the river and shoppers in the stores and markets.

Memorial Park & Theatre

Start at small ❶ **Dr Sun Yat-sen Memorial Park** where stone lions flank the road. Walk northeast to the restored neoclassical ❷ **Hawaii Theatre** then continue around the corner.

The Walk: Go southwest on Nu'uanu Ave.

Nu'uanu Ave

As you cross ❸ **Hotel Street**, look north to the block that was once one of the city's most notorious, when it was lined with bars and clubs catering to sailors from Pearl Harbor (p112). Continuing on Nu'uanu Ave, note the many characterful cafes and shops such as ❹ **Tin Can Mailman** (p108), a small vintage collectibles shop selling curated tiki wares, Hawaiiana books, silk aloha shirts and vinyl LPs.

The Walk: Cross S King St.

Historic Newspaper Building

The impressive 1898 Romanesque stone building at ❺ **928 Nu'uanu Ave** bears the name of an early tenant, 'The Nippu Jiji,' which was a newspaper serving the large

THEODORE TRIMMER/SHUTTERSTOCK

Wo Fat Building

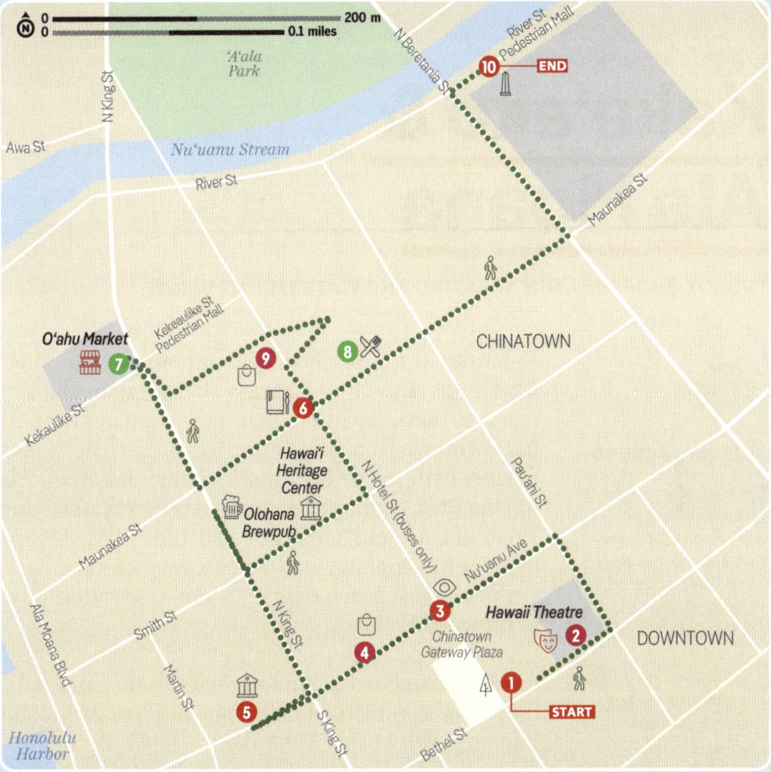

Japanese community of immigrant agricultural workers. It was a force for its readers' rights and won many victories against the powerful growers. Later, with assimilation, the paper became the English-language *Hawaii Times*.

The Walk: Stroll north on N King St, pausing at **Olohana Brewpub** if you're thirsty, and hang a right on Smith St to pass the **Hawai'i Heritage Center** (p69). Turn left into historic Hotel St.

Wo Fat Building

At the corner of Maunakea St, the ornate facade of the partially restored ❻ **Wo Fat Building** resembles a Chinese temple. The building – and, incidentally, also the villain in *Hawaii Five-0* – is named after Honolulu's first restaurant, which opened here in 1882.

The Walk: Head back to King St, and continue past the red pillars coiled with dragons at Bank of Hawai'i to the corner of N King and Kekaulike Sts.

Chinatown's Markets

Visit Chinatown's most compelling markets, starting with the buzzing 1904 ❼ **O'ahu Market** (p67). Cross the road and wander up the pedestrian mall with open-air stalls, then head into ❽ **Maunakea Marketplace** (p66) for a break at a food stall. Across N Hotel St, ❾ **Sun Chong Grocery** has aisles jammed with dry goods and its specialty: dried, sugared and spiced crack seed (Chinese preserved fruit).

The Walk: Heading *mauka* (toward the mountains) on Maunakea St, you'll pass fragrant lei shops (p69). Take Pau'ahi St to River St, passing old shopfronts in various stages of renovation.

Dr Sun Yat-sen Statue

By the river, the ❿ **Dr Sun Yat-sen Statue** stands over senior citizens playing mahjongg. An early Chinese revolutionary, he arrived on O'ahu in 1879 and later attended the same school that would educate Barack Obama nearly a century later.

Kaka'ako & Ala Moana

TRENDY SHOPPING, GREAT EATING AND WATERFRONT PARKS

GETTING AROUND

Individual areas – such as around specific developments – are walkable but mostly the district is just a bit too spread out, and sidewalks too lacking, to be walkable.

Street parking can be scarce on weekdays, though the major malls all have free or cheap parking, as do the parks. Buses linking Waikīkī with Downtown run frequently along S Beretania St, S King St, Kapi'olani Blvd and Ala Moana Blvd.

The Skyline train from the airport and points further west is not due to arrive until 2031 at the earliest.

TOP TIP

You won't want to make a day of it walking in the hot sun along the mostly shade-free streets, so be ready to take refuge in the many breweries, cafes and shops. Ala Moana is close to Waikīkī, especially if you stroll along the waterfront.

Kaka'ako means to 'chop, beat or prepare thatching,' which refers to the *pili* grass that grew in the salt marshes that once covered this now-popular area next to Downtown Honolulu. Immediately east, Ala Moana means 'Path to the Sea' and its namesake road, Ala Moana Blvd, connects the coast between Waikīkī and Honolulu. Although many people think of Ala Moana only for its shopping mall, Ala Moana Regional Park, O'ahu's largest beach reserve, is a relaxing alternative to crowded Waikīkī.

A wave of development continues to transform these neighborhoods with hip loft-style condos and faux-industrial commercial developments replacing light industry. Salt at Our Kaka'ako is a block-sized open-air mall that mixes local shops and restaurants. The area is also a delight for eating and drinking. Grounded in Hawai'i's heritage and fueled by the huge tourist numbers from across the Pacific, Ala Moana in particular boasts excellent Japanese restaurants.

Oceanfront Parks with Views

Beaches, surfing and lazing

Ala Moana Regional Park *(honolulu.gov/dpr/ala-moana-regional-park/)* boasts a broad, golden-sand beach nearly a mile long, buffered from passing traffic by shade trees. Ala Moana is hugely popular, yet big enough that it never feels too crowded. This is where Honolulu residents go running after work, play beach volleyball and enjoy weekend picnics. The park has picnic tables, restrooms, outdoor showers and lifeguards. **Kewalo Basin** is home to tour boats (p84) and sublime waterfront walking. There's good surfing offshore (p78).

Near Downtown, **Kaka'ako Waterfront Park** feels far away from the urban jungle, attracting experienced surfers in the morning and picnickers in the afternoon. In-line skaters roll along the rock-fringed promenade, offering clear views of Diamond Head and Honolulu Harbor. It's not a safe swimming spot and there's no sandy beach, but Point Panic (p78) is offshore.

RUTHIE ARORA/SHUTTERSTOCK

Salt at Our Kaka'ako

A Magical Island

Swimming and sunsets

Envisioned as a second Waikīkī, the big blob jutting into the sea south from Ala Moana Regional Park was created in the early 1960s as a base for a thicket of high-rise hotels and condos. But the same early wave of environmental activism that stopped freeways from destroying more of urban America took hold in Honolulu and stopped the development. Fittingly called **Magic Island** (no one uses the formal name Aina Moana), the artificial peninsula is now part of the park and is a fantastic escape from the city's hubbub. It has a superb swimming cove with a fine beach. Walk the shore for the city's best sunset views.

Honolulu's Splendid Art Museum

Masterpieces, movies and lunch

The exceptional **Honolulu Museum of Art** *(honolulumuseum.org; adult/child $25/free)* is among the best fine-arts museums anywhere. The collection is effectively a 'best of' summary of major art movements globally over the last several centuries (eg the Impressionist room includes a Van Gogh, a Monet, two

continued on p78

A DEPTH OF ART

The Honolulu Museum of Art, dating to 1927, has a classical facade, with galleries branching off a series of garden and water-fountain courtyards. Beautiful exhibits include one of the country's finest Asian art collections, featuring everything from Japanese woodblock prints by Hiroshige and Ming dynasty–era Chinese calligraphy and painted scrolls to temple carvings and statues from Cambodia and India.

Another highlight is the striking contemporary wing with Hawaiian works on its upper level (don't miss the surfboard crafted by the legendary CJ Kanuha), while the modern art includes Georgia O'Keeffe's Hawai'i work. You'll be bewitched by the Pacific and Polynesian artifacts, such as ceremonial masks, war clubs and body adornments. The courtyard features spectacular sculptures by Jun Kaneko.

EATING & DRINKING IN KAKA'AKO & ALA MOANA: SWEET CHOICES

Fancy Fresh Food Shop: Popular juice bar with luscious smoothies and crates of fruit stacked everywhere; near Honolulu Museum of Art. *10am-6:30pm* $

Waiola Shave Ice: Dates to the 1940s – and looks it. Old-style shave ice: superfine powder flavored with syrup. Try the luscious banana cream. *11am-6pm* $

Castaways: Old-timey ice-cream parlor with house-made treats, from waffles to ice-cream sandwiches to cookies. Get the fresh whipped cream. *2-10pm* $

Lin's Hawaiian Snacks: One-stop shop for sweet Hawaiian faves like crack seed and shave ice, plus milkshakes, fresh fruit smoothies and more. *10am-7pm* $

HIGHLIGHTS
1 Ala Moana Regional Park
2 Honolulu Museum of Art
3 Magic Island
4 South Shore Market

SIGHTS
5 Elvis Statue
6 Hawaii Children's Discovery Center
7 Kaka'ako Waterfront Park
8 Kewalo Basin
9 Obama Hawaiian Africana Museum

ACTIVITIES
10 Kewalos
11 Point Panic & Flies

SLEEPING
12 Ala Moana Honolulu by Mantra
13 Central Y Residences
14 Pagoda Hotel

EATING
15 53 By The Sea
see 19 Arvo Cafe
16 Castaways
17 Epi-Ya Boulangerie & Patisserie
18 Hamada General Store
19 Highway Inn Kaka'ako
20 Joy Cup Noodles Mean
21 Kaka'ako Farmers Market
see 8 Kewalo Basin Foodtrucks
22 Mai Masubi
23 Merriman's Honolulu
24 MW Restaurant
25 Southern Love
26 Sushi Sasabune
27 Waiola Shave Ice
28 Yangi Sushi

DRINKING & NIGHTLIFE
29 Aloha Beer Co
30 Beer Lab Hawaii
31 Bevy

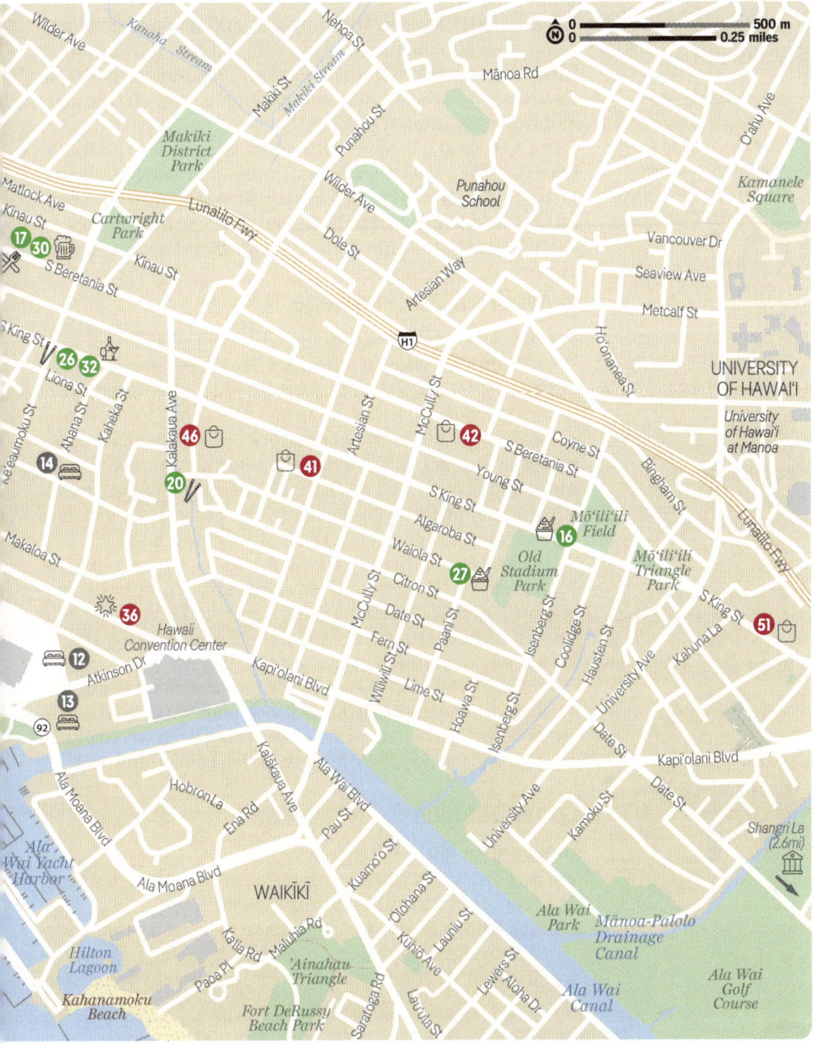

32 Chez Kenzo Bar & Grill
33 Fancy Fresh Food Shop
34 Hana Koa Brewing Co
see 50 Moku Kitchen
see 31 Village Bottle Shop & Tasting Room

ENTERTAINMENT
35 Hawai'i Symphony Orchestra
36 Hawaiian Brian's
37 Neal S Blaisdell Center
38 Republik

SHOPPING
39 Ala Moana Center
see 4 Always A.Line
40 DeStash Hawai'i
41 Fujiya Hawaii
see 4 HiLife
42 Hō'ili'ili Market by Farm Link
see 4 Jules & Gem Hawai'i
43 Kamaka Hawaii
44 KoAloha Ukulele
45 Lin's Hawaiian Snacks
see 50 Lonohana Chocolate Tasting Bar
46 Manuheali'i
47 Nā Mea Hawai'i
48 Reyn Spooner
49 Sake Shop
50 Salt at Our Kaka'ako
see 4 Salvage Public
51 Surf Garage
52 T&C Surf Designs
53 T&L Muumuu Factory

SURFING HONOLULU

Surf breaks dot the Honolulu shoreline, and Kaka'ako and Ala Moana's offer some notable contributions. Renting a surfboard here is easy.

Point Panic & Flies: Just off Kaka'ako Waterfront Park (p74), these breaks are popular with beginner to intermediate surfers in summer. Point Panic is also a legend with bodyboarders.

Kewalos: Off its namesake basin, Kewalos draws intermediate surfers. It's the westernmost of many breaks off Ala Moana Park (p74).

T&C Surf Designs: For stylish surf gear, sells goods bearing its distinctive yin-and-yang logo.

Surf Garage: Boards, gear and rentals, and offers storage.

Used Surfboards Hawaii: A warehouse near the airport with choices for any style and budget.

continued from p75

Gauguins etc). Plan on spending a couple of hours at the museum, possibly combining a visit with lunch at the **Honolulu Museum of Art Café**, which features dishes made with O'ahu-grown ingredients, a decent selection of wines by the glass and tropically infused desserts.

The **Art Shop** sells superb Hawaiian artworks and crafts. On offer are books, stationery, prints, posters and works by Hawai'i artisans. The **Doris Duke Theatre** shows an array of experimental, alternative, retro-classic and arthouse films. Check for special events, art lectures, film screenings and music concerts.

Hawai'i's Black Heritage

Surprises at the Obama Hawaiian Africana Museum

The **Obama Hawaiian Africana Museum** *(obamahimuseum.org; by donation)* tells the stories behind President Barack Obama's childhood on O'ahu in the 1960s and 1970s. It also presents forgotten or unknown stories about the Black experience in Hawai'i. Few know that a formerly enslaved man, Anthony Allen, arrived on O'ahu in 1810 and soon became an advisor to Kamehameha the Great. He was gifted a swath of land in Waikīkī and opened the first lodgings there.

Also largely forgotten is the 1944 West Loch Disaster (p116) at Pearl Harbor, when ammunition ships exploded, killing scores of mostly African American sailors, who had been ordered to work in unsafe conditions. (The Port Chicago disaster in California two months later repeated this tragedy.)

Housed in a long, wide spot in an office building hallway, the museum is like a life-sized scrapbook and is run by the irrepressible Deloris Guttman, who is working tirelessly to finally get a proper memorial built for the West Loch dead.

Local Designs

Shopping for top O'ahu goods

You can find an excellent range of goods from local designers and vendors in Kaka'ako and Ala Moana.

South Shore Market is an oasis of Hawaiian brands surrounded by the big box stores of Ward Village mall. The shops are small but the ambitions of the owners/designers are huge.

DRINKING IN KAKA'AKO & ALA MOANA: OUR PICKS

Bevy: Trendy bar with an airy terrace serving classic cocktails, plus tasty small-plate food. At Salt at Our Kaka'ako. *5pm-midnight Tue-Sat*

Village Bottle Shop & Tasting Room: If it's brewed in the islands, you'll likely find it on offer at this cheery Salt at Our Kaka'ako spot. *noon-9pm*

Chez Kenzo Bar & Grill: Sake heaven. Generous pours of house sake, cocktails, sake-tinis, shots and flights, plus comfort food. *5pm-1am*

Hana Koa Brewing Co: A rollicking rooftop, a party vibe and a large brewing area with tours. Live music on weekends. *noon-10pm Tue-Sun*

Aloha Beer Co: Big open-fronted brewery with award-winning house beers on offer. Tasty bar food, from snacks to meals. *11am-10pm*

Moku Kitchen: This huge gastropub is another winner for drinks at Salt at Our Kaka'ako, with dozens of microbrews and superb garlic fries. *11am-10pm*

Beer Lab Hawaii: Run by nuclear engineers with a mad-scientist ethos for beer. Has a cool vibe and a terrace. Excellent poke. *2-10pm*

Arvo Cafe: Just look for the queue stretching from the window at this cafe with coffee and matcha drinks. Healthful bites too. *8am-2pm*

JEFF WHYTE/SHUTTERSTOCK

Honolulu Museum of Art (p75)

Among the highlights: **HiLife** for goods and T-shirts enmeshed in local lore; **Always A.Line** for custom aloha wear sewn in Kaka'ako; **Jules & Gem Hawai'i** for home and personal scent products; and **Salvage Public** for casual wear with a twist.

Hawaiian musicians often sport bold-print silk aloha shirts from **Manuheali'i**. Flowing synthetic print and knit dresses and wrap tops take inspiration from the traditional *mu'umu'u*. Or just go to a source: **T&L Muumuu Factory** creates bold-print *mu'umu'u* for women that come in sizes for any island queen. On the men's side, aloha shirt sizes run from XS up to 6XL.

For vintage classics, try the popular and ever-expanding **De-Stash Hawai'i**. **Nā Mea Hawai'i** sells beautiful, silk-screened fabrics, koa-wood bowls, Hawaiian quilts, fish-hook jewelry and hula supplies.

Melodic Creations

Check out 'ukuleles, Hawai'i's instrument

Kamaka Hawaii *(kamakahawaii.com)* specializes in gorgeous, handcrafted 'ukuleles made on O'ahu since 1916, with prices

BEST LIVE MUSIC

Hawaiian Brian's: The 500-person Crossroads Concert Hall at this rambling club draws acts of all kinds, especially blues, soul and rock. Although sizable, the venue is buried in a parking garage.

Neal S Blaisdell Center: Huge performing arts and convention center stages opera, ballet, hula competitions and big touring musical acts. Elvis once sang 'Blue Hawaii' here in a 1973 TV concert, honored in a statue of the King out front.

Republik: Honolulu's most intimate concert hall for touring and local acts – indie rockers, punk and metal bands.

Hawai'i Symphony Orchestra: Much-lauded orchestra dating to 1900 and highlighting sounds from around the Pacific.

Merriman's Honolulu: Nightly acoustic and jazz at happy hour.

EATING IN KAKA'AKO: OUR PICKS

53 By the Sea: Sublime views and top-end seafood makes this a top destination for special occasions. *5-9:30pm Wed-Sun* **$$$**

Hamada General Store: Unbeatable choice for plate lunches. Family-run for generations, the menu changes daily. *9am-2pm Mon-Sat* **$**

Yangi Sushi: This festive sushi joint serves tempura to boisterous crowds well past midnight. *11am-1am Mon-Sat* **$**

Kewalo Basin Foodtrucks: Ever-changing lineup of vendors serving excellent meals; picnic in nearby parks. *hours vary* **$**

Highway Inn Kaka'ako: The Waipahu original opened in 1947; this modern version serves trad Hawaiian classics. *9:30am-8pm* **$$**

MW Restaurant: James Beard Award–winning MW is run with wit by a chef couple with decades of top-notch experience. *5-9pm Mon-Sat* **$$$**

Southern Love: As shambolic as a family in a Faulkner novel; the place for shrimp, grits, greens and classic Southern cooking. *10am-8pm* **$$**

Mai Musubi: Stop early at this Japanese deli with splendid *musubi* and bento combos. When the day's supply sells out, that's it. *7am-1pm Tue-Sat* **$**

KAKA'AKO & ALA MOANA'S BEST FOOD VENDORS

Lonohana Chocolate Tasting Bar: A highlight at Salt at Our Kaka'ako. The cocoa beans used here are grown on O'ahu's North Shore. Book a tour at the nearby factory.

Hō'ili'ili Market by Farm Link: Like a daily farmers market, this storefront has produce and prepared goods from across O'ahu. Also sells pizza, deli sandwiches and baked goods.

Sake Shop: A gold mine for those interested in Japanese sake.

Kaka'ako Farmers Market: Every Saturday morning, over 110 vendors sell beautiful fruit, baked goods, hand-pulled noodles and a whole lot more. Enjoy a meal on the grassy green in Kaka'ako Waterfront Park.

Fujiya Hawaii: A treasure! Windows look onto the busy factory area of this mochi-maker. Choose from many flavors. Banana stickers make great gifts.

THEODORE TRIMMER/SHUTTERSTOCK

Ala Moana Center

starting at around $1000. Reserve online for free 30-minute factory tours.

KoAloha Ukulele *(koaloha.com)* modestly proclaims that it's the source of the finest handmade 'ukuleles in the world. See for yourself on a free weekday workshop tour at 1pm.

Survive Ala Moana Center

Mall with hundreds of stores

Bewildering and always crowded, **Ala Moana Center** is the world's largest open-air shopping mall. It's encased by gloomy covered parking areas that you have to penetrate to reach the 340-plus stores – mostly chains. A handful of Hawai'i specialty shops are thrown into the mix, including **Reyn Spooner** ('reverse print' aloha shirts) and O'ahu-native **T&C Surf Designs**, beloved vendor of gear, wear and fabled boards.

Rainy Day Fun

Children's Discovery Center

The hands-on **Hawaii Children's Discovery Center** *(discoverycenterhawaii.org; $12)* is just the place for young visitors when the skies open up, flooding their beach dreams. Fun exhibits bring Hawai'i's culture and natural world to life. And if the skies clear, Kaka'ako Waterfront Park is across the street.

EATING IN ALA MOANA: OUR PICKS

Merriman's Honolulu: An originator of Hawai'i Regional Cuisine, this place serves locally sourced fare. Excellent bar with music at happy hour. *11am-9pm* $$$

Epi-Ya Boulangerie & Patisserie: Grab a tray and choose pastries and treats at master baker Yukikazu Sato's French-accented bakery. *6am-6pm Wed-Mon* $

Joy Cup Noodles Mean: Beef-bone soup, piquant Sichuan noodles – choose your spiciness level. There are other good choices on the same strip. *10:30am-9pm Wed-Mon* $$

Sushi Sasabune: *Omakase* (chef's tasting menu) meals at Honolulu's pick for serious sushi aficionados are the gold standard for sushi and sashimi. *5:30-10pm* $$$

Waikīkī

RESORTS, BEACHES AND THE HOLIDAY LIFE

Once a swampy Hawaiian royal retreat, Waikīkī now revels in its role as a retreat for the masses. This famous strand of sand moves to a rhythm of Hawaiian music at beachfront high-rises and resorts. In this pulsing jungle of modern hotels and malls, you can, surprisingly, still hear whispers of Hawai'i's past, from the chanting of hula troupes at Kūhiō Beach Park to the legacy of Olympic gold medalist Duke Kahanamoku.

Take a surfing lesson from a talented instructor, then spend a lazy afternoon lying on Waikīkī's golden sands, or go for a stroll to quieter beaches just minutes from the center. Before the sun sinks below the horizon, hop aboard a catamaran and sail off toward Diamond Head. Sip a sunset mai tai and be hypnotized by the lilting harmonies of slack key guitar, then mingle with the vibrant residents, many of whom have made this their lifetime playground.

GETTING AROUND

Waikīkī is entirely walkable.

Most stops for TheBus in Waikīkī are found inland along Kūhiō Ave. Bus 13 is handy: it runs down Kūhiō Ave and Kapahulu Ave and serves Chinatown and Downtown.

Waikiki Trolley *(waikikitrolley.com)* runs three circular bus routes designed for tourists.

From the airport, you can reach Waikīkī via TheBus route W. Buses run frequently along Kūhiō Ave. Taxis and rideshares cost $40 to $50.

TOP TIP

The best way to get around this bustling tourist area is on foot. Follow the shoreline and enjoy the views. Inland, every street has interesting cafes and shops that enliven your walk. Waikīkī still has plenty of intriguing hidden corners you'll only discover on a stroll.

A Wealth of Sandy Delights

Waikīkī's top beaches

Visitors quickly learn that **Waikīkī Beach** is not one swath of sand, but many. Here are the best, roughly north to south.

Fronting the Hilton Hawaiian Village, large **Kahanamoku Beach** is Waikīkī's westernmost beach. It's named for Duke Kahanamoku (1890–1968), the legendary Waikīkī' surfer whose family once owned the land where the resort now stands. Hawai'i's champion surfer and Olympic gold medal winner learned to swim here.

Less crowded, adjoining **Fort DeRussy Beach** is an often-overlooked beauty. The water is usually calm and good for swimming. Windsurfers, bodyboarders and board surfers all play here.

Kahaloa & Ulukou Beaches, the narrow beaches between the Royal Hawaiian and Moana Surfrider hotels, are Waikīkī's busiest sections of sand and surf, making it great for people-watching. **Kūhiō Beach Park** offers everything from protected

ONE BEACH FROM MANY

The 2-mile collection of sandy beaches that everyone calls Waikīkī Beach changes names and personalities along its undulating length. Quiet in the morning, by midmorning, the day's action is underway.

If you want to walk the length of the beach (p90), you'll find it impossible to do it all on sand due to the separation of individual beaches and beach erosion. For instance, **Gray's Beach** has always been isolated, with a long gap to the southeast all the way to the Royal Hawaiian.

And remember, though the core beaches get crowded, there's much more open sand to be found at Fort DeRussy Beach (p81), and as you stroll south along Kapi'olani Beach Park (p82).

swimming to outrigger canoe rides. You can spend hours watching surfers of all types riding the curls. **Kapahulu Groin** is one of Waikīkī's hottest bodyboarding spots.

Queen's Surf Beach is a great place for families: the waves are gentle for young kids while older kids can swim out to the larger breakers. **Kapi'olani Beach Park**, backed by a green space of banyan trees and grassy lawns, offers a relaxing niche with none of the frenzy found on the beaches fronting the Waikīkī hotel strip.

At the Diamond Head edge of Waikīkī, **Kaimana Beach** is a prime triangle of sandy oceanfront that's far from the frenzied tourist scene. A shallow reef close to shore and a breakwater make for wave-free, protected waters and provide good snorkeling.

Find Your Favorite Mai Tai

A taste that says 'Waikīkī'

Sun, sand and mai tais: all critical ingredients for the perfect Hawai'i trip. Since introduced at the Royal Hawaiian (p84) in 1953, the sweet and fruity drink has been served in countless numbers to tens of millions of delighted visitors.

Satisfying versions are served up and down the beach as well as at bars, from divey to tiki to posh, in backstreets and resorts. Whether $10 or $40 (an absurdly over-priced version at the Royal Hawaiian), the best mai tais overlay fresh pineapple and lime juices with quality rum, orange curaçao and the one ingredient often missing from mediocre versions: orgeat syrup. Try the surprising **Koa Oasis** or the Moana Surfrider's **Beach Bar**.

See Fireworks!

Spectacular Friday night shows

Every Friday night at 7:45pm, fireworks explode in a light show over Kahanamoku Beach (p81). Sponsored by Hilton Hawaiian Village, the booming show is a huge hit with visitors and residents alike, despite its under-five-minute length. Although it's done in conjunction with a touristy lūʻau (Hawaiian feast) near one of the pools, the actual show is over the water in front of the beach.

Fort DeRussy Beach (p81) affords good views: at the water's edge, get as close as possible to the ropes strung along the north end of the beach. Or, before the crowds clog the sidewalks, loop around to the west end of Kahanamoku Beach near the stalls selling food and drinks. There's often impromptu hula dancing among the light-hearted crowd of residents.

Surf's Up!

Where riding waves began

Waikīkī, where surfing began, is good for riding the waves year-round, with the largest waves rolling in during winter. Gentler summer surf breaks are best for beginners.

Right offshore, **Canoes** is famous and often busy with surfing classes. It's an easygoing mix of left and right breaks with a crowd from around the world enjoying long, consistent rides.

Queens is the perfect break for beginners who've mastered Canoes. It's an all-around great wave that's a longboard dream and is usually crowded.

Techniques date to the 1930s when Waikīkī surfers developed hollow boards in order to execute the maneuvers needed to surf these breaks. Previously, the cumbersome, heavy redwood boards couldn't be used here.

Surfing lessons and rentals of surfboards, stand-up paddleboards (SUPs) and bodyboards can be arranged at the many

ROYAL HAWAIIAN BAND CONCERTS

The Kapiʻolani Park Bandstand is the perfect venue for the time-honored **Royal Hawaiian Band** *(rhb-music.com)* that performs classics from the Hawaiian monarchy era. It's a quintessential island scene that caps off with the audience joining hands and singing Queen Liliʻuokalani's 'Aloha ʻOe' in Hawaiian. The setting is lush amid the swaying palms and spreading shade of the monkeypod and ironwood trees.

Among the most affecting (and remembered) lyrics of this beloved song are: *Until we meet again sweet memories come back to me.*

Check the band's website for details on performances at special events and festivals across Oʻahu. The orchestra's Friday noontime concerts (p60) at ʻIolani Palace are a treat.

EATING & DRINKING IN WAIKĪKĪ: BEACHFRONT

Barefoot Beach Cafe: Shady tables with views and island-accented breakfasts, lunches and snacks just south of Queen's Beach. Plus good drinks and live music. *8am-8:30pm* $

Koa Oasis: Barebones, sand-in-your-toes, self-proclaimed 'booze shack.' Great cheap mai tais served with aloha. Free sunscreen, grand views and $4 juice drinks. *noon-6pm* $

Duke's Waikiki: A raucous, surfing-themed scene, especially when concerts spill onto the beach, at the remodeled Outrigger Waikiki Beach Resort. In the heart of the action. *7am-midnight* $$

Hau Tree Lanai: Sweeping views under namesake trees at the New Otani Kaimana Beach Hotel. Hawaiian flavor amid casual flair; great breakfasts, romantic dinners. *8am-9pm* $$$

WAIKĪKĪ'S ROYAL HISTORY

Less than 150 years ago, Waikīkī was almost entirely wetlands filled with fishponds and *lo'i kalo* (taro fields). Fed by mountain streams from the Mānoa Valley, Waikīkī (Spouting Water) was once one of O'ahu's most fertile farming areas.

In 1795 Kamehameha I became the first *ali'i* (chief) to successfully unite the Hawaiian Islands under one sovereign's rule, bringing his royal court to Waikīkī.

Later in the 19th century, Queen Kapi'olani had two homes here. One grander palatial estate was at the southeast end of today's Ala Wai Canal, near where her namesake park is today. Another more modest home was on the waterfront. She spent her days here writing poetry and working to preserve ancient forms of hula.

beach concession stands. **Hans Hedemann Surf** *(hhsurf.com)* offers high-end lessons near Queen's Surf Beach. **Quality Surfboards Hawaii** *(qualitysurfboardshawaii.com)* offers lessons, rentals, sales and more. Centrally located **Stoke Drift Surf School** *(stokedrift.com)* is also popular.

As your model for Waikīkī wave-riding, check out the dashing **Surfer on a Wave Statue** at Queen's Surf Beach.

Go Ride a Boat

Booze, views and thrills

Hop aboard a boat for a jaunt to see the sights from the water. Some waterfront surf outfits offer **outrigger-canoe rides** (from $180 for four people) that take off from the beach and ride the tossin' waves home while paddlers row furiously.

Several **catamaran cruises** leave right from Waikīkī Beach – just walk down to the sand, step into the surf and hop aboard. Some sailings are 1½-hour, all-you-can-drink 'booze cruises.' Reservations are recommended for sunset sails, which sell out fast.

Of the many large boats for touring, the **Vida Mia** *(thevidamia.com; from $140)* is an attractive restored wooden motor yacht that offers more intimate group voyages. It docks at Waikīkī's Ala Wai Small Boat Harbor. Other large boats leave from Kewalo Basin in Kaka'ako.

Savor a Historic Beachfront Resort

No room key required

Moorish-style turrets and archways define the 1927 **Royal Hawaiian Hotel**. Don't miss the stylized map of Hawai'i by Ernest Clegg. Painted directly on the plaster, it has been a permanent feature outside the elevators in the original building since the hotel opened.

The Beaux Arts, plantation-style **Moana Surfrider** hotel opened in 1901. The famed *Hawaii Calls* radio show was once broadcast live from the banyan-tree-shaded courtyard and helped plant the dream of Hawai'i in generations of listeners. Take a load off on one of the rocking chairs on the veranda overlooking Kalākaua Ave.

Construction began on the 3300-room **Hilton Hawaiian Village** in 1955 and has never really stopped. The iconic Rainbow Tower has the world's largest (again!) ceramic-tile mosaic, a 286ft-tall rainbow. In 1961 Elvis Presley filmed *Blue Hawaii* here.

EATING IN WAIKĪKĪ: TOP END CHOICES

Roy's Waikiki: Roy Yamaguchi's O'ahu-born chain is perfect for a flirty date or just celebrating the good life. Menu and service are memorable. *11:30am-9:30pm* **$$$**

Michel's at Colony Surf: Enjoy timeless classics prepared tableside – many flambéed – and beautiful water views through huge windows, Waikīkī glowing in the distance. *5-9pm* **$$$**

Hy's Steakhouse: Meat masters cook up an array of succulent cuts of beef in view of a clubby dining room with an old-school leather and wood fit out. *5-9pm* **$$$**

La Mer: At the Halekulani resort, the French menu features fresh local ingredients. Superb beach views, rigorous dress code and fine wines. *5:30-8:30pm Tue-Sat* **$$$**

Note the strict dress code and book well ahead.

HIGHLIGHTS
1 Fort DeRussy Beach
2 Royal Hawaiian Hotel

SIGHTS
3 Don Ho Statue
4 Gray's Beach
5 Kahaloa & Ulukou Beaches
6 Moana Surfrider

ACTIVITIES
7 Aisawan Thai Spa & Massage
8 Moana Lani Spa
9 Stoke Drift Surf School
10 Waikiki Wind Spa Massage

SLEEPING
11 Coconut Waikiki Hotel
12 Halekulani
13 Laylow Waikiki
14 Moana Surfrider
15 Ohia Waikiki Studio Suites
16 Regency on Beachwalk Waikiki
17 Royal Hawaiian
18 Sheraton Waikiki Beach Resort

EATING
19 Donut King
20 Henry's Place
21 La Mer
22 Liliha Bakery
23 Monkeypod Kitchen
24 Nature Waikiki
25 Roy's Waikiki
26 Stix Asia
27 Topped Waikiki

DRINKING & NIGHTLIFE
28 Arnold's Beach Bar & Grill
29 Beach Bar
30 Cuckoo Coconuts
31 Duke's Waikiki
32 Genius Lounge
33 Hideout
34 Koa Oasis

ENTERTAINMENT
35 Blue Note Hawaii
36 Cirque du Soleil 'Auana
37 House Without a Key
38 Kani Ka Pila Grille

SHOPPING
39 Duke's Marketplace
40 House of Mana Up
41 International Market Place
42 Island Slipper
43 Royal Hawaiian Center
44 Ukulele PuaPua

HIGHLIGHTS
1 Queen's Surf Beach

SIGHTS
2 Duke Kahanamoku Statue
3 Kaimana Beach
4 Kapahulu Groin
5 Kapi'olani Beach Park
6 Kūhiō Beach Park
7 Makua & Kila Statue
8 Prince Kūhiō Statue
9 Princess Ka'iulani Statue
10 Queen Kapi'olani Statue
11 Surfer on a Wave Statue

ACTIVITIES
12 Canoes
13 Hans Hedemann Surf
14 Honolulu Zoo
15 Nā Ho'ōla Spa
16 Queens
17 Waikīkī Aquarium

SLEEPING
18 'Alohilani Resort Waikiki Beach
19 Aston at the Waikiki Banyan
20 Beach Waikiki Hostel by ALOH
21 Castle Bamboo Waikiki Hotel
22 Hotel Renew
23 Kaimana
24 Lotus Honolulu at Diamond Head
25 Polynesian Hostel Beach Club
26 Royal Grove Waikiki
27 Waikiki Beachside Hostel

EATING
28 Barefoot Beach Cafe
29 Blue Ocean
30 Hau Tree Lanai
31 Hy's Steakhouse
32 Michel's at Colony Surf
33 Musubi Cafe Iyasume
34 Rainbow Drive-In
35 Shimazu Shave Ice
36 Tonkatsu Tamafuji
37 Uncle Bo's Pupu Bar & Grill

DRINKING & NIGHTLIFE
38 Hula's Bar & Lei Stand
39 Wang Chung's

ENTERTAINMENT
40 Kūhiō Beach Torchlighting & Hula Show

SHOPPING
41 Bailey's Antiques & Aloha Shirts

Live Music Everywhere

Free performances nightly

On any given night, Waikīkī offers first-rate live music, mostly for free or for the price of a drink. Traditional and contemporary Hawaiian music features mellow duos or trios playing slack key guitars and ʻukuleles. More numerous are vocalists and cover bands, which can be heard at many bars, lounges and restaurants nightly.

Don't miss **House Without a Key**. Named after a 1925 Charlie Chan novel set in Honolulu, this open-air lounge sprawls beneath a nearly 140-year-old *kiawe* tree at the waterfront Halekulani resort. A genteel crowd gathers here for sunset cocktails, excellent Hawaiian music and hula dancing. Get here right at 5pm to secure a seat; to reserve a seat, you must have dinner.

Blue Note Hawaii *(bluenotejazz.com)* in the Outrigger Waikiki Beach Resort is a sophisticated music venue that draws top acts performing blues, jazz, pop, rock and Hawaiian.

The Outrigger Reef Waikiki Beach Resort is another good location for live entertainment. At poolside, **Kani Ka Pila Grille** hosts excellent, laid-back live-music shows after sunset. Across the pool, waterfront Monkeypod Kitchen has vocalists in the bar from noon through dinner.

Fun for All Ages

Waikīkī for families

Waikīkī defines family-friendly. Start at the beach – in just an hour or so, the older kids can learn how to surf or bodyboard.

Want to see the world from beneath the waves? Don a snorkel and peer at the colorful fish at Queen's Surf Beach (p82). The **Waikīkī Aquarium** *(waikikiaquarium.org; $12)*, with its kaleidoscopic array of tropical fish, giant clams and reef sharks, has lots of fun just for *na keiki* (children). The small **Honolulu Zoo** *(honoluluzoo.org; adult/child $21/13)* has a petting zoo – where children can get eye-to-eye with tamer creatures – and lots of activities and games for kids.

Everyone enjoys the spectacle at **Cirque du Soleil ʻAuana** *(cirquedusoleil.com/auana; from $85)*, which is an 80-minute Hawaiian-themed show featuring local legends told through incredible feats of acrobatics. Ticket deals abound.

WAIKĪKĪ'S BEST PUBLIC ART

Duke Kahanamoku Statue: 'The father of modern surfing' is always draped in lei. A Hawaiian hero, Duke won Olympic medals and much more.

Makua & Kila Statue: A bronze charmer shows a young surfer (Makua) with a monk seal (Kila). Inspired by a children's book about love and respect.

Princess Kaʻiulani Statue: Heir to the throne when the Kingdom of Hawaiʻi was overthrown in 1893. The princess visited Washington but couldn't prevent the coup.

Prince Kūhiō Statue: Celebrates the prince when the kingdom was overthrown. Known for his efforts to preserve and strengthen Hawaiian culture.

Queen Kapiʻolani Statue: The Queen was a beloved philanthropist and loved children. The near-life-size statue is always covered with fresh lei.

EATING IN WAIKĪKĪ: CASUAL CHOICES

Liliha Bakery: Sublime pies, Coco Puff doughnuts, quality diner fare and upscale plate lunches on the International Market Place rooftop. Full bar, outside seating. *7am-10pm* $$

Stix Asia: Browse the choices at this underground Japanese food court with nearly 20 authentic stalls and restaurants. It's like a tunnel to Tokyo! *11am-10pm* $$

Nature Waikiki: Quiet backwater location with a shady lānai amid a large quiet garden. Creative modern Hawaiian tasting menus with vegan options. *5:30-10pm* $$

Monkeypod Kitchen: A casual, creative island-accented menu of comfort classics and live music in the bar in a waterfront place of honor at the art-filled Outrigger Reef resort. *7am-11pm* $$

VIDAHAWAII/SHUTTERSTOCK

Royal Hawaiian Center

Waikīkī's Best Free Show

Top-flight hula and Hawaiian traditions

It all begins with the sounding of a conch shell and the lighting of torches after sunset. The **Kūhiō Beach Torchlighting & Hula Show** is one of Waikīkī's best traditions. It takes place at the Kūhiō Beach Hula Mound, under the branches of a huge banyan tree. The hour-long shows start at 6:30pm; check at your hotel to see what days they're on.

This is a truly authentic Hawaiian music and dance show. There's no bit of tourist fluff either, as top talent regularly performs, including much-lauded hula experts from the University of Hawai'i.

Savor Hawai'i's Culture

Free demonstrations of hula and more

The **Royal Hawaiian Center** *(royalhawaiiancenter.com)* offers free cultural classes and demonstrations that are great introductions to Hawaiian arts and crafts. Try lei-making or

EATING IN WAIKĪKĪ: CHEAP EATS

Food Truck Park: Top-notch, well-run pod with a dozen vendors of diverse foods. At Kalākaua Ave and Niu St. There's another on Uluniu Ave. *7am-10pm* $

Blue Ocean: Seafood in all forms; the spicy garlic shrimp po' boy is fab and the salmon dishes excellent. Picnic tables under umbrellas. *8am-10pm* $

Musubi Cafe Iyasume: Popular and cluttered hole-in-the-wall makes fresh onigiri (rice balls) and silky and warm Spam *musubi*. Delicious and addictive. *7am-2pm* $

Topped Waikiki: Korean fare served from a ramshackle stand perched at the entrance to the Cuckoo Coconuts bar. Goes by 'hood standards. *11am-11pm* $

hula dancing. Within the mall and adjoining Royal Grove venue, there are Hawaiian music and hula performances by top local talent many nights.

Catch hula dancing several evenings each week at the big open-air mall **International Market Place** *(shopinternationalmarketplace.com)*. It also has good displays on Hawaiian culture scattered throughout. Boomers and Gen Xers get misty-eyed at the **Don Ho Statue**, modeled on the famed crooner's appearance on one of *The Brady Bunch* episodes set in Hawai'i.

Avoid those flimsy souvenir 'ukuleles and find the real deal at **Ukulele PuaPua** *(ukulelepuapua.com)*, a serious little shop in the Sheraton Waikiki. You can join a free group beginner lesson daily at 4pm and learn about this traditional Hawaiian instrument and music ('ukulele provided).

Find Your Shopping

Malls and international chains

Bailey's Antiques & Aloha Shirts over on Kapahulu Ave might be unremarkable outside but it has the finest aloha-shirt collection on O'ahu, possibly the world. Racks are crammed with thousands – from vintage rarities to modern bargains.

Shopping within Waikīkī tends to center on major chains as local designers and boutiques prefer to have shops in Kaka'ako and Ala Moana, where they can draw on the local market, which shuns the resort hubbub.

Among the several big malls, Royal Hawaiian Center houses over 80 top-end stores. Seek out **House of Mana Up**, which supports the nascent entrepreneurial dreams of local designers and artisans. Browse decor items, prepared foods, apparel and cosmetics. **Island Slipper** is unmatched for ultra-comfy suede and leather sandals – all made in Hawai'i since 1946.

Across Kalākaua Ave (dubbed the 'Vegas strip of Hawai'i'), chain-filled International Market Place is worth a visit for the huge 100-year-old banyan tree and cultural displays.

Finally, **Duke's Marketplace** is the place for vendors hawking the tackiest (but at times irresistible) souvenirs – think plastic hula dancers holding signs reading 'Life's a Beach!'

WAIKĪKĪ'S BEST SPAS

Nā Ho'ōla Spa: At this ocean-view spa, *limu* (seaweed) wraps detoxify, *kele-kele* (mud) wraps calm sore muscles, and *ti*-leaf wraps soothe skin. At the Hyatt Regency Waikiki.

Moana Lani Spa: Views through palm trees onto the sand are the hallmarks of this luxury spa with rooms for couples. In the historic Moana Surfrider resort.

Aisawan Thai Spa & Massage: This Thai-style spa offers massages along with extras such as hot stones, potions and lotions. Enjoys a big local following.

Mandara Spa: With roots on Bali, Waikīkī's largest spa has its own pool and deep tropical traditions. Part of Hilton Hawaiian Village.

Waikiki Wind Spa Massage: Long-running indie spa emphasizes various massage styles (Swedish, Shiatsu, sports etc) in one- to two-hour sessions. Also offers facial and body treatments.

EATING & DRINKING IN WAIKĪKĪ: OFFBEAT PICKS

Henry's Place: Whole and cut fresh fruit, house-made rich sorbet and ice cream in obscure tropical flavors, bananas in many forms and irreverent signs. *11am-9pm* $

Genius Lounge: Like a Japanese speakeasy, this third-floor, candlelit hideaway serves East-West tapas bites, retro jazz and electronica. *5pm-midnight* $$

Green Lady Cocktail Room: Bartender wizards create drinks with flair that lure residents and tourists. Great outdoor seating. Try a Supernova Girl, a Cool Haircut etc. *8pm-1am* $$

Donut King: Best doughnuts in Waikīkī. New choices arrive fresh all day; a bite into a cream-filled longjohn is a bite you'll remember. *7am-8pm* $

WALKING TOUR

Waikiki Beach Walk

Waikīkī originally had few beaches. But the $2 billion that tourism generates each year – and surveys showing that 60% of visitors wouldn't visit if there was no beach – keep sand-pumping efforts going to preserve the existing, mostly artificial, beaches. The 2.1-mile, two-hour Waikiki Beach Walk covers much of the waterfront. Since the sand isn't contiguous, the route has inland detours, which add interest.

Kahanamoku Beach & Fort DeRussy

Start at ❶ **Kahanamoku Beach** (p81), a large patch of sand that exists thanks to the curving breakwaters. Follow the beach southeast past Hilton Hawaiian Village (p84). The line of beachfront high-rises is broken at the usually less-crowded ❷ **Fort DeRussy Beach** (p81), the sandy front yard of Fort DeRussy Military Reservation. The 'fort' today is mostly green grass and home to the ❸ **US Army Museum of Hawaii** *(hiarmymuseumsoc.org; free)*. It has excellent displays about life in Honolulu during WWII, plus a lot of interesting military paraphernalia.

The Walk: At the Castle Waikiki Shore hotel, hang a left. At Kalia Rd, turn right. Follow a path into the gargantuan Sheraton Waikiki (p119) and cross into the lush open area.

Royal Hawaiian Hotel

Wander the gardens to the 1927 art deco ❹ **Royal Hawaiian Hotel** (p84). This gorgeous landmark is dubbed the 'Pink Palace.' It's worth exploring.

The Walk: Exit to the beach and turn left at the sand.

Kahaloa & Ulukou Beaches

Look left up the ❺ **Waikiki Surf Alley** where residents lock up their surfboards between rides. These are ❻ **Kahaloa & Ulukou Beaches** (p81), the busiest swaths of Waikīkī sand. The soaring banyan tree is in the courtyard of the 1901 ❼ **Moana**

Kūhiō Beach Park (p81)

Surfrider (p84) hotel, where local tourism began.

The Walk: Continue along the sand in the direction of Diamond Head.

Kūhiō Beach Park

You're entering 8 **Kūhiō Beach Park** (p81), where Waikīkī's beach and surfing culture thrives. Just south and away from the water are the mysterious 9 **Stones of Life of Kapaemahu & Kapuni**. Signs tell their intriguing story. Next is the 10 **Duke Kahanamoku Statue** (p87), where selfies rule. At the 11 **huge banyan tree**, look for demonstrations of coconut splitting. Continue to the 12 **Prince Kūhiō Statue** (p87), who was prince when the Kingdom of Hawai'i was overthrown in 1893.

The Walk: Shift to the water and the people-watching hot spot Kapahulu Groin (p82). Continue to where Kalākaua and Kapahulu Aves meet.

Queen's Surf Beach

Look for two works of public art near the sand: the 13 **Makua & Kila Statue** (p87) and the 14 **Surfer on a Wave Statue** (p84). Pause on the sand at 15 **Queen's Surf Beach** (p82), one of Waikīkī's most pleasant. Look for the stone 16 **marker** that recalls that this was a gathering place for LGBTIQ+ people in the 1970s and that Honolulu's first gay Pride parade was held here in 1974.

The Walk: Continue along Kapi'olani Beach Park (p82).

Kaimana Beach

Pause in front of the 17 **Waikiki Natatorium War Memorial**, a once-grand monument that's crumbling due to bureaucratic inaction. End your walk at the welcoming sand of relaxed 18 **Kaimana Beach** (p82), a favorite with residents.

QUEEN LILI'UOKALANI READING LIST

Queen Lili'uokalani of the Kingdom of Hawai'i was overthrown on January 17, 1893, in a colonial coup that still sparks outrage today. She spent much of her time in Waikīkī at two properties, one by today's Ala Wai Canal and the other at Kūhiō Beach Park.

Chinatown's Native Books at Arts & Letters (p71) in conjunction with Ala Moana's Nā Mea Hawai'i (p79) has created a reading list of books they sell about this remarkable woman.

Lili'uokalani: By playwright Aldyth Morris, who researched the queen's life in 1929.

Diaries of Queen Lili'uokalani of Hawai'i, 1885–1900: The queen's life in her own words, including her time in prison after the coup leaders jailed her for treason.

The Queen's Songbook: Lili'uokalani wrote music, including the iconic 'Aloha 'Oe.'

Rollicking Nights Out

Mai tais, karaoke and friends

Waikīkī doesn't party late – streets are quiet by midnight – but there are lots of lively places for drinks dotted around the backstreets with loads more character than the hotel bars.

Cuckoo Coconuts is a legend despite – or because of – its mismatched wobbly tables under a canopy of canvas and ragged umbrellas, plus a menagerie of potted tropical plants. Every night, hard-working cover bands perform classics out of the *Proud Mary* songbook.

Arnold's Beach Bar & Grill has a grass-shack vibe and the best cheap mai tais in Waikīkī. Or down a stiff 'Tiki Tea' while pretending the bar's naked mannequins don't freak you out. Closer to Ala Moana, **Suzie Wong's Hideaway** is a gregarious dive in an open-sided barn of a building hidden down an alley.

Legendary **Hula's Bar & Lei Stand** is an LGBTIQ+ venue with dance tunes and spectacular views of Diamond Head from a breezy balcony. **Wang Chung's** is a happy-go-lucky, gay-friendly karaoke bar that goes late. It's behind the lobby of the Stay Hotel Waikiki.

With a Vegas vibe, **Hideout** has a big roof deck where you can get lit while gazing at the lights of the surrounding towers, which echo with lounge acts at the surrounding venues.

EATING IN WAIKĪKĪ: KAPAHULU AVE

Rainbow Drive-In: Rainbow-colored neon provides glow for Plate Lunch 101 cuisine. A fave of teenage Obama. There's a gift shop too. *7am-9pm* $

Tonkatsu Tamafuji: Katsu, the deep-fried Japanese cooking method that coats pork and chicken in a crispy exterior, stars. *11am-9:30pm Wed-Mon* $$

Uncle Bo's Pupu Bar & Grill: Boisterous groups graze the encyclopedic list of fusion *pupu* (snacks) crafted with island flair. Reserve ahead. *4-10pm Tue-Sat* $$

Shimazu Shave Ice: Soaring portions and offbeat flavor choices such as red velvet and crème brûlée; you can even get the notorious durian. *noon-7pm Thu-Tue* $

WAIKĪKĪ'S TOURISM HISTORY

Tourism began in 1901 when Waikīkī's first luxury hotel, the Moana (p84), opened on a former royal compound and the one part of the shoreline with a beach.

Tiring of the mosquitoes that thrived in Waikīkī's wetlands, early tourists demanded that the 'swamps' be drained. The Ala Wai Canal was dug to divert the streams that irrigated what had been taro and rice fields.

In the Roaring '20s, the Royal Hawaiian Hotel (p84) opened to serve passengers arriving on luxury ocean liners from San Francisco. The Depression and WWII put a damper on tourism.

As late as 1950, surfers could still park on the beaches. In the 1960s huge mega-resorts proliferated, priced for the masses arriving on jets.

Waikīkī Beach (p81) and Royal Hawaiian Hotel (p84)

JESS LOITERTON/SHUTTERSTOCK

Diamond Head & Kaimukī

THRILLING NATURE AND NEIGHBORHOOD DELIGHTS

GETTING AROUND

In Kaimukī, street parking is always at a premium, though you need to park just once, as the entire area is walkable. There is a larger parking area back behind 11th and 12th Aves, but competition for those spots is fierce as well. However, it's easy to get here by rideshare or taxi from Waikīkī.

You can easily bike into Diamond Head State Monument from Waikīkī.

Kaimukī is one of Honolulu's most appealing neighborhoods for strolling. There's always a new little shop or offbeat eatery to discover amid long-running treasures.

A dramatic backdrop for Waikīkī Beach, Diamond Head is one of the best-known landmarks in Hawai'i. Ancient Hawaiians called it Le'ahi, and at its summit they built a *luakini* heiau, a temple dedicated to the war god Ku and used for human sacrifices. Ever since 1825, when British sailors found calcite crystals sparkling in the sun and mistakenly thought they'd struck it rich, the sacred peak has been called Diamond Head. Today it affords a memorable climb with breathtaking views. At its base are a series of uncrowded beaches.

An easy walk from Waikīkī at the base of Diamond Head, Monsarrat Ave boasts some fine eateries. The affluent seaside suburb of Kahala includes the tiny peninsula of Kupikipiki'o (Black Point), home to one of O'ahu's top attractions: Shangri La.

Diamond Head's Quiet Beaches

Unmatched views and serenity

Dotted around the base of Diamond Head like a string of pearls are a series of uncrowded pocket beaches a short walk or cycle ride from the Waikīkī frenzy. Heading southeast from **Kapi'olani Regional Park** along Diamond Head Rd, the first one is **Mākālei Beach Park**. Like all of these beaches, it has a few perfectly placed palm trees, a fine strip of sand and uninterrupted views out to sea. Past a few apartments and surprisingly modest homes (given the location), **Lē'ahi Beach Park** adds a blissful expanse of lawn to the mix.

Somewhat squat **Diamond Head Lighthouse** is a historic landmark dating to 1917. **Diamond Head Beach Park** borders the lighthouse. The rocky beach draws surfers, snorkelers and tide-poolers, plus a few picnickers. Immediately

TOP TIP

Diamond Head State Monument is a pretty 2-mile walk from Waikīkī. It's even easier to reach the Diamond Head beaches, the Monsarrat restaurant strip and the eateries along Kapahulu Ave by foot from Waikīkī.

HIGHLIGHTS
1 Diamond Head Lookout
2 Diamond Head Summit
3 Shangri La

SIGHTS
4 Amelia Earhart Marker
5 Diamond Head Beach Park
6 Diamond Head Hike Lookout
7 Diamond Head Lighthouse
8 Diamond Head State Monument Parking Lot
9 Diamond Head State Monument Ridge
10 Ka'alawai Beach
11 Kapi'olani Regional Park
12 Kuilei Cliffs Beach Park
13 Lē'ahi Beach Park
14 Mākālei Beach Park

EATING
15 Ars Cafe & Gelato
16 Bogart's Cafe
17 Diamond Head Market & Grill
18 Pioneer Saloon

east, **Kuilei Cliffs Beach Park** is a long and narrow sandy beach. Experienced windsurfers flock here when the trade winds are blowing.

Up on the road, which runs above the beach, **Diamond Head Lookout** has sweeping views of surfers and out to sea, plus a marker recalling Amelia Earhart's solo flight from Hawai'i to California (p98). Finally, often-empty **Ka'alawai Beach** provides a glimpse of the Shangri La estate.

EATING IN KAPAHULU: OUR CHOICES

Aburiya Ibushi: Menu pictures plaster the exterior: smoky grilled pork, chicken and sausage on small plates, plus silky vegetables. Japanese home-style goodness. *5-10:30pm* $$

'Ono Seafood: Poke served the way you want. It's fish first, sauce second, so you can customize, choosing from white or brown rice and many toppings. *9am-4pm Tue-Sat* $

Waiola Shave Ice (p75): Superfine shave ice since 1940. There are 20-plus flavors of syrup and toppings like azuki beans or spicy-sweet *li hing mui* (crack seed). *11am-6pm Wed-Mon* $

Leonard's Bakery: This bakery is famous for *malasadas* (sweet Portuguese-style fried rolls), attracting crowds of tourists. It has an eye-catching 1950s neon sign and a gift shop. *6am-7pm* $

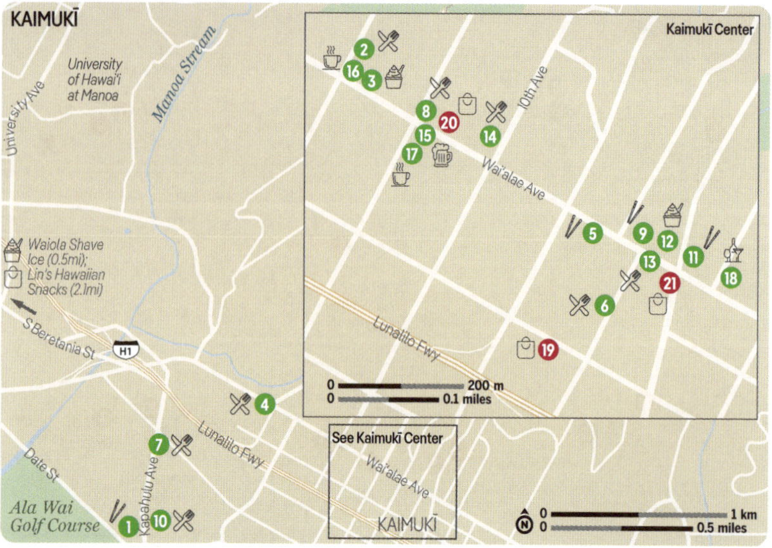

EATING
1 Aburiya Ibushi
2 Breadshop
3 Chillest Shave Ice
4 Higoto Japanese Eatery
5 Kim Chee II
6 Koko Head Cafe
7 Leonard's Bakery
8 Mud Hen Water
9 Okata Bento
10 'Ono Seafood
11 Pig & the Lady
12 Pipeline Bakeshop & Creamery
13 Surfing Pig
14 Tamura's Fine Wine & Liquors

DRINKING & NIGHTLIFE
15 Brew'd Craft Pub
16 Curb
17 Leahi Health Kaimuki
18 Vintage Books

SHOPPING
19 Da Shop
20 Island-Boy
21 Kaimuki Crack Seed Store
see 20 Keep it Simple
see 20 Local General Store

Doris Duke's Shangri La

Sublime seaside beauty

Doris Duke had a lifelong passion for Islamic art and architecture, inspired by a visit to the Taj Mahal during her honeymoon at the age of 23. During that same trip in 1935, the heiress stopped at O'ahu, fell in love with the island and decided to build a seasonal residence, **Shangri La** *(shangrilahawaii.org; $49)*, on Black Point in the shadow of Diamond Head. You can visit this extraordinary home as part of a tour, but you must book well in advance.

For over 60 years Duke traveled the globe from Indonesia to Istanbul, collecting priceless Islamic art objects. Duke

EATING IN MONSARRAT AVENUE: OUR PICKS

Diamond Head Market & Grill: Best take-out near Waikīkī. Made-to-order plate lunches. Ready-made *musubi* and salads; sublime banana cream pie. *7:30am-8:30pm* $

Pioneer Saloon: Wildly popular for Japanese-fusion plate lunches, with dozens of choices including *yakisoba* (fried noodles). Fab shave ice too. *11am-8pm* $$

Ars Cafe & Gelato: Avocado toast two cuts above the cliche and other stylish bites. Also a gallery for local artists with rotating exhibits. Excellent coffee. *6:30am-4pm* $

Bogart's Cafe: Beloved for breakfast. Regulars crave the taro-banana pancakes; the avocado-and-spinach Benedict is also a winner. Reserve ahead. *7am-3pm* $$

appreciated the spirit more than the grand scale of the world wonders she had seen, and she made Shangri La into an intimate sanctuary rather than an ostentatious mansion. One of its true beauties is its harmony with the natural environment. Interiors open to embrace gardens and the ocean, with one glass wall framing Diamond Head.

Duke's extensive collection of Islamic art includes vivid gemstone-studded enamels, glazed ceramic paintings and silk *suzanis* (intricate needlework tapestries). Art often blends with architecture to represent a theme or region, as in the Damascus Room, the restored interior of an 18th-century Syrian merchant's house.

Shangri La can only be visited on a guided tour departing from the Honolulu Museum of Art (p75), where you'll travel as a group by minibus to the estate.

Take a Stroll in Kaimukī

Cool shops and appealing streetscapes

The old neighborhood of Kaimukī matches Chinatown for creativity and the two bookend the core of Honolulu. Wander Wai'alae Ave, from 7th Ave to Koko Head Ave, for a smorgasbord of appealing businesses.

In the morning, start at a sidewalk seat outside **Breadshop**, munching on the beautiful, fresh bread and pastries. Note the schedule showing what's fresh from the oven when.

Shops abound in the 100-year-old shopfronts. **Keep It Simple** bills itself as the 'Honolulu Zero Waste' store. It carries fashion and gear produced locally with a green ethos. **Island-Boy** has an exquisite collection of housewares, gifts and clothing that are both produced in-house and made by other Hawai'i designers.

The luscious ice cream at **Pipeline Bakeshop & Creamery** is Honolulu's best. Over-the-top flavors include 'M&M overload.' Other options include fresh *malasadas* (like a doughnut without the hole). Most indulgent are the 'cake bombs,' a sort of huge, filled cupcake.

A literal hole in the wall, **Okata Bento** sells scrumptious and fresh takeaway Japanese boxed lunches in myriad variations.

DORIS DUKE'S RICH LIFE

Shangri La is captivating not just for its beauty but also for the unique glimpse it provides into the life of tobacco heiress Doris Duke (1912–93), once nicknamed 'the richest little girl in the world.'

She was eccentric and reclusive. Duke's inherited fortune allowed her to do as she pleased, which included two very public divorces.

In Hawai'i, she became the first white woman to surf competitively, learning from Olympic gold medalist Duke Kahanamoku. The movie *Bernard and Doris* (2006) stars Susan Sarandon as Duke and Ralph Fiennes as her butler, Bernard Lafferty.

Lafferty was the sole executor of her fortune, which Duke decreed be spent supporting the arts and fighting cruelty to children and animals.

EATING IN KAIMUKĪ: TOP PICKS

Mud Hen Water: Comfort foods drawn from Honolulu's many cultures and made to harmonize. *5-9pm Tue-Sun* $$

Surfing Pig: Gastropub vibe, with a long drinks menu. Mains are a meaty mix of burgers, steaks and seafood with island accents. *4-9pm* $$

Pig & the Lady: Award-winning, imaginative Vietnamese fusion restaurant. Book well ahead. *11am-2:30pm & 5-9:30pm Tue-Sun* $$

Kim Chee II: Old-school booths welcome diners to this long-running, family-run Korean restaurant. *10:30am-7:30pm Wed-Mon* $$

Higoto Japanese Eatery: Top source for *musubi* in variations from Spam to cheeseburger, with a few healthier varieties. *11am-4pm Wed-Sun* $

Koko Head Cafe: Get your place in the queue online for this popular brunch spot. American classics meet Asian standards. *8am-2pm* $$

Tamura's Fine Wine & Liquors: Best poke on the island? Spicy 'ahi and the smoked marlin are a feast for the eyes. *9:30am-8pm* $

Chillest Shave Ice: Shave ice based on the 8th-century Japanese-style *kakigōr*. Served with unique syrups. *11am-6pm Thu-Tue* $

AN INCREDIBLE FLIGHT

The ongoing mystery of her disappearance at age 39 in the Pacific Ocean overwhelms the extraordinary life Amelia Earhart lived as a pilot.

Her achievements were many. In 1932 she became the first woman to cross the Atlantic solo. Only three years later, she accomplished something even greater, when she became the first pilot to fly solo from Hawai'i to California.

The journey was over 2400 miles long, almost entirely over water. Numerous people had died in previous years, either attempting the flight or while trying to rescue those who failed. Earhart piloted her single-engine plane alone for 19 hours and landed in Oakland on January 12, 1935.

Today, an artful marker below Diamond Head recalls her accomplishment.

VIBBILY/ALAMY

Kaimuki Crack Seed Store

Local General Store bakes Hawai'i's best croissants and it stocks the best O'ahu-sourced foods.

Over on Harding Ave, **Da Shop** is one of Honolulu's best bookstores. Run by a local publisher, the curated selection of books includes staff recommendations and Hawai'i titles.

The Mysteries of Crack Seed

Honey kumquat or licorice ginger?

Crack seed, the traditional treat loved in Hawai'i, confounds visitors. Is it sweet? Sour? Salty? What is it? Answers to all these questions can be found at **Kaimuki Crack Seed Store**, a timeless crack-seed paradise. This tiny mom-and-pop candy store vends overflowing glass jars of made-from-scratch crack seed, plus addictive frozen slushies spiked with *li hing mui* (dried plums in rock salt). Sample your way through the versions – note the helpful illustrated poster in the window that lays out the 129 varieties on offer. Another good shop is Lin's Hawaiian Snacks (p75) in Ala Moana.

DRINKING IN KAIMUKĪ: TOP PICKS

Brew'd Craft Pub: Gastropub with good pub food and a large and inviting patio. The knowledgeable staff help you navigate the long beer list. *11am-10pm* $$

Curb: Buzzy cafe with good smells from coffee (made with locally roasted beans), sensational cookies (killer chocolate chip) and breakfast toasts. *7am-2pm* $

Leahi Health Kaimuki: Come for the smoothies in many variations, stay for the kale. Has fresh health tonics and juices, and good coffee plus cold brew. *8am-6pm* $

Vintage Books: Kaimukī's most atmospheric restaurant features its namesake decor. Dark and stylish bar for creative cocktails and a good wine list. *4-11pm* $$

DIAMOND HEAD HIKE

One of O'ahu's top hikes, the climb to the windy summit of Diamond Head affords fantastic 360-degree views.

START	END	LENGTH
Diamond Head State Monument parking lot	Diamond Head State Monument parking lot	1.6mi; 1½ hours

Begin at the 1 **Diamond Head State Monument parking lot** and follow the signposted trail. The first set of 74 2 **concrete steps** is followed by a curving 225ft-long tunnel. At the 3 **T-junction**, turn left and follow the trail along the rim, enjoying the views into the sun-blasted crater, where almost all the WWII buildings are now gone. The Hawaiian name for the crater, Le'ahi, means 'wreath of fire.' Don't miss the 4 **lookout**, which has impressive views. On a clear day, you may spot the islands of Moloka'i, Maui and Lāna'i. In winter, watch for passing humpback whales.

Ascend the 82 metal steps to the 5 **crater rim**; most of the bunkers you see were built in 1915. Finally, a set of 54 metal stairs takes you to the top. You're now at the 6 **crater summit** and the top level of the Fire Control Station (761ft). The station was built to direct artillery fire out to sea from batteries at Fort DeRussy in Waikīkī and Fort Ruger outside Diamond Head crater. Enjoy the city view and the blue Pacific!

Loop back around to the lower level of the fire-control station. Duck inside and descend the lighted spiral staircase until you exit to a set of 99 steep steps down to the T-junction. Retrace the route back to the parking lot.

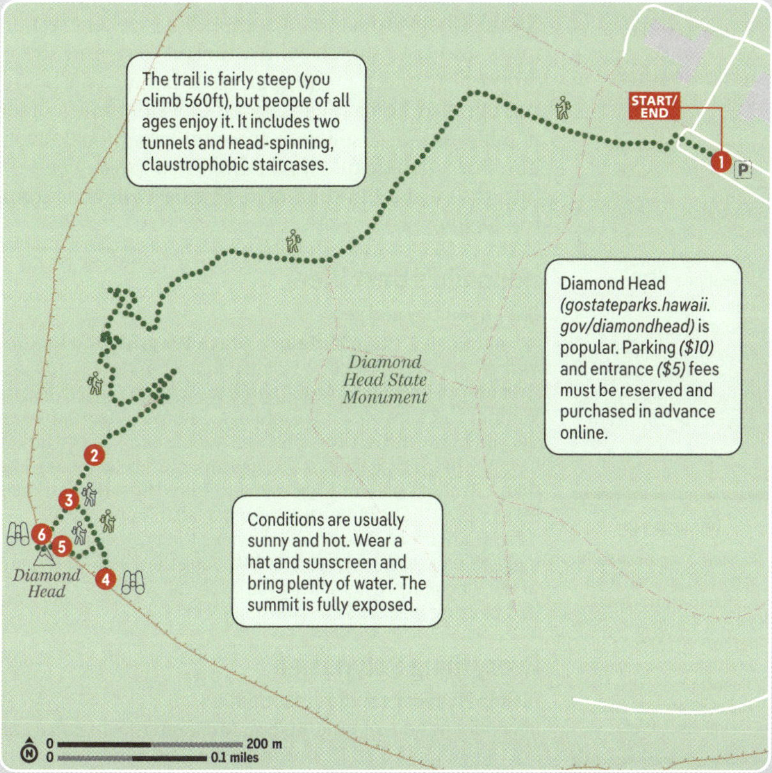

Greater Honolulu

MOUNTAIN HIKES, MUSEUMS AND PLATE LUNCHES

GETTING AROUND

Greater Honolulu is spread out. Consider renting a car for a day or two to explore. With the notable exception of Mānoa Falls, few trailheads are easily reachable by TheBus. Kalihi is spread out with no definable center and unpleasant walks past warehouses and box-store parking deserts.

Reaching much of Greater Honolulu using TheBus from Waikīkī will require one or more transfers. Route 2 does come fairly close to the Bishop Museum and Rapid Bus W does pass through Kalihi.

TOP TIP

Plan on having lunch early at the classic lunch spots scattered across Greater Honolulu. On weekdays they get busy and parking can be a challenge on narrow neighborhood roads. Also, the most popular menu items sell out.

Away from the beaches of Waikīkī and the bustling flatlands in the commercial center is another Honolulu, one where emerald *pali* dominate shadow life, where hiking trails weave through the solitude of the forests and waterfalls around the city. Some of Oʻahu's most popular hiking trails lead into the lush, windy Koʻolau Range just above Downtown. This great Honolulu arcs around the center in a crescent. Oʻahu's top museum is also here, as are old royal landmarks.

Toward the airport, the industrial neighborhood of Kalihi is home to scores of humble but excellent restaurants and plate-lunch joints, tucked here and there. Stop off at one for a proper meal before you board the big bird home. Scattered about Honolulu's older neighborhoods elsewhere are some great local favorites. For a delightful – and edible – surprise, head up into the verdant and affluent Mānoa Valley for some top local eats.

Honolulu's Best View

Gaze upon city and sea

At the hillside **Puʻu ʻUalakaʻa State Wayside Park** *(dlnr.hawaii.gov/dsp/parks/oahu/puu-ualakaa-state-wayside)*, sweeping views extend from Diamond Head on the left, across Waikīkī and Downtown Honolulu, to the Waiʻanae Range on the right. The airport is visible on the coast and Pearl Harbor beyond that. The Pacific is a backdrop to everything. It's less than 2.5 miles up Round Top Dr from Makiki St to the entrance. Signs detail the area's history as a macadamia nut farm.

Pro tip: park at the picnic area near the park entrance and make the short and rewarding walk along the shrub-lined path to the viewpoint. This spares you from the scrum for the limited parking places at the viewpoint.

Everything Polynesian

Bishop Museum's endless fascination

Spend a few hours at the **Bishop Museum** *(bishopmuseum.org; adult/child $39/31)*, one of the world's finest Polynesian

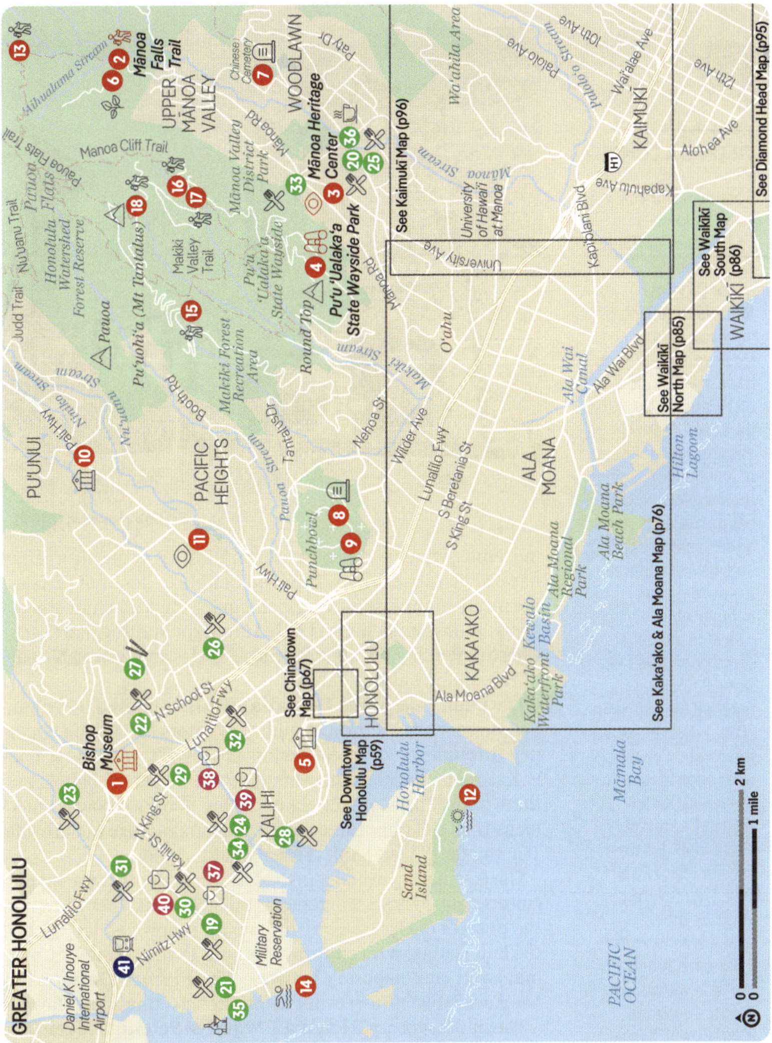

★ **HIGHLIGHTS**
1 Bishop Museum
2 Mānoa Falls Trail
3 Mānoa Heritage Center
4 Pu'u 'Ualaka'a State Wayside Park

● **SIGHTS**
5 Hawaiian Music Hall of Fame
6 Lyon Arboretum
7 Mānoa Chinese Cemetery
8 National Memorial Cemetery of the Pacific
9 Punchbowl Overlook
10 Queen Emma Summer Palace
11 Royal Mausoleum State Monument
12 Sand Island State Recreation Area

● **ACTIVITIES**
13 'Aihualama Trail
14 Jet Ski Oahu
15 Makiki Valley Trailhead
16 Mānoa Cliff Trailhead
17 Moleka Trailhead
18 Pu'u 'Ohi'a Trailhead

● **EATING**
19 Alicia's Market
20 Andy's Sandwiches & Smoothies
21 Best Drive In
22 Helena's Hawaiian Food
23 Kalihi Bar-B-Q Drive-Inn
24 Kamehameha Bakery
25 Lady Elaine
26 Liliha Bakery
27 Natsunoya Tea House
28 Nico's Pier 38
see 20 Off the Hook Poke Market
29 Palace Saimin
30 Pongo's Kitchen
31 Ray's Cafe
32 Tamashiro Market
33 Waioli Kitchen & Bake Shop
34 Young's Fish Market

● **DRINKING & NIGHTLIFE**
see 37 Honolulu Beerworks
35 La Mariana Sailing Club
36 Morning Glass Coffee

● **SHOPPING**
37 Lion Coffee
38 Na Lima Mili Hulu No'eau
39 Nisshodo Candy Store
40 Sun Noodle

● **TRANSPORT**
41 Kahauiki/Kalihi Transit Center

SKYLINE: THE TRAIN'S A COMIN'

Speedy trains soaring over Honolulu's coagulated traffic is the promise of the **Skyline** *(honolulutransit.org)* light-rail system. However, trouble has been a waystation on this ticket to paradise. Years of missed deadlines and blown budgets (once touted as costing $4 billion, $10 billion has been spent to date and it's still – literally – nowhere near complete).

Skyline did generate some good news when it finally reached the airport in 2025; however, except for a station on the west edge of Kalihi (**Kahauiki/Kalihi Transit Center**), the entire line runs west to Kapolei via Pearl City. This severely limits Skyline's usefulness to visitors.

Not until 2031 will the final – and most useful – portion (Chinatown, Downtown and Kaka'ako) open. Stops near Ala Moana and Waikīkī were cut to save money.

MICHAEL VI/SHUTTERSTOCK

Bishop Museum (p100)

museums, which showcases a remarkable array of cultural and natural history exhibits. Founded in 1889 in honor of Princess Bernice Pauahi Bishop, a descendant of the Kamehameha dynasty, it originally housed only Hawaiian and royal artifacts. These days it honors all of Polynesia and is an unmissable part of Honolulu's cultural fabric.

The main gallery, the **Hawaiian Hall**, is housed in a dignified three-story Victorian building. Visitors embark on a journey through the different realms of Hawai'i. On the 1st floor is Kai Akea, which represents Hawaiian legends, beliefs and the world of pre-contact Hawai'i. One floor up, Wao Kanaka focuses on the importance of the land and nature in daily life. The top floor, Wao Lani, is the domain of gods.

The fascinating exhibits in the **Pacific Hall** cover the myriad cultures of Polynesia, Micronesia and Melanesia. They show how the peoples of Oceania are diverse, yet deeply connected, and the hall is filled with cultural treasures such as canoes, woven mats and contemporary artwork. The **Picture Gallery** features evocative 19th-century paintings depicting a lost Hawai'i.

The multi-sensory **Richard T Mamiya Science Adventure Center** explores Hawai'i's environment. The **Hawai'i Sports Hall of Fame** has photos and memorabilia from Hawaiian sports legends starting with the ubiquitous Duke Kahanamoku.

The well-marked **Na Ulu Kaiwi'ula Native Hawaiian Garden** features species important to Hawaiian culture, ranging from endemic plants to imports like breadfruit, which were brought to Hawai'i by Polynesians centuries ago.

The **planetarium** has an ever-changing range of shows, including an engaging demonstration of traditional Polynesian methods of navigation.

The **gift shop** sells books on the Pacific not easily found elsewhere, as well as high-quality Hawaiian art, crafts and souvenirs. The on-site cafe **Tūt'ū's Place** is run by the renowned Highway Inn (p79) and serves traditional foods.

A Beach Hiding in Plain Sight

Sand Island State Recreation Area

A barely visited half-mile ribbon of fine-grain sand hides in plain sight from much of Honolulu. Industrial Sand Island, sitting between the airport and the port, is home to **Sand Island State Recreation Area** *(dlnr.hawaii.gov/dsp/parks/oahu/sand-island-state-recreation-area)*. The beach is backed by vast lawns dotted with trees. Watch planes taking off and enjoy views of hulking cruise ships pulling into port backed by the high-rises of Downtown and Waikīkī. In 2026 the State of Hawai'i began the process to change the name of Sand Island back to its Hawaiian name of Mauliola, which means 'breath of life' or 'power of healing.'

On the way to the park entrance, stop off for a thrill at **Jet Ski Oahu** *(jetskioahu.com; 45min rental from $110)*. Zip across the smooth waters of the Ke'ehi Channel and around tiny islands dotted with fishing shacks.

Surprising Kalihi

Treasures among warehouses

Between Downtown and the airport, semi-industrial Kalihi has top-notch shops and places to eat you won't want to miss, dotted amid the warehouses.

Lion Coffee *(lioncoffee.com)* roasts local coffee in varied flavors, ranging from straight-up strong to off-the-wall (caramel, toasted coconut). Take a tour, have a taste and buy some beans.

The industrial exterior of **Nisshodo Candy Store** *(nisshodomochicandy.com)* is home to freshly made, succulent mochi (chewy Japanese rice cakes). Coconut is a fave; peanut butter sells out early.

At **Na Lima Mili Hulu No'eau** *(featherlegacy.com)*, a skilled family keeps alive the ancient craft of feather lei-making at this simple shop, whose name means 'the skilled hands that touch the feathers.' Check for opening hours or to schedule an appointment for a personalized lesson.

The Sweet Melodies of Hawai'i

Hear the incredible musical heritage of the islands

With over 100 inductees, the **Hawaiian Music Hall of Fame** *(hmhof.org; free)* encompasses an extraordinary wealth of talent. See their stories at the hall's gallery in the Design Center. Panels tell a compelling range of stories, such as that of Mary Kawena Puku'i, who wrote more than 50 songs as well as co-authoring

HAWAI'I'S UNIQUE 7-ELEVENS

Think 7-Eleven on the mainland and you'll likely picture a Big Gulp or a Slurpee. If it's food, you might imagine the high-fat charms of Slim Jim beef jerky or the ultra-processed pleasures of a bag of Cheetos.

Stop into a 7-Eleven in Hawai'i *(7elevenhawaii.com)*, and you can indeed find the items above, plus all the other expected snack foods. But look further and you'll discover a bevy of food items unlike any you've seen at any mainland 7-Eleven. Fresh sushi, bento boxes, lovely salads, authentic noodle soups that don't need boiling water, trays of dim sum and tempting *musubi* (for only $2!).

That's because Hawai'i's 7-Elevens are affiliated with Japan's, which are renowned for their wide selection of fresh food.

EATING & DRINKING IN KALIHI: SURPRISING PICKS

Kamehameha Bakery: Beloved, no-frills bakery selling pastries, rolls, breads. Try the poi-glazed doughnut. Many doughnuts sell out by noon. *2am-4pm* $

Ray's Cafe: Diner facade hides plates groaning with excellent hunks of prime rib priced for the masses. Also a range of steaks and full menu for breakfast. Cash only. *6am-5pm* $$

Honolulu Beerworks: This warehouse microbrewery is one of O'ahu's best. Taste the seasonal beers in the sweet little beer garden. *noon-8pm Tue-Sat* $$

La Mariana Sailing Club: Thatch-walled, tiki-themed 1950s waterfront joint filled with modern-day sailors. Mai tais are as killer as the other tropical potions. *11am-8pm* $$

the landmark *Hawaiian Dictionary*. The hall regularly inducts new members – many multi-talented veterans of the lounges of Waikīkī – and it hosts live shows by top local talent.

Royal Refuges

Quaint palace and stately chapel

The old Pali Hwy passes two significant royal Hawaiian sites. In the heat and humidity of summer, Queen Emma (1836–85), the wife and royal consort of Kamehameha IV, used to slip away from her formal Downtown Honolulu home to a cooler hillside retreat in Nu'uanu Valley.

On a self-guided tour of the compact **Queen Emma Summer Palace** *(daughtersofhawaii.org/queen-emma-summer-palace; adult/child $14/5)*, Hānaiakamalama in Hawaiian, you can appreciate treasures such as the cathedral-shaped koa cabinet displaying a set of china given by England's Queen Victoria, brightly colored feather cloaks and capes once worn by Hawaiian royalty. Built in Greek Revival style, the exterior has a columned porch and high ceilings. Stroll the serene gardens.

Known as Mauna 'Ala (Fragrant Hills) in Hawaiian, the **Royal Mausoleum State Monument** *(dlnr.hawaii.gov/dsp/parks/oahu/royal-mausoleum-state-monument; free)* is the final resting place of Hawai'i's two prominent royal families, the Kamehamehas and the Kalākauas. Completed in 1865 for Prince Albert, the mausoleum is home to the remains of most of Hawai'i's monarchs, their consorts, and various princes and princesses. A sacred place to all Hawaiians, the manicured grounds are peaceful and the Gothic Revival chapel is on the National Register of Historic Places.

Punchbowl's Fields of Sacrifice

Historic final resting place

Northeast of Downtown Honolulu is a bowl-shaped crater, nicknamed the Punchbowl, formed by a long-extinct volcano. Hawaiians called the crater Puowaina (Hill of Human Sacrifices). It's believed that at an ancient heiau (temple) here, the slain bodies of *kapu* (taboo) breakers were ceremonially cremated upon an altar. Today, the remains of ancient Hawaiians sacrificed to appease the gods share the crater floor with the bodies of well over 50,000 soldiers at the **National Memorial Cemetery of the Pacific** *(cem.va.gov/cems/nchp/NMCP.asp)*.

The remains of Ernie Pyle, the legendary war correspondent killed during the final days of WWII, lie in section D, grave

BEST OFFBEAT FESTIVALS

Waikīkī Spam Jam *(spamjamhawaii.com)* This street festival in April is devoted to Hawai'i's favorite tinned meat product.

Shinnyo Lantern Floating Hawai'i *(lanternfloatinghawaii.com)* On Memorial Day, souls are honored with a Japanese Shinnyo floating lantern ceremony in Ala Moana Regional Park (p74).

Queen Lili'uokalani Keiki Hula Competition *(keikihula.org)* In July, children's hula troupes compete at the Neal S Blaisdell Center.

Hawaii Dragon Boat Festival *(chinesechamber.com)* In July, colorful 21-person dragon boats race to the beat of island drummers. It's held in Ala Moana Regional Park.

Hawaiian Slack Key Guitar Festival *(waikikiaquarium.org)* A day-long celebration of traditional Hawaiian slack key guitar and 'ukulele music. Held at the Waikīkī Aquarium in August.

EATING IN KALIHI: PLATE LUNCHES

Best Drive In: On the way to Sand Island and its hidden beach, stop in at this unadorned Korean-style cafe serving spicy fare like kimchi-redolent pork. *5am-3pm Mon-Sat* $

Kalihi Bar-B-Q Drive-Inn: Best-selling chicken katsu in portions good for one, two or three meals. Secret-recipe katsu sauce, plus Chinese classics. *10am-7pm* $

Pongo's Kitchen: Combo plates are the specialty. There's simple seating inside and out. The walls are plastered with menus and food descriptions. *10am-2pm Mon-Fri* $

Young's Fish Market: Serving popular plate lunches since 1951. Known for traditional *laulau* (pork and fish steamed in leaves with poi). *9:30am-7pm Mon-Sat* $

DOUGLAS PEEBLES PHOTOGRAPHY/ALAMY

National Memorial Cemetery of the Pacific

109. Five stones to the left, at grave D-1, is Ellison Onizuka, the Hawai'i (Big Island) astronaut who died in the 1986 *Challenger* space shuttle disaster. Longtime US senator and WWII Medal of Honor winner Daniel K. Inouye (section D, grave 391A) is also here. Look up grave site locations at the **visitors center**.

Note the iconic 30ft-tall statue *Columbia* on the central tower, which features in the opening credits of *Hawaii Five-0*.

The **Punchbowl Overlook** offers Honolulu's best views, from the airport to Diamond Head, with the Pacific shimmering in the distance. The walkways are lined with memorials to various military units, many with poignant stories attached.

The Green Mānoa Valley

Lush beauty, history and good eats

Roads into the upper **Mānoa Valley** enter a lush land dripping with water, framed by rainbows, laced with hiking trails and where green carpets climb the steep *pali*.

The valley also holds many attractions, including the Mānoa Heritage Center (p108) and one of O'ahu's best hikes to Mānoa Falls (p108). Founded in 1852 amid a backdrop of mountains, the large **Mānoa Chinese Cemetery** is an evocative place for a stroll among the memorials and grave sites.

To top it all off, there are excellent eateries, including top cafe Waioli Kitchen & Bake Shop (p109).

BEST HIKING TRAILS

The mountains behind Honolulu are laced with trails. See maps and options at hawaiitrails. *ehawaii.gov/trails* and *alltrails.com*. The road trip on Tantalus and Round Top Drive (p106) passes many of these trailheads.

Makiki Valley Trail: This 2.5-mile trail links three trails through lush tropical forest. Expect mud, so wear shoes with traction.

Pu'u 'Ohi'a Trail: Littered with fragrant *liliko'i* (passion fruit). Contemplative forest hikes combined with city views.

Mānoa Cliff Trail: Runs 2 miles each way along a ridge with good views. Links to trails that reach Pu'u Ohi'a.

Moleka Trail: A good taste of the mountains, this 2.3-mile loop begins and ends at a parking area.

'Aihualama Trail: Starts near Mānoa Falls, ascending high up the Ko'olau Range, with steep *pali* visible all around.

EATING IN GREATER HONOLULU: CLASSIC CHOICES

Liliha Bakery: The original 1950 location of a local mini-chain. Old-school island bakery and diner known for Coco Puffs (chocolatey cream puffs). *6am-10pm* $

Natsunoya Tea House: Traditional family-run teahouse on a hillside; used by Japanese spies before Pearl Harbor. Little has changed in decades. *11am-9pm Wed-Sun* $$

Helena's Hawaiian Food: Legendary 1946 institution. James Beard Award winner gets the details right on its plate lunches. Lines form early. *10am-7:30pm Tue-Fri* $$

Palace Saimin: The name sums up this simple 1946 storefront. Saimin (a Hawaiian take on Japanese noodle soup) comes in many delicious forms here. *10am-8pm Tue-Sat* $

DRIVING TOUR

Punchbowl, Pu'uohi'a & Round Top Drive

Head up into Honolulu's backdrop of lush, green mountains for a grand break from sand and surf. Few fail to be startled by the prolific tropical vegetation, the elevation gained and the stupendous panoramas on this adventurous 16-mile, three-hour drive up Pu'uohi'a (aka Mt Tantalus). Stop along the way and stroll one of the many hiking trails, or just marvel at the views and nature along this swath of O'ahu.

1 Punchbowl (Puowaina)

Just to the east of Downtown Honolulu, Punchbowl (Puowaina) is an extinct volcanic tuff cone. Today, it's the site of the National Memorial Cemetery of the Pacific (p104). Hawaiians called the bowl-like crater 'Puowaina' (Hill of Human Sacrifices). Today the remains of ancient Hawaiians share the crater floor with the bodies of nearly 50,000 soldiers, many of whom were killed in the Pacific during WWII.

The Drive: Leaving Punchbowl, turn right and join Tantalus Dr. The road climbs into hillside Honolulu and you'll pass many suburban houses with enviable views.

2 Makiki Valley Trailhead

The road passes many vantage points with sweeping city vistas. The roughly U-shaped route has pullouts for numerous hiking trails through the dense rainforest, ridges and water-riven valleys. At a sharp bend, the Makiki Valley Trailhead (p105) starts a trail that traverses small gulches and crosses gentle streams bordered by patches of ginger and guava trees while offering glimpses of the city below.

The Drive: Tantalus Dr now begins a series of sharp uphill switchbacks into the Makiki forest reserves. Go slow and watch for daredevil cyclists careening downhill.

LILLIAN K/SHUTTERSTOCK

Mānoa Cliff Trail (p105)

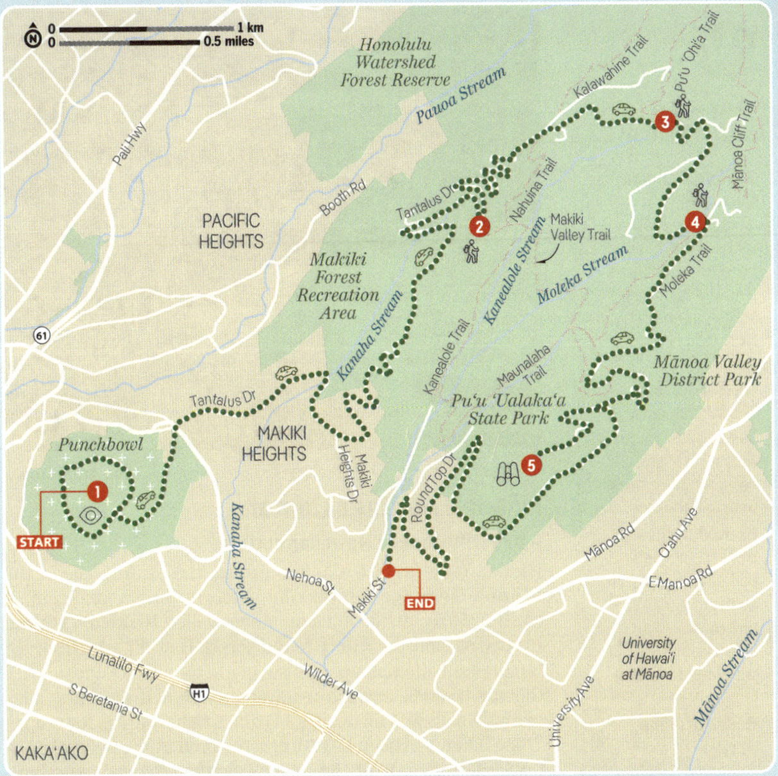

❸ Pu'u 'Ohi'a Trailhead

Pu'uohi'a (2014ft), aka Mt Tantalus, is the heart of what's literally an urban jungle. Just a few minutes ago, you were in the sun-dappled city. Now you're in the clouds, where rain is either falling or about to fall. Near the top of the road, the Pu'u 'Ohi'a Trailhead (p105) leads to the summit on a 4-mile out-and-back jaunt. You'll feel the high humidity and fragrant warmth of the dense living and rotting vegetation in your bones.

The Drive: From its high point, Tantalus Dr turns into Round Top Dr for its gentler descent down the eastern side of the mountain.

❹ Mānoa Cliff & Moleka Trailheads

Trailheads for two popular trails are here. Mānoa Cliff Trail (p105) follows the ridge north for a challenging hike that ends at Pu'uohi'a (Mt Tantalus). The looping Moleka Trail (p105) goes south and boasts startling views of Diamond Head, which looks otherworldly rising above the surrounding urban sprawl and the Pacific.

The Drive: Flowering trees such as jacaranda and African tulips add to the visual stimulation as you continue your Round Top Dr descent.

❺ Pu'u 'Ualaka'a State Wayside Park

One of O'ahu's underappreciated treasures, Pu'u 'Ualaka'a State Wayside Park (p100) is worth the stop. Its viewpoint presents sweeping views of Waikīkī and Honolulu from Diamond Head in the east to the Wai'anae Range in the west. Waikīkī high-rises jut up like the teeth of an alligator.

The Drive: It's 2.5 miles down Round Top Dr in ever-increasing suburbia to Makiki St at the foot of the mountain.

BEST FOR QUALITY HAWAIIAN GIFTS

Tin Can Mailman: Cute little Chinatown shop with a wonderfully curated selection of Hawaiiana goods, some decades old. Browsing is half the fun.

Nā Mea Hawai'i: This Ala Moana shop has goods from top Hawai'i artisans and creators, plus rare and unusual books.

Honolulu Museum of Art: Luxe and stylish goods inspired by the museum's fine Hawaiian art collection (p75), plus scholarly tomes on local culture.

House of Mana Up: Waikīkī store celebrates Hawaiian start-ups, who design and make housewares, apparel, gift items, edibles and artworks.

Bishop Museum: The shop at the famous museum (p100) covering Polynesian culture has goods inspired by the fabled collections, along with an excellent book section.

BLOODBERRY/SHUTTERSTOCK

Lyon Arboretum

Mānoa's Heritage Center

A beautiful look at Hawaiian culture

Hidden on a private 3.5-acre estate, the centerpiece of the **Mānoa Heritage Center** *(manoaheritagecenter.org; adult/child $25/free)* is the ancient, stone-walled **Kūka'ō'ō Heiau**. It's one of thousands once found across Hawai'i, which served hundreds of different uses. This is one of the smaller ones and it's thought it served agriculture given its view of the Mānoa Valley below, which was once one of O'ahu's richest areas for crops.

The heiau has been beautifully restored at the behest of the Cooke family (one of the major colonizing clans), who built the incongruous mansion that looms behind and also funded the heritage center.

Today you can visit on a **guided tour** booked well in advance. Docents go deep into Hawaiian lore and traditions. They explain the gardens where rare native and Polynesian-introduced plants grow in profusion and the air is redolent with hibiscus.

Hike to Mānoa Falls

Popular, beautiful but buggy

Honolulu's most rewarding short hike, the **Mānoa Falls Trail** *(hawaiitrails.ehawaii.gov/trails)* is a 1.6-mile, two-hour round-trip trail that runs above a rocky stream bed before ending at a pretty little cascade. Tall tree trunks line the often muddy

EATING IN GREATER HONOLULU: GOOD BETS

Sun Noodle: For sublime DIY Japanese noodles, hit the factory outlet of Hawai'i's top noodle producer; some come with sauce mix. *9am-3pm Tue-Sat* $$

Tamashiro Market: Fish vendor sells prepared foods and poke with many options, including various spices. Take-out only. There are also grocery items. *8am-3pm* $

Alicia's Market: Neighborhood market selling excellent poke and smoked meat. Prepared Asian meals and packed picnic lunches too. *10am-2pm Mon-Sat* $

Nico's Pier 38: Sprawling patio overlooking a fishing fleet. Chef Nico blends his classical French training with plate lunches; daily seafood specials. *6:30am-9pm* $$

and slippery path. Wild orchids and red ginger grow near the falls, which drop about 100ft into a small, shallow pool. Note that it's illegal to venture beyond the established viewing area.

The trail has an 800ft elevation and features many plants, including four kinds of tree ferns. Falling rocks and the risk of leptospirosis (a waterborne bacterial infection) make entering the water dangerous. One caveat for visitors: the hike is very popular. Mornings and all-day weekends see a frenzy of visitors. Come on a weekday afternoon and try for the off-season.

The cacophony of 'no parking' signs in the area indicates the problems the neighborhood faces from the crowds. You can park for a fee (if space is available) 100m from the entrance. Or take bus 5 to the end of the line from where it's a half-mile walk uphill to the trailhead. And bring bug spray – although the parking attendant can sell you some.

A Garden of Soulful Plants

Lush Lyon Arboretum

See all of Hawai'i's key plants in one place at **Lyon Arboretum** *(manoa.hawaii.edu/lyon; free)*. During an hour-long visit, get up close and personal with *'ulu* (breadfruit), *kalo* (taro) and *ko* (sugarcane), which were brought by early Polynesian settlers. Other green notables include *kukui* (candlenut trees), once harvested to produce lantern oil; and *ti*, which was used for medicinal purposes during ancient times and for making moonshine after Westerners arrived.

The office has a good selection of books for sale, as well as insect repellent. The gardens are near the Mānoa Falls trailhead, which means access is a hassle; get there early to snare one of the few spaces. Otherwise, park in the lot for the falls or ride bus 5 to the end of the line and make the 0.6-mile walk uphill.

An Alluring, Historic Cafe

Enjoy Waioli Kitchen & Bake Shop

Set in a vintage compound amid enormous trees, the sublime **Waioli Kitchen & Bake Shop** cooks delicious breakfasts and lunches. Sit out on the gracious Craftsman-style 1920s veranda of what was once a girls' orphanage. Today, many of the staffers are residents learning a trade. The menu has daily specials, but stalwart items include fantastic macadamia nut pancakes, avocado toast, excellent scones, burgers and more. The coffee is excellent, too – with free refills! The biggest challenge on a visit is finding the will to leave and get on with your day in paradise.

HONOLULU HIKES & INFO

Hawai'i Nature Center *(hawaiinaturecenter.org)* Inside the Makiki Valley State Recreation Area, this small nonprofit runs environmental education programs, day camps and guided weekend hikes for ages six and up. Best to book ahead.

Hawaiian Trail & Mountain Corp *(htmc1910.org)* This volunteer-run hiking club arranges group hikes on weekends. There's a calendar of hike and trail descriptions online.

Sierra Club *(sierracluboahu.org)* The Hawai'i chapter leads weekend hikes and outings around O'ahu, including volunteer opportunities to rebuild trails and combat invasive plants.

State Department of Labor & Natural Resources *(dlnr.hawaii.gov/recreation/nah/oahu)* Has extensive info and links to detailed OuterSpatial planning tools.

EATING & DRINKING IN THE MĀNOA VALLEY: TOP CHOICES

Off the Hook Poke Market: Lines form early for the superb poke – the spicy 'ahi is sublime and the flavor combos spot on. Has sidewalk tables. *10am-6pm Mon-Sat* $

Andy's Sandwiches & Smoothies: This take-out spot gets packed. Superb sandwiches, smoothies and salads; try the green-chili-melt sandwich. *7am-4pm Mon-Fri* $

Morning Glass Coffee: Small, open-air coffee bar with mountain views serves terrific food. Good bet: macaroni and cheese pancakes. *7am-2pm Tue-Sun* $$

Lady Elaine: Creative, cliche-busting Med fare that changes with the seasons. Appealing dining room and a shady terrace. The valley's most alluring bar. *11am-9pm Mon-Sat* $$

Pearl Harbor & 'Aiea

MEMORIES OF WWII

TOP TIP

The main Pearl Harbor National Memorial sites have basic concession stands. For lunch, the Hanger Café at the Pearl Harbor Aviation Museum has the best menu (sandwiches etc), although it's rather gloomy. Security requirements preclude bringing a picnic onto the visitor center grounds. Fortunately, there are some excellent choices nearby and in 'Aiea.

Still an active military base, Pearl Harbor has a resonance for all Americans. The site of the December 7, 1941, attack that brought the US into WWII is accessible, evocative and moving. Every year, more than two million people visit Pearl Harbor's memorials and museums, including the USS *Arizona* Memorial, making it the most visited site in Hawai'i. The events of over 85 years ago are recalled even as the last veterans have died.

Just north of Pearl Harbor lies the suburb of 'Aiea, a slice of modern island life and a gateway to O'ahu's green interior. In the misty Ko'olau Range above the harbor, explore an ancient Hawaiian temple and the wonders of 16th-century Hawaiian healthcare (think aromatic plants for a start). A loop walk reveals the lush beauty just beyond the city's edge.

'Aiea is also a center for great – and cheap – meals. Kamehameha Hwy has numerous delicious hole-in-the-wall and Asian eateries. Continuing west is strip-mall-filled Pearl City.

Aloha Stadium Swap Meet & Marketplace

From tacky to treasures

The hugely popular **Aloha Stadium Swap Meet & Marketplace** *(alohastadiumswapmeet.net; $2)* draws hundreds of vendors and thousands of shoppers from morning

GETTING AROUND

The Pearl Harbor National Memorial is off the Kamehameha Hwy (Hwy 99); there's plenty of paid parking. From Waikīkī, bus 42 is the most direct, taking just over an hour each way.

Bus routes from Honolulu serving 'Aiea include 40, 42 and 51.

The Skyline Hālawa/Aloha Stadium Station is a 15-minute walk from the Pearl Harbor National Memorial. It's also close to the Aloha Stadium Swap Meet & Marketplace (bus 42 also passes close by from Waikīkī).

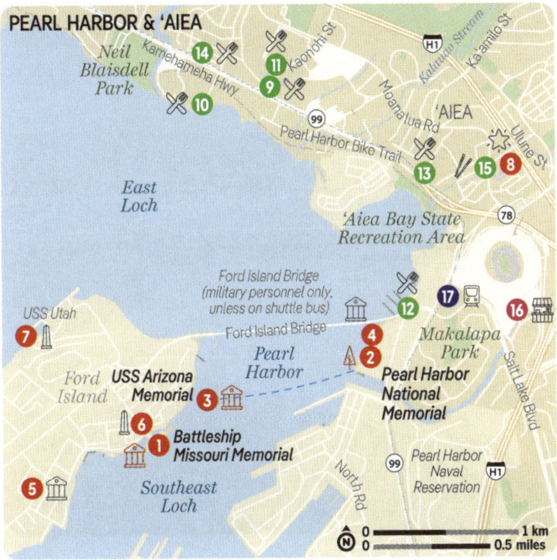

HIGHLIGHTS
1 Battleship Missouri Memorial
2 Pearl Harbor National Memorial
3 USS Arizona Memorial

SIGHTS
4 Pacific Fleet Submarine Museum
5 Pearl Harbor Aviation Museum
6 USS Oklahoma Memorial
7 USS Utah Memorial

ACTIVITIES
8 'Aiea Bowl

EATING
see 8 Alley Restaurant at 'Aiea Bowl
9 Anna Miller's
10 Ige's Lunchwagon
11 Kehau's Kitchen
12 Restaurant 604
13 Ryder's Poke & Shave Ice
14 Shiro's Saimin Haven
15 Sushi Spot

SHOPPING
16 Aloha Stadium Swap Meet & Marketplace

TRANSPORT
17 Hālawa/Aloha Stadium Station

to mid-afternoon every Wednesday, Saturday and Sunday. Your eyes will cross at the plethora of gaudy souvenirs, cheap T-shirts, loudly patterned clothes in unnatural fibers, plastic orchids, phone cases and fad foods (think creatine). Amid it all, though, are interesting handmade items and fresh fruit vendors. Note: many vendors don't get set up until after 9am.

The replacement building could open in 2029 as part of a massive redevelopment, but the marketplace will likely live on.

Score a Strike

Fun times at 'Aiea Bowl

Throw a strike at **'Aiea Bowl** *(aieabowl.com)*, in the aging 'Aiea Shopping Center. It's a lively, old-school bowling alley with a full slate of special events and lots of diversions like arcade games for non-bowlers. It also has an excellent restaurant and bar, the Alley Restaurant, with tables overlooking the lanes.

EATING AROUND PEARL HARBOR & 'AIEA: TOP PICKS

Alley Restaurant at 'Aiea Bowl: Try the *furikake* 'ahi sandwich or Asian braised pork at this bowling alley diner. Tables have views of the lanes. *10am-9pm* $$

Kehau's Kitchen: Superb plate lunches at a simple storefront. *Kālua* pork and *lomi lomi* salmon (minced salmon with veg) made in-house. Huge combo plates. *10am-8pm* $$

Shiro's Saimin Haven: Specializing in its namesake soup since 1969. Fresh noodles and other options keep the crowds coming. In a restaurant-filled strip mall. *7am-9pm* $$

Restaurant 604: Pearl Harbor views over a yacht marina. Weekend brunch, comfort food and a busy bar. It's a 10-minute walk north from the visitor center. *10:30am-9pm* $$

U.S. NAVY PHOTO/JOHANS CHAVARRO, VIA WIKIMEDIA COMMONS

Above: Ford Island; Right: USS *Arizona* Memorial

TOP EXPERIENCE

Pearl Harbor

The rallying cry 'Remember Pearl Harbor!' once mobilized an entire nation. It was here that the surprise Japanese attack on December 7, 1941, hurtled the US into war in the Pacific. The iconic offshore shrine at the sunken USS *Arizona* is the focus while other unmissable museums and memorials tell the story of the attack and the larger war.

DON'T MISS

- National Memorial Museum
- USS *Arizona* Memorial & boat ride
- Battleship *Missouri* Memorial
- USS *Oklahoma* Memorial
- Pearl Harbor Aviation Museum
- Pacific Fleet Submarine Museum & USS *Bowfin*

Pearl Harbor National Memorial

One of the USA's most significant WWII sites, the National Park Service (NPS) **Pearl Harbor National Memorial** recounts the history of the Pearl Harbor attack and commemorates the dead. The visitor center at the main entrance is the hub for visits to Pearl Harbor's sites and museums.

The free memorial grounds and **NPS Visitor Center** are more than just a boat dock for the USS *Arizona* Memorial. Be sure to stop at the superb **museum**, where engaging displays bring to life the war in the Pacific through photos, films, graphics and oral histories. A shoreside walk passes signs illustrating how the attack unfolded in the now-peaceful harbor.

Historic **Ford Island** can be visited via official buses to the USS *Missouri*, the Pearl Harbor Aviation Museum and on certain tours. The rest of the island is off-limits to tourists.

Practicalities

● nps.gov/perl/planyourvisit ● 7am-5pm ● Free

TROPICALPIXSINGAPORE/GETTY IMAGES

ONE WAR, THREE MAIN SIGHTS

Besides the USS *Arizona* memorial, there are two other important historical sites nearby: the USS *Bowfin* submarine (aka the 'Pearl Harbor Avenger') and museum, and the huge battleship USS *Missouri*, where the Japanese surrender at the end of WWII was accepted. These military sites represent the beginning, middle and end of the war for the US.

Besides special events on Memorial Day (last Monday in May) and Veterans Day (November 11), Pearl Harbor Day (December 7) is the focus of weeklong memorials and ceremonies.

USS *Arizona* Memorial

The somber **USS *Arizona* Memorial** is one of the USA's most significant WWII sites, commemorating the destruction of the USS *Arizona* and its dead with an iconic offshore monument reachable by boat.

The memorial was built over the midsection of the sunken *Arizona*, with deliberate geometry to represent initial defeat, ultimate victory and eternal serenity. In the furthest of three chambers inside the shrine, the names of the 1177 crew killed in the attack are engraved onto a marble wall. In the central section, cutaways reveal the skeletal remains of the ship, which still oozes about a quart of oil each day into the harbor, where you can see sea turtles and fish. In its rush to recover from the attack, the US Navy left over 900 servicemen inside the sunken ship; they remain entombed in its hull. In recent decades, some surviving *Arizona* veterans opted to have their cremated remains added to those of their shipmates.

During a 15-minute visit to the memorial, try to step away from others and contemplate the size of this ship and what was lost. Look at the model of the wreckage back at the museum to understand what's below.

Free **boat tours** to the memorial depart from 8am until 3:30pm (weather permitting). The 45-minute tour must be reserved online via recreation.gov up to 56 days before your visit. Tickets are also available on the website one day before, beginning at 3pm Hawai'i time - but these are very limited. There is also an optional 23-minute documentary film about the attack.

TOP TIPS

- Reserve early!
- Dedicate a full day to visiting all the Pearl Harbor sites.
- Strict security measures mean you can't have any items that allow concealment (eg larger purses, fanny packs, daypacks, diaper bags etc). Phones and cameras are allowed. There is a paid storage facility near the visitor center entrance.
- Private boat tours of Pearl Harbor only pass by the USS *Arizona* memorial and don't dock.
- There are basic refreshment choices; see p116 for the best options.
- On the shuttle buses to Ford Island, seats on the left side have the best views.

REMEMBRANCE CIRCLE

Take time to stroll the memorial grounds. By the water, the Remembrance Circle has plaques that explain the historic Pearl Harbor sites. Movingly, panels record the names of the 2403 Americans killed in the attack. Besides military personnel, it lists the 49 civilians killed, one only two months old. Many died by 'friendly fire' from US antiaircraft shells.

Battleship *Missouri* Memorial

The last battleship built by the US (it was launched in 1944), the **USS *Missouri* Memorial** *(ussmissouri.org; from adult/child $40/28)* provides a historical 'bookend' to WWII. Nicknamed the 'Mighty Mo,' this decommissioned battleship saw action during the late WWII battles of Iwo Jima and Okinawa.

The USS *Missouri* is now docked on Ford Island, just a few hundred yards from the sunken remains of the USS *Arizona*. On a **self-guided audio tour**, you can explore portions of the ship and stride across the deck where General MacArthur accepted the Japanese surrender on September 2, 1945. The huge ship was decommissioned in 1955, but was heavily modified and put back into service in the 1980s during the military buildup near the end of the Cold War.

To visit the *Missouri*, board the mandatory Ford Island visitor bus from the NPS Visitor Center.

Pearl Harbor Aviation Museum

The **Pearl Harbor Aviation Museum** *(pearlharboraviationmuseum.org; adult/child $30/18)* covers WWII and the conflicts in Korea, Vietnam and beyond. Exhibits include the Pearl Harbor attack and the pivotal Battle of Midway, when the tides of WWII in the Pacific turned in favor of the Allies. Restored planes on display here include a Japanese Zero and a Navy Dauntless dive bomber.

Another hangar has planes used in conflicts since WWII. Out on the tarmac, in the shadow of the famous old control tower (which visitors can ascend at added cost for sweeping views), you can imagine what it was like in this same spot on December 7, 1941. To visit the museum, use the mandatory Ford Island bus.

JEFF WHYTE/SHUTTERSTOCK

USS *Missouri* Memorial

Pacific Fleet Submarine Museum

Adjacent to the Pearl Harbor visitor center, the **Pacific Fleet Submarine Museum** *(bowfin.org; adult/child $26/15)* harbors the moored WWII-era submarine USS *Bowfin* – you can explore its tight confines. The museum traces the development of submarines from their origins to the nuclear age. The park has waterside exhibits on every US submarine lost during the war.

Launched on December 7, 1942, one year after the Pearl Harbor attack, the *Bowfin* sank 44 enemy ships in the Pacific by the end of WWII. The US undersea war against Japan was a major contribution to winning the war in the Pacific and is often overlooked.

USS *Oklahoma* Memorial

After the USS *Arizona,* the second-largest number of lives lost on December 7, 1941, was aboard the battleship USS *Oklahoma.* Numerous Japanese torpedoes struck the ship early in the attack and it capsized at dock, trapping hundreds of men below decks. Ultimately, 429 of the crew died. The *Oklahoma* was eventually salvaged and towed away. Many of her dead were buried in mass graves at the Punchbowl, the National Memorial Cemetery of the Pacific (p104).

The **USS *Oklahoma* Memorial** has full details about the ship and one thin white marble column for each man who died. You can visit on a free 1½-hour bus tour from the Pearl Harbor visitor center. There are three tours a week and seats are limited. Reserve online up to 14 days in advance at recreation.gov. Tours include a stop at the **USS *Utah* Memorial** (it was a training ship also sunk on December 7).

A Surprise Attack

December 7, 1941 – 'a date which will live in infamy,' President Franklin D Roosevelt later said – began at 7:55am with a wave of more than 350 Japanese planes swooping over the Koʻolau Range, headed toward the unsuspecting US Pacific Fleet in Pearl Harbor. The battleship USS *Arizona* took a direct hit and sank in less than nine minutes, with most of its men killed in the explosion that destroyed the ship. The average age of the 1177 men who died in the attack on the ship was just 19 years. It wasn't until 15 minutes after the bombing started that US antiaircraft guns began to shoot back. Twenty other US military ships were sunk or seriously damaged and 347 airplanes were destroyed during the two-hour attack.

Ultimately, the greatest cost of the Pearl Harbor attack was human. Except for three ships sunk that day – the *Arizona*, the USS *Oklahoma* and the USS *Utah* – almost all the rest of the navy ships damaged were repaired and fought in WWII. And while the damage of the US battleships was massive, events soon proved that such vessels were already obsolete. The war in the Pacific was fought by aircraft carriers, none of which were in Pearl Harbor during the attack. And the attack was ultimately a disaster for Japan as it led to the destruction of the empire and the devastation of the homeland.

PEARL HARBOR IN FILMS

Tora Tora Tora (1970) This accurate American-Japanese production presents the attack from both sides. It lets the incredible events around December 7 drive the story. How the US continually missed clear indications that an attack was coming is still relevant today.

From Here to Eternity (1953) Set on Oʻahu just before the attack, the film evocatively captures the languor of prewar life. It includes the oft-parodied scene – shot at Hālona Cove in southeast Oʻahu – of Burt Lancaster and Deborah Kerr getting it on in the surf.

Pearl Harbor (2001) The movie *not* to watch. The overwrought script is inaccurate and cringeworthy, plus the digital effects haven't aged well. *Midway* (2019) is not much better.

WEST LOCH DISASTER

The second deadliest disaster at Pearl Harbor during WWII was the largely forgotten West Loch disaster. On May 21, 1944, an explosion occurred while ships were being loaded with ammunition for invasions in the Central Pacific.

Explosions continued for the next 24 hours, resulting in six ships sunk, 163 sailors killed and nearly 400 injured. It was a disaster at a critical time in the war, and it was entirely preventable. Safeguards were frequently overlooked, as they were at West Loch.

In the segregated US armed forces during WWII, Black soldiers were largely relegated to support roles such as the dangerous job of loading ammunition. Just two months later, 320 mostly Black sailors were killed in a similar disaster in Port Chicago, California.

A Temple for Healing

Explore Keaīwa Heiau State Recreation Area

In the mountains north of Pearl Harbor, **Keaīwa Heiau State Recreation Area** *(dlnr.hawaii.gov/dsp/parks/oahu/keaiwa-heiau-state-recreation-area; free)* protects Keaīwa Heiau, an ancient *ho'ola* (healing or medicinal) temple. It was used by *kahuna lapa'au* (healers who used plants for medicine), who used hundreds of medicinal plants and grew many on the grounds surrounding the heiau.

Among those found here are *noni*, whose pungent yellow fruits were used to treat heart disease; *kukui*, whose nuts are an effective laxative; *'ulu*, whose sap was used to soothe chapped skin; and *ti* leaves that were wrapped around a sick person to break a fever. Not only did the herbs have medicinal value, but the heiau itself was thought to possess life-giving energy, and the kahuna was able to draw from the powers of both the temple and the plants.

Near the park entrance and guarded by roaming chickens, the stone heiau may date to the 16th century. The 4ft-high terraces are made of stacked rocks that enclose an approximately 16,000-sq-ft platform.

Today, people wishing to be healed still place offerings within the heiau. The offerings reflect the multiplicity of Hawai'i's cultures: rosary beads and sake cups sit beside flower lei and rocks wrapped in *ti* leaves. You can also visit the even older Kūka'ō'ō heiau at Mānoa Heritage Center (p108) in Honolulu.

The 334-acre state park also contains picnic facilities and the enjoyable 'Aiea Loop Trail, which is a good introduction to the densely forested hills that tower over much of Honolulu (plus it has lush views across O'ahu). From Downtown Honolulu, bus 74 ('Aiea Heights) stops about 1 mile downhill from the park entrance.

EATING AROUND PEARL HARBOR & 'AIEA: CASUAL CHOICES

Ige's Lunchwagon: Hidden spot with lunches that change daily: watch for pork teriyaki, Korean fried chicken and savory *laulau. 9:30am-5pm Tue-Fri* $

Anna Miller's: An authentic 1970s-chic vibe and classic diner fare including 21 types of pie (get the banana cream!). *8am-3pm* $$

Sushi Spot: Family-run storefront serving up great made-to-order hand rolls and sushi, all impeccably fresh. Katsu and tempura too. *10:30am-9pm Tue-Sat* $$

Ryder's Poke & Shave Ice: Small but busy outlet with best poke on the west side. Choose from many options and dine under a tree. Also, shave ice. *11am-4pm* $

HIKE THE 'AIEA LOOP TRAIL

The scenic 'Aiea Loop Trail offers a lush visual feast, including sweeping vistas of Pearl Harbor, Diamond Head and the Ko'olau Range. The trail begins in the Keaīwa Heiau State Recreation Area.

START	END	LENGTH
Trailhead	Trail End Point	4.8mi

The 1 **'Aiea Loop Trailhead** is at the top of the park's paved loop road. Set out amid lemon eucalyptus trees, which give the air a lemony scent. There are also Norfolk pines, with their strange otherworldly appearance. Look for a granite plaque honoring the crew of a B-24 bomber that crashed near the trail in 1944.

A little over a mile in, you'll see a 2 **small side trail** that loops to a waterfall. Benches and logs for sitting are scattered along the path and are good for picnics. You also might be able to snack your way along the trail, as there is a lot of fruit growing wild, including tiny strawberry guava and passion fruit.

About midway is 3 **Pu'u Uau**, the highest point on the trail (1656ft). Just past this, you'll have a sweeping 4 **H-3 Hwy View** curving through the vibrant green mountain valleys. Beginning about 500yd beyond here, keep a sharp eye out for the few remaining scattered pieces of the 5 **crashed bomber remains**. The greenish aluminum blends in with the forest.

There are some steep, sometimes muddy switchbacks near the 6 **trail end point**, which finishes at the lower car park on the loop road.

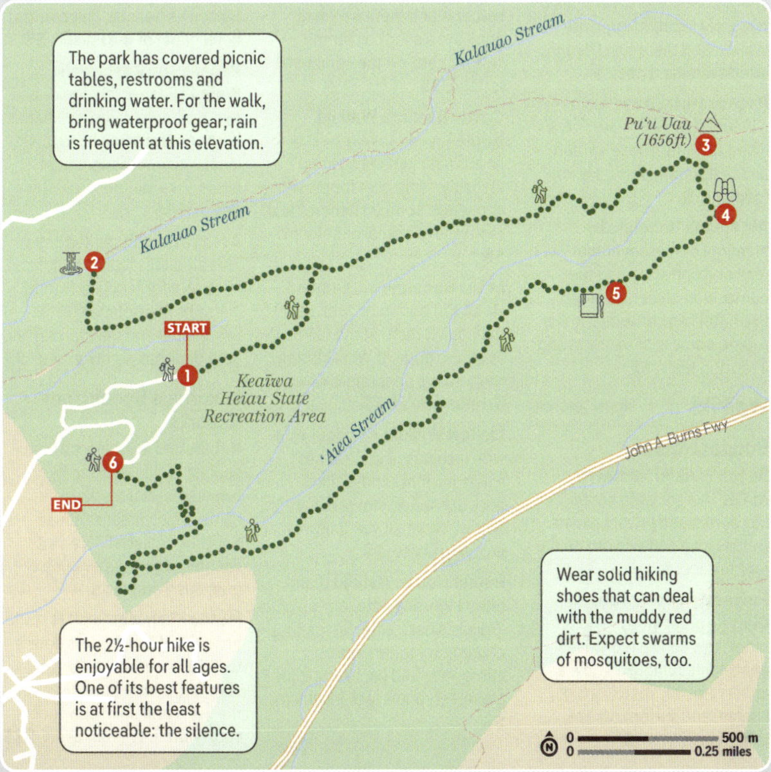

Places We Love to Stay

$** Budget **$$** Midrange **$$$ Top End

Downtown

MAP p59

Aston at the Executive Centre Hotel Geared for business travelers and extended stays; large, modern suites with floor-to-ceiling windows in a 41-story tower. **$$**

AC Hotel Honolulu A newish, modest mid-rise hotel with 112 rooms and prices that reflect its near-monopoly status downtown. **$$$**

Kaka'ako & Ala Moana

MAP p76

Central Y Residences Unfussy budget YMCA rooms on single-sex or co-ed floors. Very basic but great location opposite Waikīkī and there's an Olympic-sized swimming pool. **$**

Pagoda Hotel Basic rooms in a 1960s-style high-rise. There's a beautiful Japanese garden and restaurant, plus daily koi feedings. **$**

Ala Moana Honolulu by Mantra Looming over the mall and convenient to the convention center, this high-rise hotel has corporate-style rooms, some with balcony, and a rooftop deck. **$$**

Waikīkī

MAPS p85, p86

Budget Hotels

Beach Waikiki Hostel by ALOH This sociable hostel has dorms and private rooms. Guests love hanging out on the roof terrace. **$**

Polynesian Hostel Beach Club An older study in concrete block, this converted small apartment complex is now a cheery hostel. There's a big kitchen and surfboards are available for rent. **$**

Royal Grove Waikiki No frills but plenty of aloha characterize this kitschy, candy-pink, six-story hotel with a loyal snowbird following. Book far ahead. **$**

Waikiki Beachside Hostel In southern Waikīkī's hostel gulch, this place attracts an international party crowd and offers plenty of perks. Like most hostels on back-alley Lemon Rd, it occupies an older apartment complex. **$**

Quiet Hotels

Coconut Waikiki Hotel The Coconut delivers a splash of mod style. Rooms all have a balcony, and there's a small pool and a sandbox for the kids (or cats) on the communal terrace. **$$**

Castle Bamboo Waikiki Hotel A meditative retreat with an intimate cabana spa and stylishly minimalist rooms with kitchenette or full kitchen. Most rooms have a lānai or balcony. **$$**

Lotus Honolulu at Diamond Head Hip boutique hotel near Kaimana Beach. At the calm southern edge of Waikīkī, many rooms have panoramic views of Diamond Head. **$$**

Laylow Waikiki A budget vibe with lashings of style. It has a narrow pool sandwiched between taller concrete towers. A good choice if you'll be out enjoying O'ahu. **$$**

Romer House Waikiki Bland, older high-rise hotel on Waikīkī's back acre. Spacious, elementary rooms have a microwave and mini-fridge; the cheapest rooms lack a balcony. **$$**

Hotel Renew Design-savvy, eco-friendly accommodations with a color palette that looks like a box of chocolates. Frills include an 'aroma concierge' who will provide a custom room scent. **$$**

Apartment-Style Hotels

Ohia Waikiki Studio Suites Basic rooms in an older high-rise in Waikīkī's rear echelon equal budget rates. All rooms have cooking facilities, and some have full kitchens. **$**

Luana Waikiki Hotel & Suites Includes studios with kitchenettes and one-bedroom condos with full kitchens. Some balconies boast a 'glimpse' (in hotel lingo) of the Pacific. **$$**

Regency on Beachwalk Waikiki Respectable one- and two-bedroom units have full kitchens and some have private lānai with peekaboo ocean views. Five minutes from the beach. **$$$**

Aston at the Waikiki Banyan This all-suites high-rise hotel is perfect for families. Roomy suites have a sofa bed in the living room and balconies. The pool deck has a playground. **$$**

Luxurious Beachfront Resorts

Halekulani Evincing modern sophistication, this family-owned resort lives up to its name, which means 'House Befitting Heaven.' It's an all-encompassing experience of gracious living. **$$$**

Moana Surfrider (p84) Historic beachfront hotel (parts date to 1901) in a grand, colonial style with Hawaiian artwork on the walls and an ocean-facing courtyard. A Westin resort. **$$$**

Royal Hawaiian (p84) The original Waikīkī luxury hotel. A pink Spanish-Moorish–style landmark loaded with vintage opulence, which is kept relevant by continuous subtle upgrades. Also, a modern high-rise tower. **$$$**

Kaimana A soothing setting right on Kaimana Beach makes this 1960s-era hotel special. No pool, but with this beach, who needs one? All rooms have balconies and fridges. **$$**

Ilikai Hotel & Luxury Suites Near the Ala Wai Yacht Harbor, this mid-century landmark is close to the Ala Moana mall and the beach. The 30th floor stars in the opening credits of both versions of *Hawaii Five-0*. **$$**

Huge Resorts

Hilton Hawaiian Village (p84) Waikīkī's largest resort hotel is a family-friendly, self-sufficient tourist fortress with 22 acres of towers, restaurants, bars, five pools and franchise shops. **$$**

'Alohilani Resort Waikiki Beach The lobby features a two-story aquarium that the hotel modestly calls the 'Oceanarium.' The pool deck is a destination itself, with a saltwater infinity pool. **$$**

Sheraton Waikiki Beach Resort This mega-hotel is ginormous enough to accommodate package-tour groups and business conferences alike. Facing a thin beach, with an adults-only pool and a family-friendly pool. **$$$**

Greater Honolulu

Hostelling International Honolulu Along a quiet residential street near UH Mānoa campus, this low-slung house has same-sex dorms and basic private rooms cooled by trade winds. Often full. **$**

Manoa Valley Inn Built in 1912, this Honolulu landmark features seven rooms filled with antiques, lovely gardens, a heated pool and a sumptuous breakfast. **$$**

Leeward Coast

Ko Olina

Four Seasons Resort O'ahu at Ko Olina Luxurious resort that's popular with couples, thanks to its charming two-person rooms and adults-only amenities. **$$$**

Aulani, A Disney Resort & Spa (p125) Kid-friendly resort filled with iconic Disney characters, waterslides and Polynesian-inspired rooms. **$$$**

JEFF WHYTE/SHUTTERSTOCK

Moana Surfrider

Marriott's Ko Olina Beach Club Family-friendly resort on a lagoon of its own, complete with three pools for added water-filled fun. **$$$**

Beach Villas at Ko Olina These independently managed oceanfront accommodations are perfect for larger groups, with up to three bedrooms per suite. **$$$**

Kapolei

Hampton Inn & Suites Oahu/Kapolei In the Ka Makana Ali'i Shopping Center, this hotel is affordable and very close to shopping and dining options. **$**

Windward Coast

Kailua

Papaya Paradise B&B Long-standing B&B with two separate suites, a saltwater pool and a breezy outdoor space. **$**

Hawaii Sheffield House Cozy B&B with a private garden and prime location in the heart of Kailua. **$$**

North Shore

Lā'ie & Kahuku

Ritz-Carlton O'ahu, Turtle Bay (p192) Luxury resort known for its two golf courses and beachfront rooms and bungalows. **$$$**

Courtyard by Marriott O'ahu North Shore Small chain hotel known for its quiet North Shore location. It's located in alcohol-free Lā'ie, so there is no alcohol sold on the property. **$$**

Pūpūkea

Backpackers Vacation Inn & Plantation Village This laid-back hostel is just across the street from Pūpūkea Beach Park and is ideal for travelers on a budget. **$**

Ke Iki Beach Bungalows Enjoy these one- and two-bedroom bungalows, just across the street from some of the world's best surfing beaches. **$$$**

Researched by
Sarah Etinas

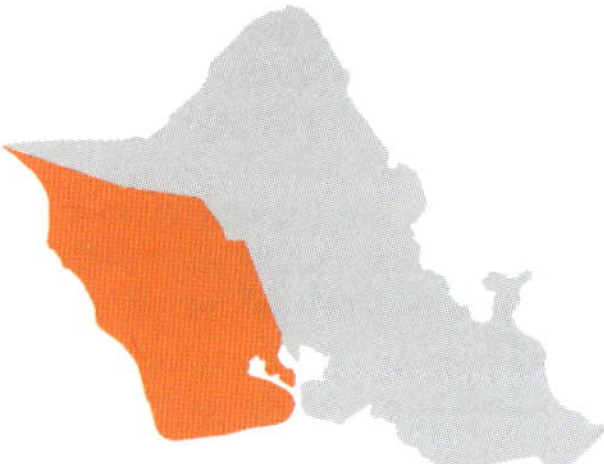

Leeward Coast

SUNSHINE-FILLED BEACH DAYS ARE CALLING

Though home to the Ko Olina lagoons and Disney's famed Aulani resort, most of the beach-filled Leeward Coast remains untouched by tourism.

Welcome to the west side of O'ahu, also known as the Leeward Coast, where you'll find more sunny days than anywhere else on the island – and lots of opportunities to spend time in the water to cool down.

DANESPRINTSHOP/SHUTTERSTOCK

Ko Olina is where the vast majority of Leeward O'ahu visitors will choose as their home base, partially for the beachfront views but mostly because this is where the coolest hotels are. The four human-made landmark lagoons were specifically created for visitor bliss, after all.

Ko Olina is technically part of Kapolei. But while Ko Olina was made for tourists, Kapolei is where O'ahu locals live, work and play. Although this residential town doesn't look like much, you'll find shopping gems and foodie finds within its unassuming strip malls.

Geographically, most of the Leeward Coast is covered by Wai'anae. While Wai'anae is officially just an itty bitty 5.4 sq miles of land, locals think of the region as comprising Nānākuli, Mā'ili, Mākaha and beyond. Basically, once you leave Ko Olina behind, you're in Wai'anae until you hit the northwestern-most tip of the island. Wai'anae is home to the highest concentration of Native Hawaiians on O'ahu – and the strong sense of cultural pride is evident everywhere.

THE MAIN AREAS

KO OLINA
Picturesque collection of artificial lagoons. p124

WAI'ANAE
Beachfront region with a large Native Hawaiian community. p129

For places to stay on the Leeward Coast, see p119

JUERGEN_WALLSTABE/SHUTTERSTOCK

Left: Māʻili Pillbox (p132); Above: Keawaʻula Beach (p131)

Find Your Way

While Leeward O'ahu is a large chunk of the island, most visitors stick to the tourist-focused Ko Olina, occasionally venturing up the coast to the beaches and hikes of Wai'anae.

Wai'anae, p129

This agriculture-focused coastal region is home to the largest concentration of Native Hawaiians anywhere on O'ahu.

Ko Olina, p124

A collection of four artificial lagoons, fantastic for calm beach days and a visit to Disney's Aulani resort.

CAR

A car is your best bet for traveling around the Leeward Coast. While roadways can be small and traffic-filled at times, there's no avoiding it, regardless of your mode of transportation.

BUS

Buses are an excellent second transportation option. You can get around Kapolei and Wai'anae (up to Mākaha) pretty easily on the public bus system, although no buses go to Ko Olina, which can be difficult if that's your home base.

TRIGGERPHOTO/GETTY IMAGES

Ko Olina lagoons (p124)

Plan Your Time

With sunny days and about 30 miles of coastline, beach days should definitely be part of the plan for your time on the Leeward side.

If You Only Do One Thing

If you don't have a lot of time, the one thing you'll want to do is go to the beach – and it doesn't matter which beach. The **Ko Olina lagoons** (p124) are great for kids, **Mākaha Beach Park** (p130) is excellent for snorkeling, and **Keawaʻula Bay** (p131) is fantastic for catching waves. And with 272 days of sunshine, the weather's practically guaranteed to be in your favor.

Five Days to Travel Around

If you have a few days, intersperse your beach time with hikes, eateries and even a bit of shopping. Tackle the trek to **Kaʻena Point** (p131), climb to the bright-pink **Māʻili Pillbox** (p132), grab a bite at **Monkeypod Kitchen by Merriman** (p125) and shop for locally made wares at Native Hawaiian–owned stores at **Ka Makana Aliʻi** (p128) shopping center.

SEASONAL HIGHLIGHTS

SPRING

Spring is busy with both Spring Break and Golden Week (Japanese holiday break). Mid- to late May is prime shoulder season.

SUMMER

Summer sunshine brings warm waters. Pack your swimwear and your snorkel gear for days in the Pacific Ocean.

FALL

Tackle the Leeward Coast's best hikes in cooler weather. Fall is also the driest time of year – prime for wildfires.

WINTER

Winter boasts the highest prices and the tallest waves, making it suboptimal for swimming but incredible for surfing.

Ko Olina

KID-FRIENDLY LAGOONS | LUXURY HOTELS | AWARD-WINNING GOLF

GETTING AROUND

Making your way around Ko Olina is easy, given its small size. If you're up for walking, you can likely get everywhere you need to go on foot. But, if multi-mile walking days aren't something you're up for, or you're planning on leaving the bounds of Ko Olina, a car is the way to go.

Fair warning: most Ko Olina hotels tack on a hefty overnight parking fee, so budget that into your calculations.

TOP TIP

Take the time to walk all four Ko Olina lagoons. You might be surprised to see how the atmosphere at each lagoon is a little different – from the activity-filled first lagoon to the fourth lagoon, a local favorite. Be sure to wear your best walking shoes for this 2.8-mile journey.

With its swaying palm trees, sunny skies and four symmetrically carved, human-made lagoons, Ko Olina was – quite literally – made to be a vacation escape. This small, 642-acre tourist hub on the Leeward side of Oʻahu is nothing like Waikīkī in scale, but it's still home to some heavy hitters in the hospitality industry, including a Four Seasons resort, a Marriott and the kid-friendly Disney Aulani resort.

While you might be tempted to spend your entire visit exploring your hotel's incredible amenities – after all, there are lūʻau (Hawaiian feasts) and waterslides galore – the lagoons will be the highlight of your stay. The calm, protected waters are an excellent place to spend a day, whether strapping on your snorkel for an underwater view, sticking to the shore for expert sandcastle-building or floating peacefully in the calm waters.

Get Out on the Water

A day at the lagoons

Given that the focal point of Ko Olina is the **lagoons** *(koolina.com)*, it only makes sense to spend an absurd amount of time around the water.

If you have little ones, the best activity is often just hanging out where the sea meets the sand. Splash around, build a sandcastle, search for little *ʻopihi* (limpet) shells and catch a glimpse of the occasional fish that speeds on by (yes, fish get that close to shore). Pack a beach picnic – with supplies from nearby **Island Country Markets** grocery store or to-go bites from **Farm to Barn Cafe & Juicery** – for a true sunrise-to-sunset beach day.

You also have the option to take things up a notch with water sports. While you can't bring personal paddleboards or canoes to the lagoons, you can use the ones available at Ko Olina. At the first lagoon, you'll find traditional Hawaiian double-hull canoe tours with **Hawaiian Ocean Adventures**

HIGHLIGHTS
1 Aulani, A Disney Resort & Spa
2 Ko Olina Golf Club
3 Monkeypod Kitchen by Merriman
4 Roy's Ko Olina

SIGHTS
5 Ko Olina Lagoons

ACTIVITIES
6 Hawaiian Ocean Adventures
7 Ocean Joy Cruises
8 Royal Hawaiian Beach Services

EATING
9 Farm to Barn Cafe & Juicery
10 Mina's Fish House
11 Noe

SHOPPING
12 Island Country Markets

(hawaiianoceanadventures.com; adult $119, child 3 and under free). Reservations must be made at the **Makiki Joe's Beach Rental Desk** at the famous resort, **Aulani, A Disney Resort & Spa**. At Lagoons 1, 2 and 3, there are a few stand-up paddleboards available for rent from **Royal Hawaiian Beach Services** *(royalhawaiianbeachservices.com; per hour $55)*. To ensure availability and ease, reserve online.

Stop by at happy hour (3:30–5pm) for the best bang for your buck.

EATING IN KO OLINA: OUR PICKS

Monkeypod Kitchen by Merriman: Enjoy farm-fresh local flavors like taro ravioli with watercress, and truffle and local mushroom pizza. *11am-10pm* $$

Noe: Savor a fancy Italian dinner at this Four Seasons O'ahu restaurant, with romantic lighting and their signature white truffle-topped tagliatelle. *5-9pm* $$$

Mina's Fish House: Enjoy oceanfront views, locally made brews and fresh seafood at this restaurant owned by celebrity chef Michael Mina. *4-9pm* $$$

Roy's Ko Olina: This Pan-Asian restaurant is owned by renowned local chef Roy Yamaguchi. Try the *misoyaki* marinated butterfish and the soufflé. *11:30am-9pm* $$$

RESPECT THE ANIMALS

Many endangered marine animals like to rest on Ko Olina's sandy shores. It's not uncommon to see *honu* (Hawaiian green sea turtles) or *'īlioholoikauaua* (monk seals) lounging around in the sunshine. If you see these animals, be sure to give them several feet of space. Not only are they wild animals looking for rest, but it's also illegal to get too close to these species, and you could be charged with a hefty fine if you're spotted near one.

Instead, enjoy these rare animals from afar. You can even actively contribute to their well-being and to *honu* and *'īlioholoikauaua* research endeavors by reporting your sightings. For *'īlioholoikauaua* sightings call the National Oceanic and Atmospheric Administration (NOAA) Marine Wildlife Hotline, and for *honu* sightings report them via NOAA's Honu Count Sighting Survey.

ERIC BRODER VAN DYKE/GETTY IMAGES

Aulani, A Disney Resort & Spa (p125)

Out into the Pacific

Ko Olina's best boat tours

While hanging out in the shallow waters of the lagoons is a great way to enjoy the salty Hawai'i waters, consider venturing a little further out on a boat tour with **Ocean Joy Cruises** *(oceanjoycruises.com; adult/child $174/154)*. For those, you'll want to head to the **Ko Olina Marina**, situated just after the fourth lagoon.

You'll hop aboard a state-of-the-art catamaran and sail up the Leeward Coast to Wai'anae. There, you'll drop anchor and enjoy an epic snorkeling adventure filled with *honu*, sea stars and spinner dolphins. In the winter, you might even spot a whale or two, spouting, breaching or waving hello with its tail.

Ocean Joy Cruises offers tours a few times a day, and each one offers something a little bit different. Mornings are when dolphins like to play, noon is when the water is at its warmest, and sunset paints views in a golden hue. Tours last around 3½ hours.

A Lū'au Crafted for Kids

The Aulani's Ka Wa'a Lū'au

There are dozens of lū'au across O'ahu, but the **Ka Wa'a Lū'au** *(disneyaulani.com/activities/luau; adult/child $190/119)* at Aulani stands out from the crowd with its kid-friendliness. After all, if there's one thing a Disney-owned property knows how to do, it's bring the magic for little ones.

The Ka Wa'a Lū'au keeps kids entertained throughout the entire three-hour experience. Before the main lū'au festivities even begin, you'll have an hour to enjoy interactive, authentic

Hawaiian pre-show activities. Try your hand at pounding *kalo* (taro) into poi (a sticky purple paste and ancient Hawaiian food staple), strum a song on the ʻukulele or get a temporary *kākau* (tattoo). A Disney character or two might even make an appearance!

Soon enough, the lūʻau will officially begin, starting with the island-inspired buffet dinner. Though not the most traditional Hawaiian spread around, it's family-friendly, delicious and still offers a taste of the islands. Kids get special bento boxes but are welcome to the buffet too!

Last but not least, there's the entertainment. And, as one would expect from Disney, it's a full-on production. Storytellers, hula dancers, fire dancers and actors all come together to bring to life some of Hawai'i's most captivating legends.

Golf Like a Pro

A world-renowned golf course

Ko Olina is home to the **Ko Olina Golf Club** *(koolinagolf.com; adult/child from $210/145)*, an 18-hole golf course designed by renowned golf architect Ted Robinson. It's as challenging as it is stunning (which is to say, very) – so much so that it has been used for international golfing competitions like the Ladies Professional Golf Association (LPGA) Hawaiian Ladies Open and the LPGA Lotte Championship. Famed pro golfer Michelle Wie West trained on this very course.

You too can test your skills on these scenic greens, spotting swaying palm trees and majestic swans along the way. But don't let the beauty fool you – slopes, bunkers and water features are just the beginning of the challenges here.

WHY I LOVE KO OLINA

Sarah Etinas, O'ahu local and Lonely Planet writer

Growing up in Kapolei, Ko Olina was always a go-to beach. It was easy enough to drive over whenever I had a free hour or two, lay my towel on the sand or grass, and take a dip in the calm water. And while the lagoons can get a little chilly in the winter for an island-raised gal, it was still always worth a visit.

To this day, I can spend hours swimming around, looking for little *'opihi* shells in the sand, or reading books in the sunshine at Ko Olina. Sometimes, my family and I might pack a meal or order a pizza to enjoy, with the salty ocean breeze and the rhythmic sound of the tide for company. Round it out with a stunning sunset, and I can't ask for anything more.

MORE UNDERWATER ADVENTURES

The Leeward Coast isn't the only place on O'ahu for underwater adventures. Go snorkeling on the **North Shore** (p182) or try submarine scootering in **Hawai'i Kai** (p143).

Beyond Ko Olina

Leave Ko Olina's lagoons behind and explore the residential town of Kapolei, with its Native Hawaiian-owned boutiques.

GETTING AROUND

To get out of Ko Olina and to Kapolei, you'll need a car of some sort – either a rental or a rideshare. It's only about a 10-minute drive, but it's all highway. Once in Kapolei, you can continue to use those two options. Parking won't be a problem, as it's nearly always available and free. Alternatively, you can opt for the affordable and sustainable public bus, which covers a large chunk of the city. There are also a couple of Skyline stops in Kapolei (Kualaka'i and Keone'ae), though they are not the most easily accessible on foot.

While most visitors to O'ahu's West Side stay in Ko Olina, they rarely venture out to Kapolei proper. Officially, Ko Olina is just one neighborhood in the larger town of Kapolei, but while Ko Olina is for the tourists, Kapolei is for the locals.

In the residential area of Kapolei you'll find all of the homey essentials, such as grocery stores and chain stores, nestled in unassuming strip malls and shopping centers. Between the necessities, though, there are all sorts of hidden gems like island-inspired eateries and locally owned boutiques. There are even a few under-the-radar hotels in the area for those who are looking to ditch the status quo and make Kapolei their home base, along with the Wet'n'Wild Hawaii water park.

Kapolei

TIME FROM KO OLINA: **10MINS**

Shop native

For the longest time, Kapolei didn't have a major shopping mall of its own – until 2016, when **Ka Makana Ali'i** opened. While it's not the busiest shopping center around, Ka Makana Ali'i is home to a surprising number of Native Hawaiian-owned stores amid the chain stores.

Head to **No'eau Designers** *(noeaudesigners.com)*, a Native Hawaiian-owned and -operated boutique, for all sorts of locally made goodies, from button-up aloha shirts to koa-wood phone grips.

Around the corner, you'll find **Sweet Honey Hawaii** *(sweethoneyhawaii.com)*, a children's clothing store filled with Hawai'i-inspired prints, like *shaka*-bedecked board shorts and dresses covered in monstera leaves. If parents want to get in on the fashion fun, there are very limited collections of men's and women's clothing, so they can match with their little ones – perfect for a beachfront family photo!

Last but not least, the **Collective by Hawaii's Finest** *(thecollectivebyhifi.com)*, a print shop and retail store, is filled with hoodies, T-shirts and baseball caps emblazoned with Hawai'i town and island names. If there's not already one on the rack, they can make a custom one for you.

Waiʻanae

BEACH LIFE | SCENIC HIKES | LOCAL EATS

Officially, Waiʻanae is a small 5.4-sq-mile area on the Leeward Coast. However, in reality, locals think of Waiʻanae as covering most of the Leeward Coast – from Nānākuli to Kaʻena Point, the northwesternmost tip of the island. In fact, the terms 'Leeward Coast' or 'Leeward side' are often used interchangeably with 'Waiʻanae Coast' or 'Waiʻanae side.'

Waiʻanae is also home to the highest concentration of Native Hawaiians on Oʻahu, and they're very proud of it. As you drive through, you'll spot Toyota Tacomas decorated with Kingdom of Hawaiʻi flags and countless weekend beach potlucks with *kālua* pig on the menu.

That said, this part of the island also has a large unhoused population. As of 2025 Hawaiʻi had about 81 unhoused residents per 10,000 residents – 3.5 times the national average. So, while on the surface Waiʻanae might sound like sunshine and rainbows (literally), many of those same sunny beaches have longtime unhoused residents.

TOP TIP

Waiʻanae is home to the largest Native Hawaiian community on Oʻahu, so be particularly respectful to the people and the land during your visit. Treat everyone with kindness, drive carefully and leave the beaches and hiking trails cleaner than you found them.

Sun, Sand & Saltwater

Time for a beach day!

Home to about 20 miles of coastline, Waiʻanae is pretty much entirely lined by golden-sand beaches. And unlike other beaches on the island, like Waikīkī Beach (p81) and Kailua Beach

GETTING AROUND

Oʻahu's public bus system can get you around a good chunk of Waiʻanae – as long as you don't go past Mākaha. (So, Yokohama Bay and the Kaʻena Point Trailhead are both inaccessible by bus.) Given those limitations, a car will likely suit your needs better. Fair warning, though – Waiʻanae's main road is one to two lanes the whole way, so a traffic jam may keep you in the area much longer than expected. Sadly, petty theft is quite common on the Leeward side, so hide your valuables (or take them with you) before you leave (and lock) your car.

HIGHLIGHTS
1 Ka'ena Point
2 Keawa'ula Beach
3 Mā'ili Pillbox Trail
4 Mākaha Beach Park
5 Poka'i Bay Beach Park

SIGHTS
6 Ka'ena Point State Park
7 Kū'ilioloa Heiau

ACTIVITIES
8 Ka'ena Point Trailhead

EATING
9 Coquito's Latin Cuisine
10 Kahumana Cafe
11 T8ste Buds
see 4 VIET808

SHOPPING
12 Wai'anae Farmers Market

(p146), Wai'anae's shorelines are rarely crowded. It's safe to say that enjoying the water on this side of the island is a must.

Mākaha Beach Park is arguably the most well-known beach in Wai'anae. Located in the middle of the Wai'anae Coast, this beach has wildly different conditions depending on the season. In summer, Mākaha Beach Park is ideal for snorkeling, with dozens of *honu* swimming in its relatively clear waters. But, in winter, a switch is flipped as 25ft waves crash onto the shores, making it a hub for many of the island's talented big-wave surfers.

EATING IN WAI'ANAE: OUR PICKS

Kahumana Cafe: Organic farm-to-table restaurant with views of the operational farm's thriving green fields. *10am-2:30pm Tue-Fri, 9am-1:30pm & 5:30-7:30pm Sat* $$

VIET808: Under-the-radar food truck near Mākaha Beach Park with Vietnamese and Thai classics like *gỏi cuốn* (summer rolls) and pad Thai. *11am-10pm* $

T8ste Buds: Elevated take-out restaurant known for its Asian flavors and fresh seafood. Try the popular spicy 'ahi (yellowfin tuna) sushi tacos. *11am-5pm Tue & Thu-Sun* $

Coquito's Latin Cuisine: Hole-in-the-wall local favorite serving up Puerto Rican, Colombian and Caribbean plates in a plantation-style building. *11am-7pm Tue-Thu, to 9pm Fri & Sat, to 3pm Sun* $$

About 4 miles from Mākaha Beach Park lies **Poka'i Bay Beach Park** *(safebeachday.com/p-ka-i-bay-beach-park)*, the calmest and most protected beach in Wai'anae. This beautiful beach is split into two sections by the ruins of an old Hawaiian temple, **Kū'īlioloa Heiau**, with the northernmost half being the more serene of the two. While there are still some surfable waves in the winter, the peaceful waters are great for families and casual swimmers the rest of the year.

At the end of Farrington Hwy, just before the Ka'ena Point Trailhead, you'll find **Yokohama Bay** *(gohawaii.com/islands/oahu/things-to-do/beaches/keawaula-beach-yokohama-beach)*. Officially called **Keawa'ula Beach** and colloquially called 'Yokes,' this secluded beach is a surfer hot spot. There are nearly always waves at this bay – with small bodyboarding waves in the summer and massive surfing waves in the winter. But, add the strong rip currents and sharp submerged rocks into the mix, and it's best to let the locals do their thing as you watch from the shore.

Trek to Ka'ena Point

O'ahu's northwesternmost point

At the very end of Wai'anae, when the main road (Farrington Hwy) no longer exists, you'll find the start of the **Ka'ena Point Trailhead** *(dlnr.hawaii.gov/dsp/parks/oahu/kaena-point-state-park)*. This 5-mile round-trip hike takes you to Ka'ena Point, a part of the island that's inaccessible by car (for the most part), filled with animals and steeped in ancient Hawaiian *mo'olelo* (stories).

There are two main *mo'olelo* associated with Ka'ena Point. The first and lesser-known one starts with the Hawaiian demigod, Maui. Known for his wild exploits, Maui decided to try to combine the Hawaiian Islands of O'ahu and Kaua'i. He cast his magical fishhook from Kaua'i, latching it onto O'ahu's Ka'ena Point. However, Maui's plan didn't come to fruition, instead leaving just a notch from his fishhook in the Ka'ena Point cliffs.

While Maui's quest offers an interesting tale, Ka'ena Point's other Hawaiian legend is much deeper. Many Native Hawaiians – both past and present – believe that the path to Ka'ena Point is the same trail that the dead use to enter their final resting place. For this reason, this hike is sacred, so be respectful when exploring it.

With these stories in mind, it's time to head to the Ka'ena Point Trailhead. Park in a roughly paved pullout and start your hike down a dusty trail. You'll quickly notice that this part of the

OTHER BIRDING OPPORTUNITIES

While Ka'ena Point is one great spot for bird-watching, **Popoi'a Island** (p153) in Kailua and the **James Campbell National Wildlife Refuge** (p194) in Kahuku (by tour only) are two other incredible birding locations to explore.

A LOCAL'S FAVORITE THINGS TO DO

Lisa Stevenson, owner of Rise Hawaii Jewelry *(risejewelry.com)*, shares some of her favorite spots in Wai'anae.

Mākaha Beach Park: One of our favorites. It's so beautiful and the water is gorgeous. I love to get in the water and snorkel or just float around. You get really awesome surf competitions in winter, too.

Wai'anae Farmers Market: There are a lot of local vendors and florists here. You have food trucks with prepared ready-to-go bowls, and people who are selling produce. It's small, but perfect if you're in the area.

Mā'ili Pillbox Trail: It's my favorite hike on the West Side, especially for sunset. My husband and I love bringing our pups up here too – it's a fairly quick up and down switchback hike.

WHAT'S A PILLBOX?

When referring to O'ahu hikes like the Mā'ili Pillbox, Lanikai Pillbox (p148) in Kailua and 'Ehukai Pillbox (p185) in Pūpūkea, the term 'pillbox' is actually a misnomer. In military terms, a pillbox is an armed defensive site, which isn't the case for any of these cement structures. Rather, they were simply used as observation stations, particularly during WWII after the bombing of Pearl Harbor (p112) on December 7, 1941.

Today, these pillboxes have been abandoned and are used as graffiti-covered landmarks on some of O'ahu's best hikes. And given their history, they make for some of the best stops and viewpoints around!

GOLDDIAMONDPHOTOGRAPHY/SHUTTERSTOCK

island is dry and there's no shade, so even though there's minimal elevation gain, bring more water than you initially think you'll need.

While the path itself is parched, the ocean is just a few feet away. After all, you're essentially following the coast to **Ka'ena Point State Park**. There, at the end of the trail, find jutting lava rocks, crashing waves and the occasional lounging *'īlioholoikauaua* or *honu*. Don't miss the tide pools for a glimpse at the tiniest crabs and snails.

If there's just one type of animal that Ka'ena Point State Park is known for, it's birds. In addition to being a state park, this remote area is also a bird sanctuary. Keep an eye out for all sorts of feathered friends, including *mōlī* (Laysan albatross), *'iwa* (great frigatebird) and *pueo* (Hawaiian short-eared owl).

Hike to the Mā'ili Pillbox

Wai'anae's bright pink landmark

As you drive along the Leeward Coast on Farrington Hwy, you might catch a flash of something bright pink sitting atop one of the oceanfront hills – that's the **Mā'ili Pillbox**.

Traditionally called Pu'u O Hulu, and colloquially called the Pink Pillbox, the trail to the Mā'ili Pillbox is one of the best hikes on the west side of O'ahu, and your goal will be to reach the top of the peak and its fuchsia-colored marker.

After finding street parking, locate the hidden start of the trail along Ka'ukama Rd between the 10th and 11th light poles. Then, follow the dusty path onwards and upwards. You'll notice that the trail forks several times on your way up, but don't

Ka'ena Point (p131)

worry, all of the trails eventually lead to the Mā'ili Pillbox (if you're unsure, you can always peek up and navigate toward the bright pink landmark).

Less than a mile from the start of the trail, you'll reach the peak and your first pillbox – although not the bright pink one you've been keeping an eye on the whole time. Stop at this initial graffiti-covered cement observation station and take in the views of the entire Leeward Coast.

In total, there are actually four pillboxes at the end of this hike, all very close together. The third in the succession is your bright pink lighthouse of sorts, the Mā'ili Pillbox. Painted pink for breast cancer awareness, the inside of the bunker is often filled with the names of cancer survivors and loved ones who have passed away from the disease. Take a few moments to read the inscribed names before retracing your steps to the start of the trail.

HIKE TO KA'ENA POINT ANOTHER WAY

There are actually two ways to hike to Ka'ena Point (p131), the other being from Mokulē'ia (p178) on the North Shore. Both hikes are about 5 miles round trip and the terrain is the biggest difference between the two. While the Wai'anae route has dry dirt paths and tide pools, the North Shore route has rocky trails and sand dunes. Each is wonderful in its own way, so it often comes down to which is more conveniently located.

WANT TO STAY ON THE LEEWARD COAST?

The Leeward Coast has hotels dotted around Ko Olina and Kapolei. Refer to the Places We Love to Stay (p119) guide for recommendations.

For places to stay on the Windward Coast, see p119

ALOHACRISHELL/SHUTTERSTOCK

Above: Kualoa Ranch (p162); Right: Makapu'u Point Lighthouse Trail (p139)

Researched by
Sarah Etinas

Windward Coast

FRAMED BY THE MOUNTAINS & THE SEA

Award-winning beaches, greenery-laden mountains, charming art galleries and institutional eateries – the laid-back Windward Coast awaits.

Nestled between the Ko'olau Mountains on one side and the Pacific Ocean on the other, the Windward Coast feels tucked away from the rest of the island. Beaches, hikes, art galleries and farms span the length of the region from Hawai'i Kai to Ka'a'awa.

EJ JOHNSON PHOTOGRAPHY/SHUTTERSTOCK

At the southeastern tip of O'ahu and the southernmost point of the Windward Coast, you'll find Hawai'i Kai. This ritzy beachfront neighborhood is technically part of Honolulu, but it feels a world away. Here you can spend your days hiking, eating and beach hopping to your heart's content.

About 10 miles north, you'll find Kailua, the most well-known town along O'ahu's eastern coast. With its art galleries and local markets, it gives off an environmental and health-focused vibe but with an island-inspired twist. It also often serves as the home base for Windward Coast explorers.

Then, there's Kāne'ohe, a sleepy neighborhood with temples, botanical gardens and mountain views hidden among its time-weathered houses. More importantly, Kāne'ohe was once home to some of the earliest Hawaiian rulers – men and women who governed even before the unification of the Kingdom of Hawai'i under the leadership of King Kamehameha I.

Much of the surrounding areas along the Windward Coast, including Waimānalo and Ka'a'awa, are home to small agricultural plots. Find some of the freshest tropical fruits to snack on or get your hands dirty with a voluntourism opportunity during your short visits to these small towns.

THE MAIN AREAS

HAWAI'I KAI
Luxury residential neighborhood with popular hikes. **p138**

KAILUA
Artsy, sustainability-focused beach town. **p146**

KĀNE'OHE
Quiet residential town on a peaceful bay. **p156**

Find Your Way

The Windward Coast is the eastern coastline of O'ahu. Navigate it by following the water's edge (and the main road). To get here, drive from the North or South Shores, or cut through the Ko'olau Range on the stunning H-3 drive.

Kāne'ohe, p156

Once the home of ancient Hawaiian rulers, Kāne'ohe is now a sleepy bayfront town, known primarily for its botanical garden.

CAR

A car is the best way to get around the Windward Coast, especially since there are so many scenic drives in this region. Don't miss the mountainous, sometimes waterfall-filled drive on H-3!

BUS

If a car isn't an option, the O'ahu public bus system offers an affordable close second. While it may take a bit more time, these buses can take you to most places along the Windward Coast.

Kailua, p146

This beachfront town is filled with many of O'ahu's eco-warriors and creatives, making it one of the most unique neighborhoods on the island.

Hawai'i Kai, p138

While primarily a plush residential neighborhood, Hawai'i Kai is also home to some of the coolest hikes and beaches on O'ahu.

0 — 10 km
0 — 5 miles

KARLOSXII/SHUTTERSTOCK

Kailua Beach Park (p146)

Plan Your Time

Be prepared to spend all of your time outdoors while you're on the Windward Coast. Beaches, botanical gardens, offshore islands and taro patches await!

Pressed for Time?

Start with a short yet sweet hike along the **Lanikai Pillbox Trail** (p148), where you can admire the view of the Mokulua Islands and the Pacific Ocean. Then grab a meal (and a cup of coffee) from **Morning Brew** (p148), a locally beloved brunch spot, before heading to **Kailua Beach** (p146) to laze a couple of hours away.

Five Days to Travel Around

Make Kailua your home base and fill your time with scenic drives, beach days and good food. Take a tour at **Kualoa Ranch** (p162), kayak your way to the **Mokulua Islands** (p152), soak up the sun in **Waimānalo** (p154), tackle the **Koko Crater Trail** (p141) in Hawai'i Kai, and get down and dirty with taro in **Kāne'ohe** (p156), just to start.

SEASONAL HIGHLIGHTS

SPRING

The slightly cooler spring weather is perfect for outdoor activities – from kayaking to hiking to taro planting.

SUMMER

The warm waters of the Pacific Ocean make for very pleasant swimming and snorkeling.

FALL

While most fruits are available year-round, rarer ones, like *liliko'i* (passion fruit) and guava, appear at farmers markets.

WINTER

The holidays bring about the highest prices of the year, so expect to pay more for a winter Windward O'ahu visit.

Hawai'i Kai

WATER SPORTS | HIKING | BEACH TIME

GETTING AROUND

Hawai'i Kai is easily accessible by both bus and car. Driving can get a little tricky during rush hour though, as traffic officials will typically cone off a lane and have cars drive on the 'wrong' side of the road to aid the flow of traffic – also called contraflow. While this can throw off visitors who are unfamiliar with the process, it's easy enough to just follow the other cars.

TOP TIP

Spend a bit of time hanging around Koko Marina Center. While there isn't a specific must-do activity here, simply taking in the turquoise water and salty breeze is refreshing. You can even enjoy a waterfront meal at one of the local restaurants as you soak in the views.

Located on O'ahu's southeastern tip, Hawai'i Kai serves as the start of the Windward Coast. While it's technically part of Honolulu, it feels like it's a world away. Instead of skyscrapers and crowds, Hawai'i Kai boasts ocean views, luxury homes and a picturesque marina.

One of the biggest draws to Hawai'i Kai is the hiking. This small neighborhood is home to some of the most iconic trails on the island, including the Koko Crater Trail, the Kuli'ou'ou Ridge Trail and the Makapu'u Point Lighthouse Trail. You'll be getting your workout in – and your fair share of jaw-dropping views – during your time in Hawai'i Kai.

After a morning hike, cool down at a nearby beach, just like the locals do. After all, the famed snorkeling spot, Hanauma Bay, calls this Windward Coast home as well.

Snorkel Beautiful Hanauma Bay

An underwater world

Head to **Hanauma Bay** *(honolulu.gov/dpr/hanauma-bay-nature-preserve; adult/child $25/free)* to experience O'ahu's underwater world. Officially known as the Hanauma Bay Nature Preserve, this protected bay is home to over 450 species of fish, as well as many mammals, crustaceans and reptiles.

Your visit will start with a short informational video, which teaches visitors how to protect the bay's delicate ecosystem and stay safe in the water. The summary: don't touch the coral or other marine animals and follow the posted safety signs. Then, hitch a ride on the free tram or walk down to Hanauma Bay.

Once you lather on your reef-safe sunscreen and grab your snorkel gear (available for rent if you don't have your own), you may want to dive right in. Instead, pause and assess the ocean safety situation – are there large waves, or strong currents? If you're unsure, it's best to ask the lifeguard.

If the conditions look good, walk along the shoreline until you come to one of the natural cutouts in the reef, officially

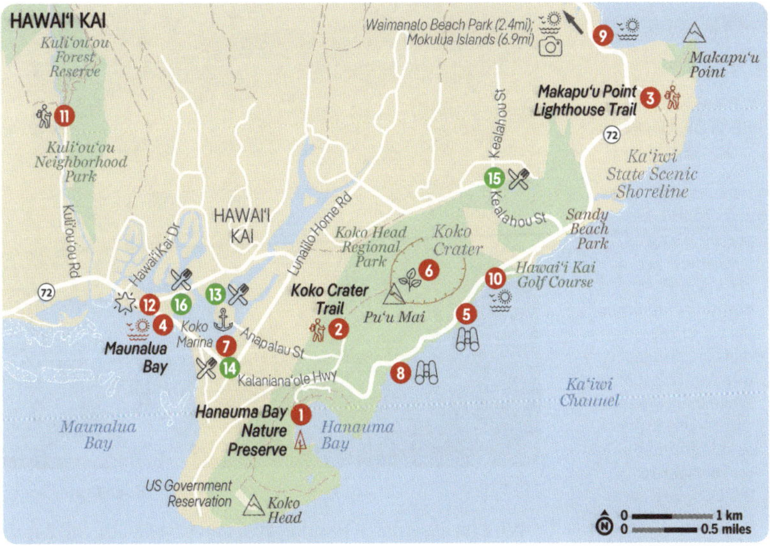

HIGHLIGHTS
1 Hanauma Bay Nature Preserve
2 Koko Crater Trail
3 Makapu'u Point Lighthouse Trail
4 Maunalua Bay

SIGHTS
5 Hālona Blowhole Lookout
6 Koko Crater Botanical Garden
7 Koko Marina Center
8 Lāna'i Lookout
9 Makapu'u Beach Park
10 Sandy Beach Park

ACTIVITIES
see 7 Big Kahuna Water Sports
see 7 Island Water Sports Hawaii
11 Kuli'ou'ou Ridge Trail
12 Mālama Maunalua

EATING
see 7 Greek Marina
13 Island Brew Coffeehouse
see 7 Kona Brewing Co
14 Leonard's Malasadamobile
see 7 Moena Cafe
15 Ono Seafood Poke Bowl Patrol
see 12 Original Roy's Hawai'i Kai
16 Paradise Poke Hawaii

called 'lagoons.' These sections allow you to reach slightly deeper waters – where most marine animals like to hang out – without having to swim over the reef the whole time. Watch out for *honu* (green sea turtles), dolphins, *he'e* (octopus) and the famed state fish *humuhumunukunukuāpua'a* (reef triggerfish).

It's important to note that Hanauma Bay requires reservations for visitors. (Locals can access the beach without a reservation.) This is to help regulate the number of people visiting the bay every day and allow the reef to thrive. Reservations become available two days prior to the intended visit date at 7am HST, so set your alarms because slots get snatched up quickly!

First Hike, Then Beach

How the locals do it

One of the best ways to experience Hawai'i like a local is to start your day with a hike and then cool off at the beach. The **Makapu'u Point Lighthouse Trail** and **Makapu'u Beach Park** are great spots to make this outdoor combination happen.

REEF-SAFE SUNSCREEN

Studies have shown that chemical sunscreen bleaches coral reefs, disrupts fish endocrine systems and stops algae growth, among other things. Instead, use reef-safe sunscreen, particularly options from local brands like Little Hands Hawai'i, Project Reef and Mama Kuleana. This simple switch will help O'ahu's marine environments survive and thrive for years to come.

CORAL RESTORATION ON O'AHU

Hanauma Bay is just one of many great places to snorkel on O'ahu. However, like many marine environments around the world, the island's reefs are struggling with coral bleaching. While there are small steps that individuals can take to help the reefs thrive, like using reef-safe sunscreen (p209) and not stepping on coral, there are also nonprofits that are doing their best to help. O'ahu's very own **Kuleana Coral Restoration** works on outplanting – or 'replanting' – dislodged coral colonies to give them a second chance at life and help the reef as a whole become happier and healthier.

Koko Crater Trail

With its designated parking area and paved path, the 2-mile round-trip Makapu'u Point Lighthouse Trail is arguably the most easily accessible hike on the island. You can find everyone from babies in strollers to active elders on this trail. Along the way, the bright blue Pacific Ocean views and salty breezes will keep you company. In the winter you might even see a few whale pals in the distance (keep an eye out for their spouts!).

The end of the hike brings you to the tip of the island. Admire the lighthouse that the trail was named after, Mānana Island (Rabbit Island), Kāohikaipu Islet Seabird Sanctuary and Makapu'u Beach Park – the latter of which is your next stop – all from this one spot.

Once you've soaked up the views and made your way back down the trail, the weather will likely have gotten warmer, and a dip at the beach will sound like bliss. Luckily, Makapu'u Beach Park is right there (though you will want to get in your car and drive there, as there isn't a good walking path between the two). If the waves are small, you can cool off with a refreshing dip in the ocean. The waves can get large at this beach, so don't go in the water when in doubt. For the best beach day, plan ahead and pack yourself a picnic lunch to enjoy on the golden sand.

EATING IN HAWAI'I KAI: OUR PICKS

Moena Cafe: Quaint brunch spot with unique plates like short rib *loco moco* and banana chantilly pancakes with toasted coconut. *7am-2:30pm* $$

Greek Marina: Casual waterfront restaurant serving up Greek dishes like lamb and beef gyros and grilled souvlaki. *11am-8pm* $$

Kona Brewing Co: Kona-brewed beer and casual all-American favorites with island twists. Grab a seat on the open-air lānai (balcony) on the marina. *11am-9pm* $$

Original Roy's Hawai'i Kai: The first Hawai'i restaurant by world-renowned local chef Roy Yamaguchi. Known for its fusion flavors. *4:30-9pm Sun-Thu, 9:30 Fri & Sat* $$$

Make it a Scenic Drive

Cruising on Kalaniana'ole Hwy

Between Hanauma Bay and Makapu'u Point, you'll find an epic scenic drive filled with winding roads and jaw-dropping ocean views. Plus, there are some fun stops along the way like the **Lāna'i Lookout**, **Hālona Blowhole Lookout** and **Sandy Beach Park**, just to start.

Take your time admiring the bright blue Pacific Ocean and spotting spouting winter whales in the distance. You can even continue your journey past Makapu'u Point into Waimānalo (p154), and further up the Windward Coast (p160) for more gorgeous beach views.

Tackle 1000 Steps to a Crater

A workout with a view

If there's one O'ahu hike that everyone has heard about, it's Koko Head. Officially known as the **Koko Crater Trail**, this challenging hike is composed of 1048 steps up a rickety railroad track. And although it's not for the faint of heart, it still manages to draw in half a million hikers every year.

This steep railroad track was originally built during WWII to shuttle supplies and people to the military bunker at the top of the crater. It was later converted into an Air Force station before being deactivated in 1966. Soon enough, the track was converted into the well-worn trail that you see today.

At first glance, Koko Crater Trail is intimidating. There's no way around it. After all, you cover about 1100ft of elevation in less than a mile, so it's practically a guaranteed thigh-burner. Just take it one step at a time. Ideally, you'll want to get an early start on the hike because there's no shade on the trail. With both the heat and the elevation gain against you, take as many breaks to rehydrate and refuel as you need to.

Once you reach the last hundred steps or so, the steepness reaches a whole new level. Lean forward and use a hand to grasp the side of the railroad track to help keep your balance.

All your efforts will be worth it once you reach the top. On clear days, you can see the entire southeastern tip of O'ahu, from Hanauma Bay to the Hawai'i Kai Marina. You might even glimpse the islands of Lāna'i and Moloka'i in the distance.

HIKING KOKO HEAD

For most hikers, getting to the top of the Koko Crater Trail takes about an hour – plus another 30 minutes or so to get back down. And that's totally OK! Pacing yourself is definitely the best move.

But some locals have made this absurdly steep hike a challenge. Since technically the hike is only 0.7 miles long, it can be done in a relatively short amount of time (ignoring the 1100ft of elevation gain, of course). The fastest recorded times hover around an impressive nine minutes!

While it may be tempting to try and compete with those times, it's a better idea to enjoy the strenuous journey at your own pace instead. After all, the view from the top looks the same whether you take nine minutes or 90 to get there.

Ono Seafood Poke Bowl Patrol: Charming take-out spot serving excellent fresh poke. Take your meal to nearby Koko Crater Botanical Garden. *10am-5pm Tue-Sat* $$

Leonard's Malasadamobile: Spin-off food truck of the famous Leonard's (p95). Get the popular doughnuts here without the crowds. Card only. *7:30am-6pm* $

Island Brew Coffeehouse: Start your day off right with 100% Hawaiian coffee and stunning marina views. If you need a bite, try an acai bowl. *6am-6pm* $

Paradise Poke Hawaii: This family-owned spot is committed to using fresh, sustainably sourced fish to make its local-style poke. *7am-8pm Mon-Fri, from 8am Sat & Sun* $$

VOLUNTEERING WITH MĀLAMA MAUNALUA

Meli James, co-founder of Mana Up *(manauphawaii.com)*, shares her experience with Mālama Maunalua.

I love working with Mālama Maunalua to pick the invasive seaweed. I grew up in that bay when the water was murky and dark, and the sand was almost like mud that you would sink into. It's been incredible to see the efforts of Mālama Maunalua's work because the bay is so pristine now.

When you're gathering all this seaweed, you put it into bags. And at the end, they pile up these 20lb bags, and you just think to yourself, 'I'm also contributing to something that others have done, and I can totally see the difference.' Yeah, that's pretty cool.

Admire Pua in Bloom

Wander through Koko Crater Botanical Garden

With the Koko Crater Trail taking up a lot of attention, **Koko Crater Botanical Garden** manages to slip under the radar. This hidden gem is home to a surprisingly long hiking trail of its own, framed by lovely plants from around the world – from African desert roses to Central American yucca plants. You'll need to lace up your hiking shoes and fill up your water bottle before taking on this dusty path.

But the best part, the **Plumeria Grove**, is right near the entrance of the botanical garden. Wander around the clustered trees and admire their bright beautiful *pua* (flowers), ranging from shades of bright white and pale yellow to striking orange and eye-popping pink.

Save the Bay

Volunteer with Mālama Maunalua

Get into the ocean and give back with **Mālama Maunalua** *(malamamaunalua.org)*. At least once per month, this incredible nonprofit organization hosts a three-hour community *huki* – or 'pulling' as it translates from Hawaiian – to remove invasive algae from the waters of Hawai'i Kai's **Maunalua Bay**. Over the years, Mālama Maunalua and its volunteers have removed nearly four million pounds of invasive algae. Without this intervention, these invasive algae species smother coral reefs and kill native algae communities, ultimately harming the bay's marine environment and making the water murky.

As for what a *huki* entails, it's exactly what the translated name implies. After being educated on which types of algae to remove – specifically gorilla *ogo* (seaweed), prickly seaweed and leather mudweed – it'll be your chance to get hands on and make a difference. Wander your way through Maunalua Bay's knee-deep turquoise waters, pulling out the designated algae species and putting them in a provided mesh bag. Every now and then, don't forget to look up and admire the bay that you're helping to restore.

Dive Down Deep

Where even more marine animals lie

You can see a great amount of marine life while snorkeling on O'ahu. You can even see quite a bit from shore (thank you, *honu*!). But to get arguably the best view of O'ahu's underwater world, you're going to want to go diving.

Hawai'i Kai's **Big Kahuna Water Sports** *(alohascuba diving.com; from $160)* makes this as easy as possible. They have options for both certified and non-certified divers, so it doesn't matter if it's your first time diving or your 10th. Once you get down deep into Maunalua Bay, keep your eyes open for tropical fish, coral, *honu* and even *he'e*. If you're a more experienced and certified diver, you can even go down 115ft to see the sunken Corsair airplane *($180)*. All participants must be at least 10 years old.

Coral reef, Maunalua Bay

'Snorkel' in a Submarine Scooter

An ideal activity for beginners

Nervous about getting into O'ahu's deeper waters? Consider booking a submarine scooter tour with **Island Water Sports Hawaii** *(islandwatersportshawaii.com; $180).*

First you'll take a boat from **Koko Marina Center** out into the beautiful waters of Maunalua Bay. After a quick intro on how to use the scooter and stay safe underwater, it's time to jump in! Simply dip your head underwater and into the 'helmet' portion of the scooter. As you do so, a member of the crew will lower the scooter, trapping the air via a scientific concept known as the Diving Bell Principle. Your head will stay completely dry the whole time, so you can continue to breathe normally.

Your body will naturally adjust to sit on the seat and grab onto the handles – which also happen to be the scooter's controls. Turtles and tropical fish will zip right on by, and all you have to do is maneuver to where you want to go.

Participants must be at least 10 years old. The scooter also makes a rather loud 'flushing'-esque noise the whole time, so it may not be ideal for those with hearing sensitivities.

THE SCIENCE BEHIND THE SUBMARINE SCOOTER

One thing that gets people about being in a submarine scooter is the air pocket inside the helmet while underwater. After all, you'll feel the waves lapping at your shoulders the whole time, but they never get any higher.

This is thanks to a scientific concept known as the Diving Bell Principle. Essentially, the principle relies on air pressure to keep water out of an open space – a concept further backed by the physics of Boyle's Law. When you submerge the scooter's helmet, the air inside is trapped because it is less dense than the water surrounding it. Since the air has nowhere to escape through the top, it creates a pressurized pocket that stays dry. The air is continuously replenished by the scooter's attached scuba tank – fresh air flows in, while CO_2 bubbles out from under the rim!

MORE VOLUNTEERING

O'ahu is filled to the brim with nature-focused opportunities to volunteer. In addition to removing seaweed with Mālama Maunalua, you can work in *lo'i* (taro fields) in **Kāne'ohe** (p158), join a community farm day in **Hale'iwa** (p172) or do some sand dune restoration at **Kahuku Point** (p193).

HIKE

Kuli'ou'ou Ridge Trail

Located 15 minutes outside of Waikīkī and downtown Honolulu, the Kuli'ou'ou Ridge Trail is an easy-to-access adventure for the most avid hikers. This challenging 4.4-mile, three-hour walk leads hikers through a series of different terrains – from forests to ridges – before finally ending at the unobstructed Kuli'ou'ou Summit in the Ko'olau Range.

1 Kuli'ou'ou Ridge Trailhead

Your Kuli'ou'ou Ridge hiking experience will likely begin with a steep walk – from your car to the trailhead. Given that the hike begins in a residential area, parking is limited and you'll likely have to park quite a distance away from the starting point. But once you've found a suitable spot, the adventure begins!

The Hike: Start the hike on a short paved trail at the end of Kāla'au Place. You'll quickly come across a fork, where you'll navigate right onto the dirt path and begin a series of switchbacks.

2 The Switchbacks

Twist and turn your way up the dry brush-covered, guava-tree-dotted mountain on a series of switchbacks, slowly making a dent in the 1666ft of elevation gain.

The Hike: While a bit dusty, this 1.25-mile section of trail is straightforward and only has a slight incline. Before you know it, you'll reach the forest.

3 The Forest

Once you've got your bearings, the terrain will change, turning into a pine forest that may seem out of place for a tropical

ALLEN.G/SHUTTERSTOCK

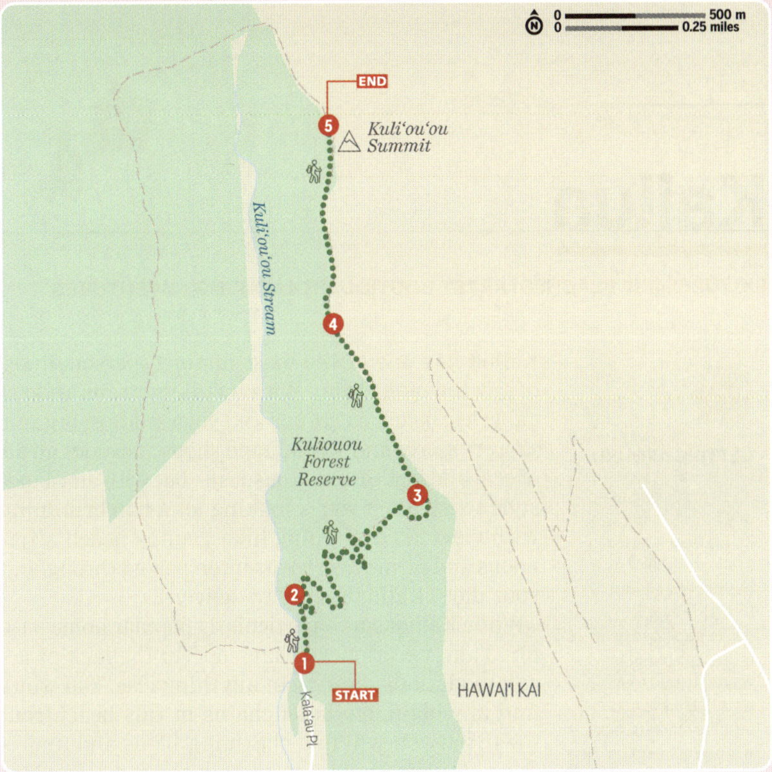

location. But the fluttering local birds like the blue-and-orange white-rumped shama and the bright yellow native *'amakihi* (Hawaiian honeycreeper) will bring you right back to the island.

The Hike: This 0.5-mile section is home to slippery, pine needle–covered slopes, so grab onto sturdy trees, watch for trail markers and make use of your high-traction hiking shoes. Luckily, those slippery pines will disappear before you reach the ridge.

4 The Ridge

Leaving the tree cover of the pines behind, you'll welcome plants that seem more in tune with the humid island air. Short shrubs of *uluhe* fern, purple-flowered vervain and rare *'ōhi'a lehua* blossoms frame the path instead. Enjoy the flora while you can, because soon enough, you'll reach the daunting 359 steps.

The best way to approach this natural stairmaster is by taking it slow. Luckily, there are lots of reasons to pause because the views from this section of the trail are epic. On one side, you'll see Hawai'i Kai (p138) and the sparkling blue marina. On the other, you'll find a unique view of Diamond Head from the back.

The Hike: These 359 steps are where you'll cover a good chunk of elevation gain – all in a relatively short 0.4-mile section. It definitely puts your muscles to work as you climb to the summit, so pace yourself!

5 Kuli'ou'ou Summit

Finally, you'll reach the end of the hike – a red dirt mound with unending views. While Diamond Head disappears behind the thriving plants, you can see from Hawai'i Kai's marina all the way to the Mokulua Islands (p152) off the coast of Kailua (p146). Spot Waimānalo Beach (p154), Koko Crater (p141) and Mānana Island (Rabbit Island). Bask in the views – and the much-needed breeze – before retracing your steps.

Kailua

PICTURESQUE BEACHES | ARTSY BOUTIQUES | KAYAKING ADVENTURES

Kailua has one of the most distinct 'personalities' of any town on O'ahu. With its hiking trails and art galleries, beach clean-ups and yoga studios, organic grocery stores and secondhand shops, it exudes an air of eco- and health-consciousness – but with an island-style twist. So, if you're looking for a trip brimming with view-filled morning hikes, sunny beach afternoons and farm-fresh treats interspersed throughout your days, Kailua is sure to deliver.

While Kailua isn't a particularly popular home base for O'ahu vacationers, that's due to the lack of accommodations more than anything else. You won't find any big-name hotel chains in this beachfront town, but you will find charming B&Bs and under-the-radar vacation rentals – talk about a cozy place to wake up to on the Windward side at sunrise.

GETTING AROUND

If you're sticking to downtown Kailua and Kailua Beach, you can likely get around by bus or even electric bike. However, if you're hoping to go a little more out of the way with food tours, waterfall hikes and farmers markets, a car will be your best bet.

While parking can be tricky at times, a spot will typically open up if you're patient enough (and avoid peak times of the day).

Hit the Beaches

Stunning shorelines await

With their turquoise waters, soft sand and views of the Mokulua Islands (p152), **Kailua Beach Park** and **Lanikai Beach** are two of the most beautiful beaches on O'ahu. In fact, this neighboring duo often makes the lists of the best beaches in the world, and there will be no question of why once you experience their natural beauty. It's also easy enough to while the day away lounging on their golden shores, swimming in their calm waters and kayaking to one of the islands nearby in the distance.

Even though Kailua Beach Park and Lanikai Beach are next door to each other, it's not so easy to get from one to the other. You can't walk along the coast, the road running between them doesn't have a designated bike lane or sidewalk – and giving up a coveted parking spot is a pretty big commitment.

Instead, choose to visit just one of the two beaches, since the experiences are quite similar. That said, if you're only going to one, the distinctions between the two make all the difference. Kailua Beach Park is the more accessible of the two, with

TOP TIP

Kailua is brimming with nature-focused volunteer opportunities. Whether it's a beach clean-up or a farm community day, there's always something happening. Consider giving back to the community and the environment during your time in town.

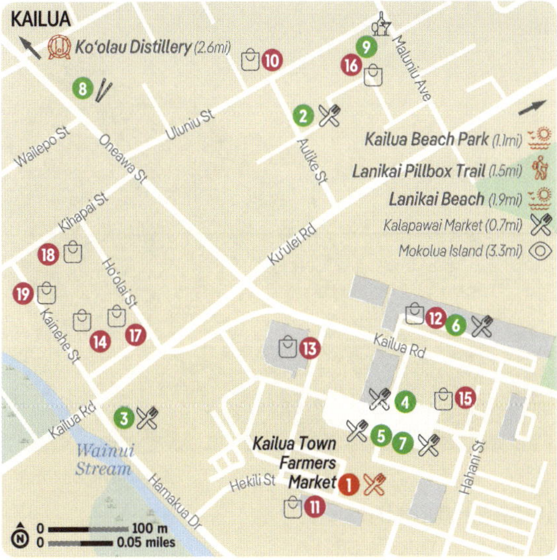

HIGHLIGHTS
1 Kailua Town Farmers Market

EATING
2 Baci Bistro
3 Easy 'Que
4 GOEN Dining + Bar
5 Kailua Farmers Market
see 13 Kono's Northshore
see 5 Middle Eats
6 Morning Brew
7 Papi's Empanadas
8 Rai Rai Ramen
see 5 The Pig & The Lady

DRINKING & NIGHTLIFE
9 Bottleheads

SHOPPING
10 Aloha Home Market
11 Aloha Kira
12 Classic Waves Boutique
13 Fighting Eel
see 11 Lauren Roth Art
14 Lexbreezy
see 10 Lōkahi Kailua Market
15 Mahina
16 Manoā Chocolate
17 Manuheali'i
18 Olive & Oliver
19 Protea Thrift

its designated parking areas, occasional paved trails, decent amounts of shade, as well as lifeguards. And while Lanikai Beach doesn't have any of those features, it has the benefit of feeling a little more removed from the world. Thanks to the barrier of beachfront houses, you won't see any cars rushing by, no matter where you are on the shoreline.

Explore the Weekly Markets

Local finds abound

While Kailua's boutique shops are great on their own, it's a real treat when there's a local market happening.

On Sunday mornings, two markets take the stage: the **Kailua Town Farmers Market** *(farmloversmarkets.com/kailua)* at Adventist Health Castle hospital and the **Lōkahi Kailua Market** *(lokahikailuamarket.com)* on Uluniu St. The former is the place to get hard-to-find tropical fruits like *liliko'i*, jackfruit, longan, guava and apple bananas, while the latter is filled with artsy creations like handcrafted shell jewelry and hibiscus-bedecked greeting cards.

On Thursday evenings the **Kailua Farmers Market** *(hfbf.org/farmers-markets/kailua/)* has its time to shine. Given its later time in the day, this market primarily serves dinner-esque foods. Savor Argentinian bites from **Papi's Empanadas**, falafel pita pockets from **Middle Eats** or Vietnamese noodle dishes from **The Pig & The Lady**. It's an international feast.

Last, but certainly not least, there's the **Aloha Home Market** *(alohahomemarket.com)*. With its sporadic schedule, it can be difficult to visit. That said, if the timing works out, you'll end up with loads of island-inspired goods to decorate your home. Monstera-leaf paintings, hand-poured beach-scented candles and flower-shaped baby sunglasses are just the beginning.

SUSTAINABLE COASTLINES HAWAI'I

Hawai'i's beaches and other landscapes don't just stay clean and stunning on their own – there's too much foot traffic for that, and trash can even wash up from across the Pacific from as far as Japan.

There are many great beach clean-up groups on O'ahu, and **Sustainable Coastlines Hawai'i** *(sustainablecoastlineshawaii.org)* is one of the most noteworthy. In 2025 alone, the local branch removed 28,000lb of debris from the islands' coastlines. They have also branched out into inland clean-ups, removing invasive fish from rivers or planting native flora.

It's easy enough to take part in a Sustainable Coastlines Hawai'i clean-up. They usually have at least a couple of events per month that are open to the public. Keep an eye on the events page on their website.

FELIX NENDZIG/SHUTTERSTOCK

Lanikai Pillbox Trail

Island Home Inspo

Welcome to Olive & Oliver

Take a bit of O'ahu home with you with some trendy, island-inspired design finds at **Olive & Oliver** *(oliveandoliverhawaii.com)*. This pair of boutiques – separated by a coffee shop – brings the best of vintage and modern, laid-back island-style and chic trends, together in the best way. Find handcrafted, rainbow-adorned mugs sitting beside aloha-embroidered sardine patches and felted wild chicken ornaments.

Hike the Lanikai Pillbox Trail

Short and steep

While there are incredible hikes all around the island, Kailua in particular has a couple of stunning hiking trails. By far the most popular hiking trail in town is the **Lanikai Pillbox Trail**. Officially known as Ka'iwa Ridge, this short, 30-minute hike looks intimidating at first, given the ropes to help you up at the very beginning, but it's doable for most visitors.

After wandering your way up the 0.9-mile inclined dirt path, you'll reach the first of the graffiti-covered pillboxes – which are actually abandoned military observation stations – in no time. Once there, all you have to do is take a seat, enjoy the breeze and soak up the jaw-dropping views of the stunning Mokulua Islands and beyond.

EATING & DRINKING IN KAILUA: OUR PICKS

GOEN Dining + Bar: This modern Roy Yamaguchi restaurant blends Asian and island influences. *4-8pm Mon-Thu, noon-8:30pm Fri & Sat, noon-8pm Sun* $$$

Kono's Northshore: This local eatery is known for its slow-cooked *kālua* pig (cooked using a traditional Hawaiian method of cooking). *7am-7pm* $$

Morning Brew: A Kailua favorite, known for its 100% Hawaiian coffee options and its tasty yet healthy breakfast and lunch menus. *6am-4pm* $

Baci Bistro: Great for a romantic night out. You can't go wrong with the *carpaccio di manzo* or the truffle gnocchi. *5-8pm Sun-Thu, to 9pm Fri & Sat* $$$

If you'd like to extend your hiking adventure, the Lanikai Pillbox Trail actually continues for another 10 minutes or so and includes one other pillbox. Although the views are essentially the same after reaching the first pillbox, you'll be able to take it all in without the crowds.

Trek to Maunawili Falls

A cascade awaits

You can swap panoramic ocean views for flowing waterfalls on the **Maunawili Demonstration Trail**. Replacing the under-repair Maunawili Falls Trail, this 7-mile round-trip trail takes you through lush forests filled with *liliko'i* trees and *naupaka* (a native Hawaiian shrub with a five-petaled white flower), and the occasional tree break gives you awe-inspiring glimpses of the greenery-covered Ko'olau Range. Three and a half miles in, you'll reach the 25ft waterfall known as Maunawili Falls, where you can take a dip in the pool at the base of the falls.

Bean to Bar

O'ahu's chocolate production

The **Mānoa Chocolate** *(manoachocolate.com; adult/child $25/15)* roastery and production facility tour is one of only a few food factory tours on O'ahu, and it's absolutely fantastic. One of Mānoa Chocolate's newest offerings, you'll get to dive into every step of the chocolate-making process, from bean roasting to wrapping each finished bar in its eye-catching label. Of course you'll also get to try plenty of chocolate samples over the 45-minute tour. If you don't have time for a full tour, Mānoa Chocolate's retail store offers a free, 15-minute tasting that takes you through a dozen of their chocolate creations.

Most Mānoa Chocolate products are made with Hawai'i-grown chocolate, with some even being made from 100% Hawaiian cacao. However, because Hawaiian cacao production is so limited, these bars are often sold for a higher price. To make most of their offerings more affordable and accessible, Mānoa Chocolate supplements Hawaiian cacao with high-quality chocolate sourced from other cacao-growing regions around the world.

It's important to note that the factory tour is located in the Kapa'a Industrial Park, not at the retail Mānoa Chocolate store in Kailua town proper. Luckily, the two are just a few miles apart.

SHOPPING FOR KEEPSAKES IN KAILUA

Lauren Roth, Kailua artist and owner of Lauren Roth Art *(@laurenrothart)*, shares some of her favorite boutiques.

Lauren Roth Art: My gallery has art from 15 local artists, so it's a great place to come if you're looking for something local to take home or to gift to somebody else.

Classic Waves Boutique: They have the most beautifully curated selection of everything from locally made treats and candles to gorgeous clothing and jewelry. It has a sophisticated feel, but it still captures the island's ocean vibes.

Aloha Kira: Stepping inside this store is like walking into a rainbow – it just explodes with color, happiness, fun clothes and gifts.

Get the Brussels sprout chips if they're not sold out!

Rai Rai Ramen: This family-owned spot has been around for decades. They've mastered the art of making fantastic ramen, so you can't go wrong. *11am-8:30pm* $

Kalapawai Market: A Kailua staple, the Kalapawai Market is known for its coffee and sandwiches. Pick up your order then walk a block to Kailua Beach. *6am-8pm* $

Easy 'Que: Get a taste of local BBQ with the brisket-heavy menu (including a brisket *loco moco*). *4-8pm Wed & Thu, to 8:30pm Fri, 9:30am-8:30pm Sat, to 7pm Sun* $$

Bottleheads: This cozy little wine bar and bottle shop is perfect for a wine night with charcuterie-like bites to nibble on. *11:30am-9pm Mon-Sat, to 8pm Sun* $$

SHOPPING FOR AN ISLAND-INSPIRED FIT IN KAILUA

Manuheali'i: This modern aloha wear brand uses authentic Hawaiian art, prints and patterns in its clothing.

Protea Thrift: This secondhand women's clothing store prioritizes high-quality, local brands. The clothes and accessories are so well cleaned and taken care of that they look like new.

Fighting Eel: Hidden in the Whole Foods area shops, Fighting Eel has island-inspired (often floral-printed) clothing for men, women and *keiki* (kids).

Lexbreezy: This modern aloha wear company is best known for its jumpsuits and dresses.

Mahina: Find both casual and classy island-inspired outfits for women at Mahina – think everything from 'Aloha'-printed sweatshirts to floor-length dresses.

Tradition Coffee Roasters

Grain to Glass

Behind the scenes at Ko'olau Distillery

Tucked away in Kapa'a Industrial Park, **Ko'olau Distillery** *(koolaudistillery.com; $25)* is the place for whiskey lovers on O'ahu. With a whiskey wizard as your guide, you'll learn all about how this spirit is distilled – from grain to glass – on a 45-minute tour. Along the way you can peek at the barrel room, the distillation equipment and the bottling process. You'll also get to sample the goods, including the distillery's other small-batch spirits, which may include gins and vodkas. Even better, you can purchase and bottle a bottle of whiskey yourself! Tours are for those 21 years old and over only.

A Cup o' Coffee

More than a caffeine boost

One of Hawai'i's most popular exports is coffee. And while much of the coffee growing is done on Hawai'i Island (the Big Island), you can still enjoy it on O'ahu.

Tradition Coffee Roasters *(traditioncoffeeroasters.com)* in Kailua's Kapa'a Industrial Park is a great place to dive even deeper into the coffee world – beyond your morning cup o' joe, that is. They have a whole slew of coffee classes, including a coffee tasting class ($47), a home barista class ($205), and a roastery tour and tasting (adult/child $26/21). Classes and tours are very limited, so be sure to book in advance.

Note, though, that if you want to drink 100% Hawaiian coffee anywhere in the islands, be sure to ask and check! Most places don't actually serve 100% Hawaiian coffee, opting to use cost-effective imported beans or coffee blends that are only partially made with locally grown beans.

AN ART WALK IN KAILUA

From adorable boutiques to brightly colored outdoor murals, Kailua is filled with artsy treasures, if you know where to look.

START	END	LENGTH
Maui Brewing Co	Oceans End Hawaii	0.5mi; 30mins

Start your stroll off right with a bite at 1 **Maui Brewing Co**. In addition to great brews, this Kailua eatery boasts two murals by renowned local artist Kamea Hadar. Meal complete, wander across the parking lot to 2 **HIC Hawaiian Island Creations**, a surf shop framed by two vibrant Sara Saffery murals on opposite sides of the building, depicting the Hawaiian history of the town.

Head down Hekili St until you hit Merchant's Row and specifically 3 **Lauren Roth Art** (p149). The colorful, whimsical creations of Lauren Roth herself – along with 15 other local artists – bring the place to life. A couple of doors down, find 4 **Aloha Kira** (p149), an equally bold and beautiful boutique with a mural painted by Kelsie Dayna. The *musubi*- and hibiscus-covered wall is the perfect backdrop to shop for all sorts of local goodies.

Arms inevitably laden with bags, turn into the Whole Foods parking lot, which will take you directly to the 5 **Nick Kuchar Art & Design Co** shop. Known for his vintage-style, island-inspired art pieces, Nick Kuchar's store showcases the best of his works on everything from beach towels to aloha shirts to prints.

Cross Kailua Rd via the crosswalk near the Bank of Hawai'i, then make your penultimate stop at 6 **Aesthetic Hawaii Gallery**, where you'll discover some of the fanciest art pieces in town. In the same building, find the flower-printed leather creations, including wallets and purses, at the locally owned 7 **Oceans End Hawaii**.

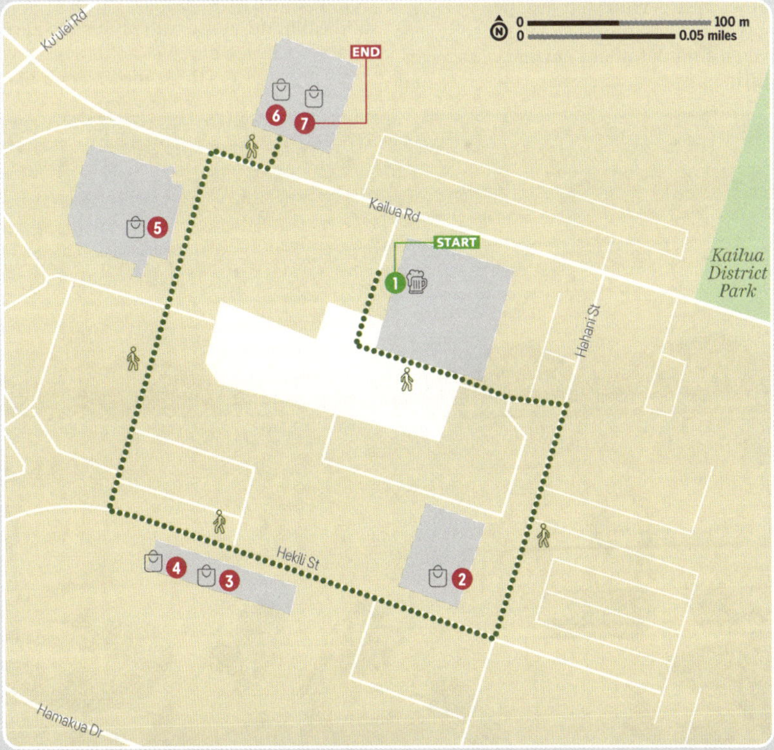

KAYAKING TOUR

Mokulua Islands

The Mokulua Islands, traditionally called Nā Mokulua and colloquially called 'the Mokes,' are a pair of islands that you can see throughout the Windward Coast – and the only way to get to them is by kayak. It's a four-hour expedition with about three hours of kayaking. If you'd like more guidance, Kailua Beach Adventures runs kayaking tours, so you can enjoy the fun without the planning.

1 Kailua Beach Adventures

To start your kayaking expedition to the Mokulua Islands, you'll need a kayak. Kailua Beach Adventures is the most convenient as it's just steps away from Kailua Beach, your launching point. As for which kayak, go for a double or triple kayak. There's no need to exert extra energy with single-person kayaks if there are other members in your group.

Your kayak rental shop is also where you'll find out about current ocean conditions (waves, currents, tides etc) and get the required permits to land on your two-island stops.

The Journey: Walking from Kailua Beach Adventures to Kailua Beach takes about five minutes. Hawai'i law states that you, as the renter, have to transport your kayak to the beach; the kayak rental-shop employees cannot help you.

2 Kailua Beach Park

Kailua Beach (p146) is filled with soft sand and calm, turquoise waters. It's the ideal spot for a beach day, just not today. Now, it simply serves as the launching point for

JUN SEITA/FLICKR/CC BY 2.0

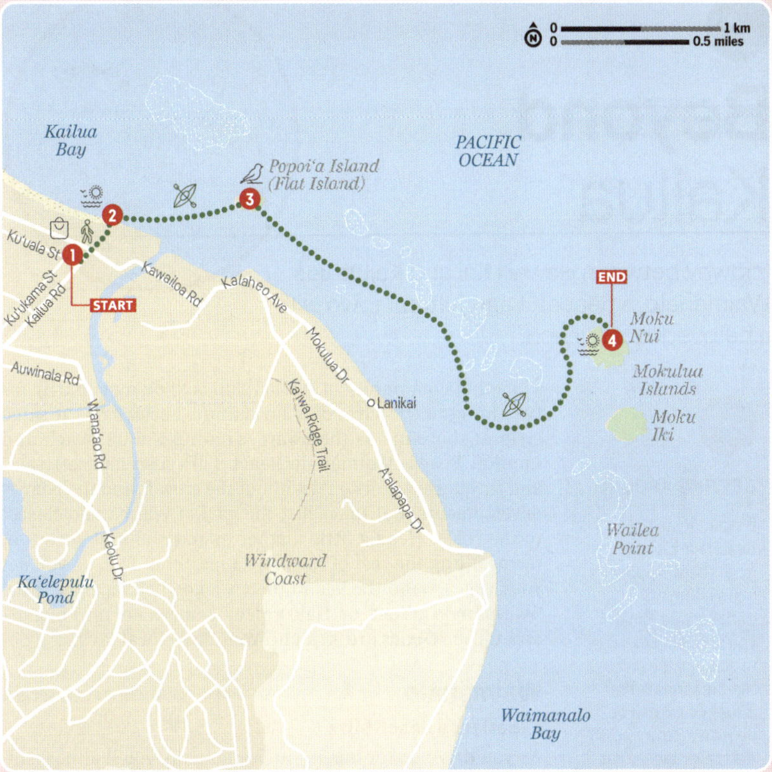

your kayaking adventure to the Mokulua Islands. And you'll be able to see your next stop – Popoi'a Island – before you even leave the shore!

The Journey: It's only a quarter mile from Kailua Beach to Popoi'a Island. The time it takes to get to the island can vary widely based on ocean conditions – expect 10 to 30 minutes.

3 Popoi'a Island

Despite being just 4 acres, Popoi'a Island – sometimes called Flat Island because of its leveled terrain – holds quite a bit of significance. For the ancient Native Hawaiians, Popoi'a Island served as a fishing shrine. Local fishers would bring a fraction of their catches to offer to the Hawaiian gods in the hopes that they would bless them with bountiful future catches.

While there isn't any fish-sacrificing going on today on Popoi'a Island, it still has importance as a State Seabird Sanctuary. Wedge-tailed shearwaters *('ua'u kani)* like to lay their eggs in the island's small sinkholes, where they lie protected until they hatch. If you happen to see these eggs while you're there, simply admire them from afar.

The Journey: From Popoi'a Island, it's easiest to head back toward the shore and calmer waters before continuing the 2-mile, 1½-hour journey onto the Mokes. This is also the section where the ocean conditions vary the most, so keep an eye out for large waves, low tides (which expose the reef) and strong currents.

4 Mokulua Islands

While there are technically two Mokulua Islands, Moku Nui and Moku Iki, only the former is accessible to the public – and luckily, it's the closer one of the two. Once you safely dock your kayak, soak up some sun on the island's little beach, keep an eye out for *honu* and monk seals, and take in the views of the Ko'olau Range from a new perspective.

Beyond Kailua

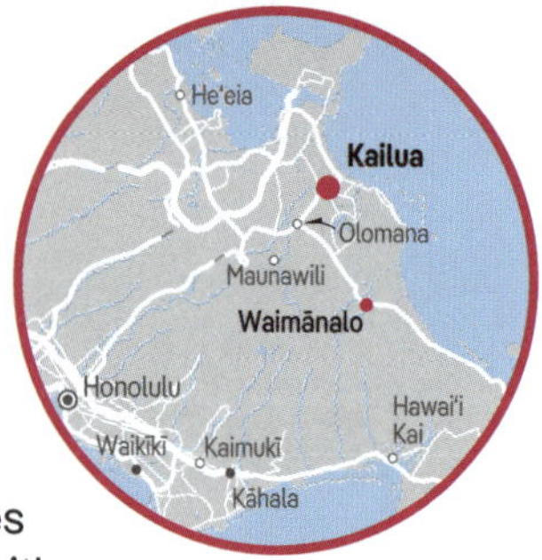

Midway between Hawai'i Kai and Kailua lies Waimānalo, a peaceful agricultural town with a beloved local beach.

GETTING AROUND

If Waimānalo Bay Beach Park is your goal, O'ahu's public bus system will definitely do. But if you're hoping to get to some of the more remote farms in the area – which can be about a mile or two off the main road – a car may come in handy.

The quiet community of Waimānalo is known primarily for two things: its beach and its agriculture. Located on the same strip of shoreline as the award-winning Kailua Beach and Lanikai Beach, Waimānalo Beach Park also has soft sand and turquoise waters, just without the crowds and the nearby developments. But that's just the part of Waimānalo closest to the coast. Head a little further inland and find dozens of farms filling the rest of town. As a matter of fact, as you eat your way around the island there's a good chance you'll see 'Waimānalo greens' or 'Nalo greens' somewhere on a menu – and those veggies are straight from these local farms.

Waimānalo

TIME FROM KAILUA: **15MINS**

Experience beach bliss

As you drive up (or bus in) to Waimānalo, you'll almost immediately be greeted by the 3 miles of teal waters and golden sand that is **Waimānalo Bay Beach Park**. Add the swaying ironwood trees into the mix – a shade-providing respite, something that's quite rare on O'ahu beaches – and there's no doubt that a beach day is in order.

Though Waimānalo Beach looks quite picture-perfect, it can get a little bit rough at times. Rather than acting as a swimming or snorkeling spot, this beach's small-to-medium-sized waves are great for bodyboarding or bodysurfing. But before you grab your board and dive in, check the shore for Portuguese man o' war, which are small, blue jellyfish-esque creatures with painful stings. If they're out and about in the water, stick to the sand instead.

A tropical fruit paradise

If you don't want to spend your whole day in Waimānalo on the beach, you can spend your afternoon exploring some of the coolest farms in town, including the beloved **Frankie's Nursery** *(frankiesnurseryllc.com)*. At this adorable farm stand you can snag some hard-to-find tropical fruits like sapote, canistels and star apples.

MARUOKAJOE/SHUTTERSTOCK

Waimānalo Bay Beach Park

Frolic amid the sunflowers

The nearly 80-year-old **Waimanalo Country Farms** *(waimanalocountryfarms.com)* started as a 'truck farming' farm – growing produce like broccoli, kai choi, sweet potato and tomatoes. But it really made a name for itself about a decade after opening as a melon farm, churning out watermelons and rarer golden melons year after year.

But as with many farms, they've had to adapt to consumer wants and needs. The produce was phased out, and in recent years, sunflowers have been brought in. Blooming intermittently throughout the year, these bright yellow blossoms are a joy to see. And all you have to do is walk around, enjoy the blooms, and take as many pictures as you want. Toward the end of the season, you are also allowed to pick your own sunflowers to take home.

It's important to note that once the sunflowers blossom, they only stick around for about 10 days. As soon as you hear about them in bloom, you'll want to go, go, go!

MORE FARM VISITS

While Waimānalo has more than its fair share of agritourism opportunities, there are a few other Oʻahu farms that are worth a visit, including **Kahuku Farms** (p194) in Kahuku, **Kahumana Farms** (p130) in Waiʻanae and the **Kōkua Learning Farm** (p174) in Haleʻiwa.

THE NATION OF HAWAIʻI

Waimānalo is home to one of the largest populations of Native Hawaiian people in the islands. It's also home to the Nation of Hawaiʻi, an independent community that functions as its own sovereign state within the islands.

Established in 1994 and led by local icon Dennis 'Bumpy' Puʻuhonua Kanahele, the Nation of Hawaiʻi serves as a living model for Hawaiian self-governance, where residents manage their own land, resources and community rules. This 45-acre area, called Puʻuhonua O Waimānalo, was established through a historic land-lease agreement with the state, marking a rare instance where the government returned land to be managed under Hawaiian authority.

Why do this? The community advocates for the restoration of Hawaiʻi's independence once again, after being unlawfully overthrown in 1893 by a group of American businessmen (p219).

Kāne‘ohe

BOTANICAL GARDENS | BEAUTIFUL BAYS | TRADITIONAL CUISINE

GETTING AROUND

A car is essentially a must for visiting Kāne‘ohe. Many of the most popular attractions, including the Byodo-In Temple and Ho‘omaluhia Botanical Garden, are a mile or two from the closest bus stop. Luckily, parking is rarely a problem.

Framed by the beautiful Kāne‘ohe Bay on one side and the lush Ko‘olau Range on the other, Kāne‘ohe is a sleepy town about halfway up the Windward Coast. While it seems unassuming today, this O‘ahu town was home to some of the first Hawaiian rulers – those who wore the metaphorical crown before King Kamehameha I united all of the islands as the Kingdom of Hawai‘i.

Today, nearly all of Kāne‘ohe's attractions embrace the town's tranquil, unhurried atmosphere, whether it's stopping to smell the flowers at a botanical garden, meditating at a hidden Japanese temple, or fishing at one of the calmest bays on O‘ahu. Simply put, be prepared to take things slow – even slower than the typical island pace – during your time in this Windward O‘ahu town.

Paddle Around Kāne‘ohe Bay

Calm waters and endless activities

With its gradient turquoise waters, curving sandbar and lush-green Ko‘olau Range backdrop, **Kāne‘ohe Bay** looks magical – which might explain why it's been used as a filming location for several movies, including *Pirates of the Caribbean: On Stranger Tides* and *50 First Dates*. But the beauty of Kāne‘ohe Bay doesn't come from its film-worthy status; rather, it comes from how locals – and now visitors – find ways to enjoy it each day.

Though Kāne‘ohe Bay looks still on the surface, there's actually a lot going on. There are five islands in the bay, including the **Kāne‘ohe Sandbar** (officially known as Ahu‘olaka Island), which occasionally makes an above-the-surface appearance, depending on the tide. It's also home to O‘ahu's only barrier reef, which helps prevent large waves from breaking in the bay, and it houses quite a bit of marine life.

Given all of these natural features, Kāne‘ohe Bay is great for all sorts of water activities. Surfing, kayaking, snorkeling and fishing are just the beginning. That said, these activities

TOP TIP

If you're hanging out on land during your time in Kāne‘ohe, spritz on some bug spray. Mosquitoes love the damp environment in this part of the island, and their bites can last weeks. If you're hanging out in the water, lather up with some reef-safe sunscreen instead.

are only great if you know the best spots in the bay for your water sport of choice. Since the locations can vary a bit based on daily ocean conditions, a guided tour – or, at a minimum, a visit to a gear rental shop – can come in handy.

Both **Captain Bob's Picnic Sail** *(captainbobspicnicsail.com; adult/child $189/167)* and **Captain Bruce** *(cptbruce.com/kaneohe-sandbar.php; adult/child $180/170)* offer prime swimming and snorkeling opportunities. Alternatively, **Kāne'ohe Bay Ocean Sports** *(kaneohebayoceansports.com; adult/child from $107/89)* has bay tours with stand-up paddleboarding, kayaking, banana boat-riding and bumper tubing.

Time with Taro

A Native Hawaiian food staple

Taro, called *kalo* in Hawaiian, has a long history in Hawai'i. According to ancient Hawaiian *mo'olelo* (stories), the legend of *kalo* begins with the Hawaiian goddess Ho'ohōkūkalani. Ho'ohōkūkalani became pregnant, but the baby, Hāloa, was stillborn. In her sadness, Ho'ohōkūkalani buried Hāloa and

HIGHLIGHTS

1 Byodo-In Temple
2 Ho'omaluhia Botanical Garden
3 K Bay Bros Fish & Ice
4 Kāne'ohe Bay
5 Waiahole Poi Factory

SIGHTS

6 Kāne'ohe Sandbar
7 Kualoa Regional Park
8 Mokoli'i
9 Nu'uanu Pali State Wayside

ACTIVITIES

see 10 Captain Bob's Picnic Sail
10 Captain Bruce
11 Kākoʻo 'Ōiwi
see 10 Kāne'ohe Bay Ocean Sports
12 Kualoa Ranch

EATING

13 Adela's Country Eatery
14 Masa & Joyce Okazuya

ROAD TRIP SNACKS

Stock up on snacks at grocery stores in Kailua and Kāne'ohe. Here are some faves.

Arare: Small, crunchy crackers seasoned with shōyu and sometimes seaweed.

Iso peanuts: Peanuts with a crunchy coating.

Li hing mui gummies: A variety of gummy candies dusted in a sweet, tangy dried plum powder. Part of a genre of local snacks called 'crack seed.'

Musubi: Made of a rectangle of rice, a slice of shōyu-seasoned Spam and nori.

Shredded ika: Dried, shredded cuttlefish.

Wasabi peas: Spicy, crunchy dried peas covered in wasabi.

LIFE ON KĀNE'OHE BAY

Glenn Pang, born-and-raised Kāne'ohe local and retired fisherman, shares stories of his times out on Kāne'ohe Bay.

When we were younger, we'd hang out in the bay – we'd swim all day, eat coconuts and mangoes, and catch fish when we could. We would hang out at the sandbar and surf at Kapapa Island all the time. The older guys made these hydroplane boats, and we used to race them in the shallows in front of our house.

Nowadays [during my retirement], I don't go out as much as I used to. My backyard is the bay – I live right on the water, so I can just sit around, watching things go by.

LEONID ANDRONOV/SHUTTERSTOCK

Ho'omaluhia Botanical Garden

watered him with her tears – until a green, heart-shaped sprout appeared: the *kalo* plant.

The history of *kalo* as told by horticulturists is a little bit different. Though the species was actually introduced to the islands, it quickly became a Native Hawaiian food staple. Different parts of the plant were pounded into poi (purple paste made by pounding taro), turned into a dessert known as *kūlolo*, and used as a wrapping (along with *ti* leaves, also known as *kī* leaves) for *laulau* (a bundle made of pork or chicken and salted butterfish, wrapped in taro and ti leaves and steamed). *Kalo* even has some medicinal properties, as ancient Hawaiians used it to treat stomachaches and infected wounds.

Today you can have your own hands-on experience with *kalo* with the nonprofit **Kāko'o 'Ōiwi** *(kakoooiwi.org)*. Each Monday, Tuesday, Wednesday and Friday, Kāko'o 'Ōiwi has *lo'i kalo* (wetland taro field) workdays. With the backdrop of the verdant Ko'olau Range, you'll get knee-deep (sometimes even waist-deep) in mud to weed, plant and harvest the *kalo*. Throughout this experience, the volunteer leaders teach the importance of *kalo* in Native Hawaiian culture, as well as the ins-and-outs of ancient Hawaiian farming practices.

EATING IN KĀNE'OHE: OUR PICKS

Waiahole Poi Factory: Authentic Hawaiian eatery known for its *kalo*-based bites. Order at a walk-up window and enjoy on one of the outdoor benches. *10am-6pm* $$

Adela's Country Eatery: Unique take-out noodle spot with house-made *kalo*-, *ube*- (purple yam) and *'ulu*- (breadfruit) based pastas. *10:30am-8pm Mon, Tue & Thu-Sat, to 3:30pm Wed* $$

K Bay Bros Fish & Ice: Very fresh take-out poke spot with both popular and hard-to-find poke flavors. Offers extra *ponzu* and *unagi* sauces on the side. *10am-6pm Tue-Sat, to 5pm Sun* $$

Masa & Joyce Okazuya: Old-school *okazuya* (sometimes translated as a 'Japanese-style delicatessen') with Hawaiian and Japanese bites. *6am-2pm Mon & Wed-Sat, from 7am Sun* $$

Sample the Roots of Your Labor

Traditional taro dishes at Waiahole Poi Factory

Enjoy the fruits (roots?) of your labor (sort of) with a trip to **Waiahole Poi Factory** *(waiaholepoifactory.com)*, just 5 miles up the road from Kāko'o 'Ōiwi. While it won't be the same *kalo* roots that you harvested, you can still sample this Hawaiian food staple. Get the tourist-favorite 'Sweet Lady of Waiahole,' a warm *kūlolo* (a *kalo*-coconut pudding of sorts) and *haupia* (coconut pudding) ice-cream dessert.

Many visitors come to the Waiahole Poi Factory just for the *kalo*-based treat, but they're missing out – this Kāne'ohe eatery has some of the best authentic Hawaiian food on the island! Order yourself a plate with beef or squid *lū'au*, *kālua* pig, chicken long rice (chicken and rice noodles in a ginger broth) or *laulau* as the entrée. With that, you'll get three authentic Hawaiian sides – poi, *lomi lomi* salmon (minced, salted salmon, diced tomato and green onion) and *haupia* – so it's an all-around Hawaiian feast.

Blooming Flowers & Mountain Views

Hang out in a peaceful refuge

As you make the mile-long drive from the entrance of **Ho'omaluhia Botanical Garden** to the parking areas, you'll already be able to tell that it's a special place. The emerald Ko'olau Range appears to rise up out of the palm-tree-lined road as you get closer to the entrance. (Note, though, that this eye-catching, greenery-framed road has been plastered across Instagram feeds so often that Ho'omaluhia Botanical Garden now explicitly prevents people from stopping their cars for photos and causing traffic jams.) But the drive in is just the beginning.

After parking, pass the Visitor Center and walk along a path lined with tropical plants, including ones from Polynesia, Melanesia, South and Southeast Asia, Africa and, of course, Hawai'i. Admire the bright red *'awapuhi* (wild ginger), ripening cacao pods and yellow heliconia, just to start. Since the trails aren't fully connected, it can be easy to completely skip a section without realizing it. Download a map of the botanical gardens in advance or pick up a hard copy at the Visitor Center to make sure you hit everything.

At some point during your wandering, you'll inevitably end up at Ho'omaluhia Botanical Garden's reservoir, officially known as **Loko Waimaluhia**. Here, you can enjoy a picturesque waterfront picnic. However, keep an eye out – there are dozens of ducks and swans that make their home in the reservoir, and they'll likely waddle on over for some food.

HAWAIIAN FOOD

While visitors often use the terms 'Hawaiian food' and 'local food' interchangeably, the two refer to completely different cuisines. Hawaiian food is the food the ancient Native Hawaiians ate before immigrants arrived to the islands. This includes a lot of the foods that you likely think of when picturing a lū'au (traditional Hawaiian feast) like *kālua* pig and poi. Local food, on the other hand, is Hawai'i's regional cuisine. It includes dishes – such as *musubi*, *manapuas* (meat-filled buns), *malasadas* (Portuguese-style doughnuts) and poke – that were created with the influence of the islands' immigrant cuisines. For more information on Hawai'i's food culture, see p204.

MORE AUTHENTIC HAWAIIAN EATERIES

The Waiahole Poi Factory isn't the only place on O'ahu to get tasty, authentic Hawaiian food. Also check out **Helena's Hawaiian Food** (p105) and **Highway Inn Kaka'ako** (p79), both in Honolulu.

CHIEF OF WAR

In 2025 Apple TV+ released the first season of the TV show *Chief of War*. Starring Jason Momoa, this show covers the story of the unification of Hawai'i from a Native Hawaiian perspective. It also features a mostly Polynesian cast and heavily features 'Ōlelo Hawai'i (the Hawaiian language).

Surprisingly, the show was mostly filmed in New Zealand, but the locations are based on real, historically significant locations in the islands, like 'Īao Valley on Maui and Pu'ukoholā Heiau on Hawai'i Island. O'ahu's Nu'uanu Pali State Wayside does not make an appearance in the plot just yet, but the show's creators and fans are hopeful that the story will continue for a couple more seasons and eventually reach the historical battle.

Take a Historic Detour

Where Hawaiian history was made

Not far from Ho'omaluhia Botanical Garden lies one of the most significant spots in Hawaiian history, the **Nu'uanu Pali State Wayside**. It was here during the 1795 Battle of Nu'uanu that King Kamehameha I finally united all of the Hawaiian Islands – a feat that many island rulers had tried to achieve.

When you visit the Nu'uanu Pali State Wayside and lookout, there's a small plaque commemorating this moment in history. Take a minute to stop and read it before you gape in awe at the sweeping views. You can see Kailua, Kāne'ohe and Mokoli'i Island, as well as miles of blue Pacific Ocean from this one stunning spot.

Take a Mini Trip to Japan

A UNESCO World Heritage Site replica

Tucked away at the back of the Valley of the Temples Memorial Park Cemetery, the **Byodo-In Temple** *(byodo-in.com; adult/child $10/6)* isn't in a spot that most people would typically explore. That said, this beautiful temple is definitely open for visitors.

Kāne'ohe's Byodo-In Temple is actually a miniature replica of the 1000-year-old Byodo-In Temple in Uji, Japan, which also happens to be a UNESCO World Heritage Site. When you visit O'ahu's small reproduction, you'll feel like you're in another world. The ringing of the **Sacred Bell** *(bon-sho)*, the backdrop of the lush green Ko'olau Range, and the peacefully swimming black swans create a serene atmosphere that urges you to take a pause.

For a closer look at the bright red temple, circle around the pond clockwise. First, you'll come across the Sacred Bell that likely caught your ear. Take your turn ringing the 5ft-tall bell with the long wooden log called a *shu-moku*. As the sound rings out, you'll be blessed with a long life filled with happiness – or so the custom goes.

From there, follow the path to the Byodo-In Temple itself. Peek inside at the 18ft-tall gold **Buddha**, where incense smoke wafts and fellow visitors offer their prayers. Finally, don't forget to pop by the gift shop, and snap a few photos of the temple from the entryway bridge on your way out.

Continue the Road Trip

Drive up the Windward Coast

Kāne'ohe is the last major town on the Windward Coast before you hit the North Shore. Why not continue the road trip up the coast? Soak up the unending ocean views and lush green Ko'olau Range. Visit Kualoa Ranch, soak up some sun at **Kualoa Regional Park**, kayak to Mokoli'i Island (p162), and keep an eye out for hidden beach swings. Soon enough, you'll reach Lā'ie and Kahuku (p190), the easternmost North Shore towns.

Beyond Kāne'ohe

Just outside of Kāne'ohe proper lies two stunning nature spots – the small community of Ka'a'awa and the little island of Mokoli'i.

At the northernmost end of Kāne'ohe Bay, you'll find the tiny town of Ka'a'awa. It is most well-known for the Kualoa Ranch, a greenery-filled, tour-focused attraction that is rich in both Hawaiian lore and movie credits. Stop in for stunning views, captivating legends and some of the freshest tropical fruit around.

Just across the water from Ka'a'awa and Kualoa Ranch (and still technically within Kāne'ohe Bay), you'll see the little island of Mokoli'i, also called Chinaman's Hat. While most visitors simply admire it from afar – specifically from the Kualoa Regional Park shoreline – you can actually make your way over via kayak or stand-up paddleboard.

Places

Ka'a'awa

TIME FROM KĀNE'OHE: **20MINS**

Ka'a'awa is one of the quietest parts of O'ahu, staunchly opposing development and keeping the region as coastal-rural as possible. You'll find houses tucked amid overflowing greenery, flanked by a two-lane main road right along the coast that's nearly lapped by the water's edge at high tide. Inland, you'll find the lush Ko'olau Range further partitioning the area from hustle and bustle. Ironically enough, this quiet town is home to one of the biggest tourist attractions on the island, Kualoa Ranch.

GETTING AROUND

Like much of O'ahu, a car is the easiest way to get to Ka'a'awa. Alternatively, Kualoa Ranch does offer hotel pick up and drop off from specific Waikīkī hotels for an additional $30 per person fee. There are also a few bus stops along the main road, but they aren't the most conveniently located in regards to attractions. You'll want to make sure you have a bit of buffer time though, as most attractions in this area require you to arrive at a specific time. Finally, once you get to Ka'a'awa, it's a short kayak or stand-up paddleboard adventure over to Mokoli'i.

For both Kualoa Ranch and Mokoli'i, you'll need to pack your day bag well. Snacks, water, reef-safe sunscreen, proper footwear and even a change of footwear are essential for both places.

THE LEGEND OF KA'A'AWA VALLEY & MOKOLI'I

According to ancient Hawaiian *mo'olelo*, Kualoa Valley came to be when the Hawaiian goddess Hi'iaka, Pele's sister, slew a massive *mo'o* ('lizard' or 'dragon'). Its body crashed onto the shore, creating the mountains that surround Kualoa Valley and modern-day Kualoa Ranch – which, by the way, aptly translates to 'long back.'

After the lizard was slain, Hi'iaka wasn't done. She cut off its tail and tossed it half a mile out into the water. This created the nearby island of Mokoli'i, which roughly translates to 'little lizard.'

MALACHI JACOBS/SHUTTERSTOCK

Film location site, Kualoa Ranch

A trip to Kualoa Ranch

There's no other attraction on O'ahu quite like **Kualoa Ranch** (*kualoa.com*). Nestled in the rugged Ko'olau Range, this vibrant green landscape offers a blend of engaging nature tours, ranging from ones featuring Native Hawaiian legends to others on the coolest movies filmed at this jaw-dropping location.

On the **Kualoa Grown Tour**, crack open cacao pods, sample tropical mountain apples fresh off the tree, and find out more about traditional Hawaiian farming practices. You'll even pay a visit to the historic **Moli'i Fishpond**, one of just four ancient Hawaiian fishponds that still exist on O'ahu today.

And while the Kualoa Grown Tour captures the attention of foodies and farms, it's the Kualoa Ranch's film history that draws the biggest crowds. Of all the movies shot at Kualoa Ranch, including *Jumanji*, *Godzilla* and *50 First Dates*, *Jurassic Park* is the most famous, making the **Jurassic Adventure Tour** one of the most popular tour options. Hitch a ride on a safari-esque vehicle to see the coolest film sites and sets from *Jurassic Park*, *Jurassic World* and *Jurassic World: Fallen Kingdom*.

If you're an all-around movie buff (not just a *Jurassic Park* fan), **Kualoa Ranch's Movie Sites & Ranch Tour** is a great choice. Cruise around on a vintage school bus and see many iconic landscapes and items from films like *Kong: Skull Island*, *Finding 'Ohana* and *Jumanji*. You'll even get to venture into an old WWII bunker filled with props, posters and other memorabilia from the hundreds of movies filmed on-site.

Mokoli'i Island

TIME FROM SHORE: **30MINS**

From Kualoa Ranch and the rest of Ka'a'awa, you'll be able to see a little island in the distance. That's Mokoli'i Island, colloquially known as Chinaman's Hat. Despite being less than half a mile from the shore, most people don't give it a second thought, snapping some pictures from the shores of Kualoa Regional Park and continuing their drive along the Windward Coast. But this little island has a couple of adventures to offer.

Paddle to a tiny island

The island of Mokoliʻi is quite close to the shore. Even better, it's still technically within the confines of Kāneʻohe Bay. Add those two facts together, and you've got yourself relatively calm waters ideal for a kayaking or paddleboarding adventure. Depending on the tide, current and starting point, your paddling journey can take between 15 and 30 minutes to get there – and all along the way, the turquoise waters and stunning Koʻolau Range will be right by your side.

Assuming you don't have a handy kayak of your own, the most difficult part of the Mokoliʻi adventure may actually be getting one. There aren't any kayak rental spots nearby, so you have a couple of different options. You can rent a kayak in Kailua, strap it onto your car and head out. Or, you can have a kayak delivered to you, right at the beach, from companies like **Hawaii Beach Time** *(hawaiibeachtime.com; per day from $74)* or **Active Oahu** *(activeoahutours.com; 4hr from $69)*.

It's important to note that baby hammerhead sharks and Portuguese man o' war are commonly found in the waters surrounding Mokoliʻi. The former usually don't cause any trouble, but keep in mind that they are still wild animals, so give them their space. The latter's stings can be painful, so if you see any on the shore before your adventure (they look like little blue-tinted plastic bags), consider rescheduling.

Then hike to the top

The journey isn't over once you reach Mokoliʻi Island. Once there, dock your kayak at the small unnamed beach, where the start of a hike awaits. Though only about 20 minutes long, the hiking trail is steep and dusty with short, scrambling sections, so it can be a bit tricky. Take your time and wear proper hiking shoes with traction. If it's a bit too steep for your liking, just slowly shuffle back down to the beach and enjoy the crystal-clear waters instead.

If you make it to the end of the hike, you'll find yourself at the top of Mokoliʻi with unobstructed 360-degree views. With the unending blue-hued Pacific Ocean on one side and the bright green Koʻolau Range on the other, it's absolutely magical.

THE HISTORY OF KUALOA VALLEY

Kualoa Valley – one of the three valleys that make up modern-day Kualoa Ranch – holds a significant place in Native Hawaiian history. For years, children of Hawaiian *aliʻi* (rulers) were brought to the area to learn the art of war, as well as Native Hawaiian history and traditions. But why here? It is believed that thousands of chiefs have been buried in the mountains surrounding the valley – and that they now haunt the grounds and are known as night-marchers in their ghostly state.

But Kualoa Ranch wasn't just a place for royalty. It also served as a *puʻuhonua*, a place of refuge, for just about everyone – warriors coming to heal, criminals fleeing from the death penalty, and women, children and elderly simply looking for safe places to live.

WANT TO STAY ON THE WINDWARD COAST?

The Windward Coast only has a handful of B&Bs and hotels. Refer to the Places We Love to Stay guide (p119) for recommendations.

Researched by
Sarah Etinas

North Shore

HISTORIC TOWNS & SURFER-FILLED BEACHES

From Mokulē'ia to Lā'ie, O'ahu's North Shore region is filled with prime surf swells, golden-sand beaches and historic relics.

O'ahu's North Shore has made a name for itself as one of the best surf regions in the world. Banzai Pipeline (at 'Ehukai Beach Park) tends to top the list with its 30ft-plus waves, but Hale'iwa Ali'i Beach Park, Sunset Beach Park and Waimea Bay Beach Park all certainly hold their own in terms of swells and surf competitions.

PPICTURES/SHUTTERSTOCK ©

Depending on the time of year, these very same beaches – and some of the ones next door – can still have calm waters that are great for all sorts of beach activities. Swimming, snorkeling and cliff jumping are just the beginning, so grab your beach bag, lather on some reef-safe sunscreen and hit the beach.

While beaches and surfing are a big part of Hawaiian life – both past and present – there's even more to this O'ahu region. To round out your island knowledge a little more, explore the nuggets of each phase of O'ahu history that can be found on the North Shore. Find ancient Hawaiian *ahupua'a* (land division) markers in Kahuku, old missionary-founded churches in Hale'iwa and sugar plantation ruins in Waialua.

On top of all that and beyond the miles of beaches, there's also a fair bit of nature in this part of the island. Hike your way to waterfalls, explore working local farms and take in-demand bird sanctuary tours.

THE MAIN AREAS

WAHIAWĀ
Weathered residential town with the Dole Plantation. **p168**

HALE'IWA
Old-school, boutique-filled surfer town. **p172**

PŪPŪKEA
Beach-filled region known for its surf competitions. **p180**

LĀ'IE & KAHUKU
Quiet towns with foodie gems. **p190**

For places to stay on the North Shore, see p119

Left: Sunset Beach Park (p183); Above: Surfing, Hale'iwa (p172)

Find Your Way

Kamehameha Hwy follows nearly all of the North Shore coastline (with the exception of Waialua and Mokulē'ia, where Farrington Hwy becomes the main road). Follow it, and you'll get anywhere you need to go!

CAR

A car is the most convenient mode of transportation on the North Shore, as there are simply so many potential stops to make. That said, parking can be a real hassle at times.

BUS

Ditch the parking fiascos and hitch a ride on O'ahu's public bus system instead. Since the vast majority of the North Shore is accessible via one main road, Kamehameha Hwy, the bus routes are quite efficient.

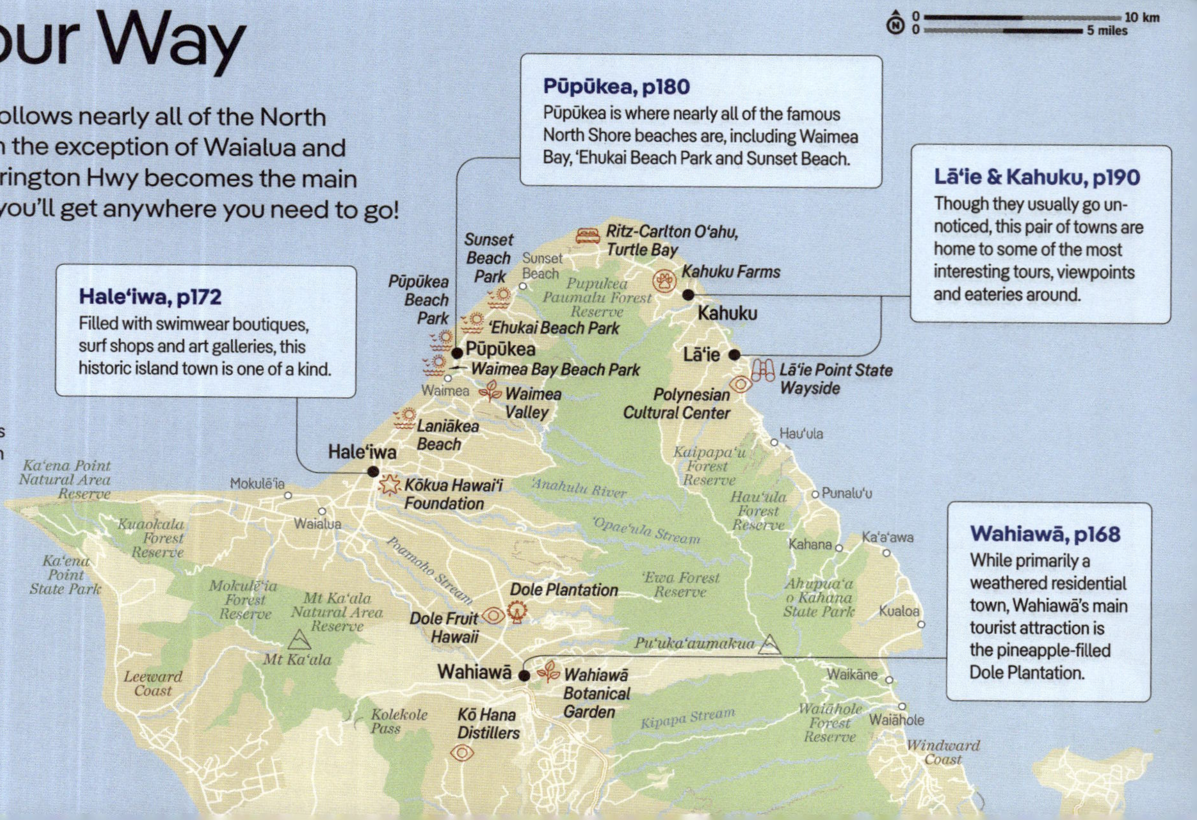

Pūpūkea, p180
Pūpūkea is where nearly all of the famous North Shore beaches are, including Waimea Bay, 'Ehukai Beach Park and Sunset Beach.

Lā'ie & Kahuku, p190
Though they usually go unnoticed, this pair of towns are home to some of the most interesting tours, viewpoints and eateries around.

Hale'iwa, p172
Filled with swimwear boutiques, surf shops and art galleries, this historic island town is one of a kind.

Wahiawā, p168
While primarily a weathered residential town, Wahiawā's main tourist attraction is the pineapple-filled Dole Plantation.

MIXA CO LTD/GETTY IMAGES

Waimea Bay Beach Park (p180)

Plan Your Time

In summer, beach time – whether that be snorkeling, swimming or suntanning – should top the list. In winter, visit those same beaches to watch incredible surf competitions.

Pressed for Time?

With limited time, fill your North Shore itinerary with beaches. Since nearly all of the beaches in this part of the island are stunning, it doesn't matter which one you visit. Simply pick the one with parking (or the one closest to a bus stop) and enjoy it! **Waimea Bay Beach Park** (p180) and **Sunset Beach Park** (p183) are just a couple of favorites. Have a swim, or just kick back and watch surfers take to the waves.

A Weeklong Stay

As well as dedicating a couple of days to the sandy shorelines, add some tours – like those offered at **Kahuku Farms** (p194) and **Gunstock Ranch** (p194) – to the schedule. Spend a day learning about island cultures at the **Polynesian Cultural Center** (p190). Eat your way through **shrimp trucks** (p193), acai bowl nooks and farm-to-table restaurants. And don't miss a visit to **Waimea Falls** (p184)!

SEASONAL HIGHLIGHTS

SPRING
Flowers bloom bright on the North Shore each spring, particularly at Waimea Valley.

SUMMER
The warm water that comes with summer demands you enjoy some prime snorkeling and swimming opportunities.

FALL
Be prepared to (literally) go with the flow in autumn. The water may be calm for swimming or wave-filled for surfing.

WINTER
The waves start to reach 20ft-plus, making winter the season to watch famed surf competitions.

Wahiawā

DOLE PLANTATION | RUM DISTILLERIES | BOTANICAL GARDENS

GETTING AROUND

A car would be ideal in Wahiawā. While there are buses, there aren't convenient stops for visiting specific attractions like Wahiawā Botanical Garden and Kō Hana Distillers.

Regardless of your mode of transportation you'll likely hit some traffic. Good surf, military vehicle transport or a regular ol' work commute are all enough to back things up. There are rarely ways to get around it, so just sit back and relax on the slower-than-usual drive.

TOP TIP

Keep an eye out for the pineapple fields as you drive near the Dole Plantation. While the silvery swaths of land on the west side of the road may not look like much at first, that's where the pineapple plants grow. You may even be able to spot a few tiny fruits.

While technically part of Central O'ahu, Wahiawā is along the main route to and from the North Shore. And while some visitors just drive on through to reach their destination, others pull over at the town's most famous attraction, the Dole Plantation, for some sweet pineapple treats.

That said, Wahiawā isn't typically a town that tourists seek out. Rather, it's a residential place whose buildings have seen their fair share of storms and whose locals have seen their fair share of military service members come and go (there's a large military base here).

While present-day Wahiawā might not seem all that exciting, this town was a particularly special spot to ancient Native Hawaiian royalty. At the (now off-limits) Kūkaniloko Birthstone State Monument, these padded ancient stones were believed to ease the pains of labor. It was here that many Native queens gave birth to the next generation of *ali'i* (rulers).

Savor the Original Dole Whip

A stop at the Dole Plantation

While the famed pineapple company started in 1901, the **Dole Plantation** *(doleplantation.com)* as a tourist attraction began in 1950 as a small roadside fruit stand nestled among the pineapple fields. Today it has grown to a pineapple-filled wonderland with quite a few pineapple-themed activities on offer.

When you first drive up to the Dole Plantation, you'll be greeted by a large pale-yellow building called the **Plantation Center**. Inside, you'll find every pineapple-inspired creation you can imagine – from pineapple candies to pineapple stuffed toys and pineapple-bedecked baby onesies.

The highlight of this attraction is tucked at the very back of the building: the original Dole Whip (from $8), a creamy (and surprisingly vegan) soft-serve-like pineapple dessert. Order it at the **Plantation Grille**. You can grab yourself a

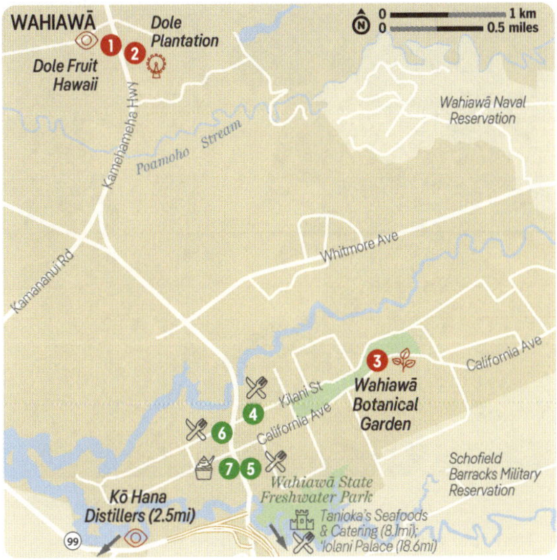

HIGHLIGHTS
1 Dole Fruit Hawaii
2 Dole Plantation
3 Wahiawā Botanical Garden

EATING
4 Barrio Cafe
5 Maui Mike's Fire-Roasted Chicken
6 Shige's Saimin Stand
7 Uber Factory

classic, ungarnished Dole Whip or top your treat with fresh pineapple and a dusting of *li hing mui*, a bright red, sweet and tangy powder.

Tour a Dole Factory

Pineapple factory behind the scenes

Though most visitors to O'ahu make a stop at the famous Dole Plantation with its iconic butter yellow Plantation Center and Dole whips, they completely miss what lies directly across the street. Officially known as **Dole Fruit Hawaii** *(dolefruithawaii.com/pages/pineapple-farm-tours)*, this sort-of second Dole is actually owned by a completely different entity than the first – though neither is owned by the original Dole Company either, but that's another story.

While the Dole Plantation is the spot for a Dole whip, Dole Fruit Hawaii is where you'll want to pick up a fresh pineapple and a gallon of the best pineapple juice you've ever had. Even better, it's where you can get a first-hand look at the pineapple factory in action on a **tour** *(adult/child $20/3)*. Watch these golden fruits get washed, food-grade waxed, sorted and boxed in a matter of minutes. You'll get to sample both the fresh pineapple and the juice at the end too.

THE DOLE FAMILY

James Dole wasn't the only famous Dole in the islands. His cousin Sanford Dole played a significant role in the overthrow of Queen Lili'uokalani, the last reigning monarch of the Kingdom of Hawai'i. After the coup, Queen Lili'uokalani was held under house arrest at **'Iolani Palace** (p58).

HAWAI'I'S PINEAPPLE HISTORY

Despite Hawai'i's strong association with pineapples, the fruit actually isn't native to the islands; rather, it was likely introduced from South America, although no one knows exactly when. The date 1813 marks the first written mention of pineapples on the islands, and in 1820, when the first missionaries arrived, pineapples were growing all over – both in the wild and in gardens.

However, pineapple as a commercial industry didn't get its start until James Dole arrived in the islands in 1899. Within just two years, he established the Hawaiian Pineapple Company in Wahiawā. Add a series of national advertisements and a speedy new canning system to the mix, and Hawai'i quickly became synonymous with pineapples and the Dole brand stamped onto the cans.

A GHOSTLY TALE

Like many Hawai'i sites, the Wahiawā Botanical Garden has a *mo'olelo* (story) behind it – although this one is particularly sad. Rumor has it that a woman, now known in these stories as the Green Lady of Wahiawā, started off as a typical mother but one with a debilitating fear of car crashes. Instead of crossing any roads, she'd take her children into the Wahiawā Gulch to avoid any potential car accidents. Unfortunately, one day while crossing the Gulch, one of the Green Lady's children got lost in the forest. She was frantic, searching high and low for her lost little one, with her other children in tow. None of them were ever seen again.

Legend has it that the Green Lady of Wahiawā now haunts the Wahiawā Gulch and Wahiawā Botanical Garden area. True to her new name, she's now a vibrant emerald hue – and she's still searching for her lost child.

WENDY CUTLER/FLICKR/CC BY-SA 2.0

Wahiawā Botanical Garden

Tours are walk-in only and typically start soon after you request them in-person at the welcome center (aka the brightly colored shipping container in the parking lot). Just keep in mind that tours are harvest-dependent – if there are no pineapples to process that day, the factory floor stays quiet and no tours will be offered.

Stroll Through Beautiful Botanical Gardens

A once-experimental success

Unlike Kāne'ohe's Ho'omaluhia Botanical Garden and Pūpūkea's Waimea Valley, **Wahiawā Botanical Garden** flies under the radar. The garden got its start in the 1930s when sugar planters made an experimental arboretum – and they succeeded. Today the 27-acre garden is filled with heliconias and gardenias, fishtail palms and bamboo groves, orange *wiliwili* flowers and red *'ōhi'a lehua* blossoms. Stroll the winding paths and admire the towering trees and blooming flowers.

Bring a Dog on Your Adventures

A dog for a day

Due to heightened agricultural concerns and animal quarantine laws, it's very difficult to bring animals to Hawai'i (p198). You'll more than likely have to leave your pets at home. But if you need a little bit of puppy love, don't worry! The Wahiawā branch of the O'ahu SPCA has an incredible **Doggy Day**

A MUST-STOP POKE SHOP

Located in nearby Waipahu, **Tanioka's Seafoods & Catering** is where locals go to get their fresh poke (cubed raw marinated fish). Simply known as Tanioka's, this long-time take-out spot has all of the classic poke flavors – spicy 'ahi (yellowfin tuna), *limu* (edible seaweed) and shōyu (soy sauce), just to start. To get the most bang for your buck, get the poke without the rice – the fish is so good, you might not need the starch anyway.

Trip Program *(oahuspca.org/doggy-day-trips)* that allows you to take a shelter dog with you on your island adventures.

To participate, you'll need to be over 21 years old, and you'll need to fill out an application with your availability, experience with dogs, and dog preferences (ie small dog, high energy, good leash manners). Aim to submit the form about a week before you'd like to participate. If you're approved, you'll be matched with a pup, who you'll pick up in the morning and return in the afternoon. You'll also be given a backpack with all of the doggie essentials – a water bowl, poop bags, treats, you name it – so you and your newest furry friend can set off on your day of fun. Take them up to the North Shore beaches (p180) or down to one of the Hawai'i Kai hiking trails (p139).

A $35 non-refundable donation is required in order to participate in the Doggy Day Trip Program. The proceeds will go toward helping other pups at the Wahiawā OSPCA. This experience is available Tuesday through Saturday.

Visit Kō Hana Distillers

From farm to glass

Just outside of Wahiawā proper in nearby Kunia, **Kō Hana Distillers** *(kohanarum.com)* is making its mark on the local rum scene. Specializing in Agricole Rum – that is, rum made from fresh-pressed sugarcane juice as opposed to industrial rum's molasses – this O'ahu distiller is reviving Hawai'i's lost sugar legacy (p178) in a whole new way.

There are a few different ways to experience Kō Hana Distillers and its fantastic products. First, you can pop into the gift shop, where you can enjoy a **walk-in tasting** *($15-30)* and pick up a bottle or two to take home.

But for an even better experience, you'll want to stick around for a one-hour **Kō Hana Distillery tour** *(adult/child $35/15)*. You'll learn the history of Hawai'i-grown sugarcane *(kō)* and how the stalks are distilled and aged into rum, and also sample a few versions of the final product. Kids get a gelato cup to enjoy.

For visitors looking to dive even deeper into the rum-making world, Kō Hana Distillers also offers a two-hour tour, only available on Fridays.

'ŌKOLEHAO: HAWAI'I'S FIRST ALCOHOLIC SPIRIT

Made from the root of the *ti* plant, 'ōkolehao is believed to be Hawai'i's only native spirit. Though there's some debate regarding who to give credit to when it comes to its invention.

First, there's the English ship captain Nathaniel Portlock (à la Captain Cook's ship) in 1780. He baked and fermented the root into a sort of make-shift beer. But it was escaped British convict William Stevenson who truly made 'ōkolehao in its final form. A decade later, he distilled the rather rough beer into a cleaner spirit, one similar to moonshine.

But 'ōkolehao's run didn't last long. Soon after, the Kingdom of Hawai'i introduced a period of prohibition, one that was closely followed by US prohibition. The spirit all but died out. In the past couple of decades, small local distillers, like **Island Distillers** and **Hanalei Spirits**, have worked to bring 'ōkolehao back to the scene.

EATING IN WAHIAWĀ: OUR PICKS

Huli-huli (or 'turn-turn') is sort of like a rotisserie.

Shige's Saimin Stand: A local favorite known for its saimin, a Hawai'i noodle dish with roots in Japanese ramen, Chinese *mein* and Filipino *pancit*. *10am-9pm Tue-Sat* $

Uber Factory: This unassuming little dessert shop is known for its *ube* treats, like the yam *haupia* tarts and the chantilly *ube* crunch tarts. Cash only. *9am-2pm Wed, Fri & Sat* $

Barrio Cafe: While Mexican food typically isn't O'ahu's strong suit, Barrio Cafe is arguably the island's best place to satisfy your taco cravings. *7am-3pm Mon-Sat* $$

Maui Mike's Fire-Roasted Chicken: Using the traditional Hawaiian *huli-huli* method of cooking, this eatery serves up some of the juiciest chicken in town. *11am-8pm* $

Hale'iwa

BEACHY BOUTIQUES | TURTLES | UNDERWATER ADVENTURES

TOP TIP

During your time in Hale'iwa, there's a good chance that you'll pass the **Lili'uokalani Protestant Church**, which was originally built by missionaries in 1832 from lumber donated by Queen Lili'uokalani. It doesn't look like much, so most people just walk on without realizing that they've just passed one of the most historic spots in town! Take an extra moment to soak up this sacred place.

The architecture in Hale'iwa takes you back in time, with many historic buildings originating from the town's sugar plantation era. But, today, rather than housing plantation workers, these structures now hold some of the best boutiques, galleries and eateries on the island.

Like much of the North Shore, surfing is a big part of Hale'iwa's local culture. Big brand surf stores like Hurley, Rip Curl and Volcom line the streets, alongside small, local surf shops. And when there's a surf competition at Hale'iwa Ali'i Beach Park, like the HIC Hale'iwa Pro, the surf-loving atmosphere still somehow manages to go up a notch.

Even when the waves aren't rolling in, the ocean is still at the heart of Hale'iwa. Rent a stand-up paddleboard (SUP) and paddle around, say hello to a few *honu* (Hawaiian green sea turtles) lounging on the shores, or dive down deep into the Pacific.

Sustainability at its Finest

Mālama 'āina (take care of the land)

A big part of living in – and visiting – Hale'iwa is learning to take care of the environment. After all, if everyone didn't do their part, those blissful beaches and emerald streams wouldn't be as healthy and stunning as they are. Founded by Kim and Jack Johnson, **Kōkua Hawai'i Foundation**

GETTING AROUND

Navigating your way around Hale'iwa can be a little bit chaotic at times. Pedestrians cross the street at random places, cars seem to pop out between buildings and scooters wind their way among the chaos. If you're sticking to the heart of Hale'iwa, it might be easiest to get into town via bus or car (park at Hale'iwa Store Lots), and then walk around the area. That said, walking does come with its disadvantages as well. For such a well-trodden neighborhood, Hale'iwa's main thoroughfare doesn't have continuous sidewalks, so it's not the most accessible.

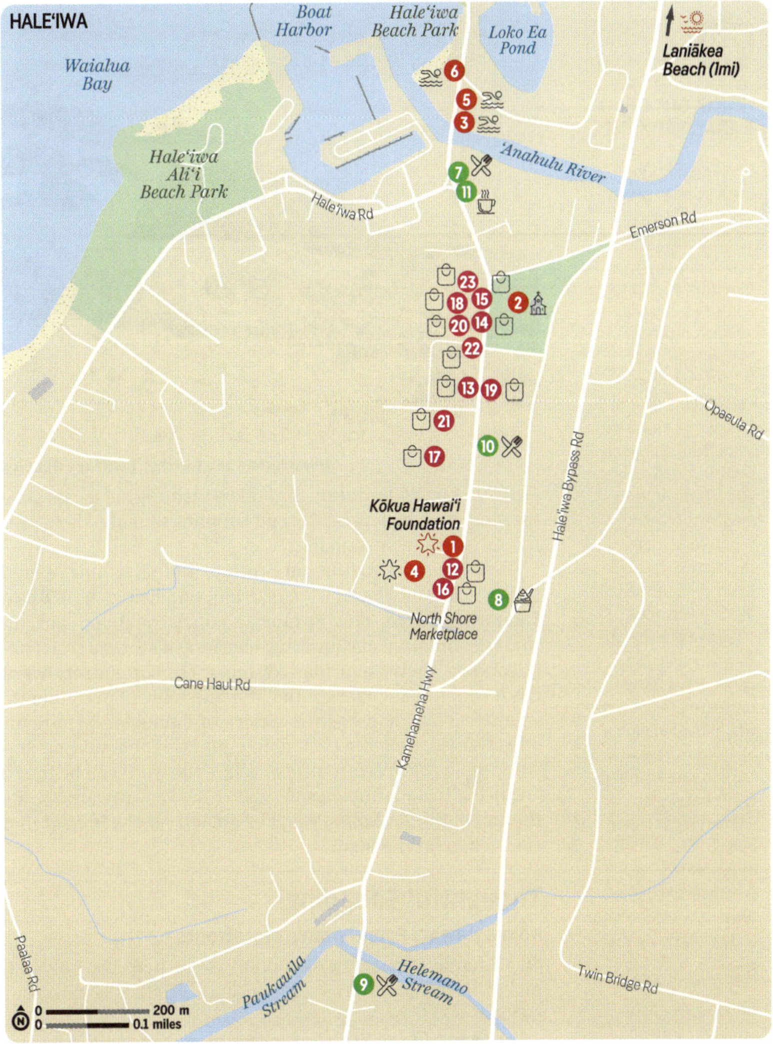

HIGHLIGHTS

1 Kōkua Hawai'i Foundation

SIGHTS

2 Lili'uokalani Protestant Church

ACTIVITIES

3 Blue Planet Adventure Company
4 Kōkua Learning Farm
5 SUPDog Hawaii
6 Surf N Sea

EATING

7 Hale'iwa Bowls
8 IL Gelato Cafe
9 Jenny's Shrimp
10 Roy's Kiawe Broiled Chicken

DRINKING & NIGHTLIFE

11 Saylor's Hale'iwa

SHOPPING

12 'Āina Farm Stand
13 Greenroom
14 Guava Shop
15 Kahala
16 Kōkua General Store
17 Longs Drugs
18 Mahina
19 North Shore Surf Shop
20 Olukai
21 Pakaloha Bikinis
22 Roger
see 14 Splash! Hawaii
23 Whalers General Store

HONU: OUT OF ENDANGERMENT

For decades, *honu* – the Hawaiian green sea turtle – were endangered. Ancient Hawaiians used *honu* as a food source for centuries, but they were careful not to overfish. When Western settlers came to the islands, they didn't enact the same care. Between 1948 and 1973, over 200,000lb of turtle meat was legally reported as 'catch' in the islands. By 1973 there were only 67 nesting *honu* left.

To save the species, Hawai'i banned the commercial harvest of turtles in 1974. In 1978, when the Endangered Species Act came to be, *honu* were added to the list. Turtle nesting areas were quickly designated as protected, and communities came together to safeguard turtles lazing on the shore.

As of 2026 the National Oceanic and Atmospheric Administration (NOAA) estimates there are 4000 nesting *honu*. And in late 2025, the International Union for Conservation of Nature officially downgraded the species from 'endangered' to 'least concern.'

REUBER DUARTEV/SHUTTERSTOCK

***Honu* (green sea turtles), Laniākea Beach**

(kokuahawaiifoundation.org) offers visitors and locals alike the chance to pick up skills and supplies to make their lives a little bit more sustainable.

There are several different projects and programs offered through Kōkua Hawai‘i Foundation, one being the **Kōkua Learning Farm**. This farm is an educational and agricultural destination, encouraging learners of all ages to actively support their local food systems. On community work days, which take place on the first Saturday of each month, volunteers participate in a variety of hands-on farm-related activities, including mulching, planting, harvesting and working in the *lo‘i* (taro fields). While the work can be tough – especially on a hot summer day – it's very rewarding. By the end of the 2½ hours, you'll be able to see the impact that you've had on the land.

Thoughtful Shopping

Kōkua Hawai‘i Foundation's storefronts

Sustainable farming is just one way to help the environment through your day-to-day actions. Another is with your purchases.

The **‘Āina Farm Stand**, another branch of the Kōkua Hawai‘i Foundation, takes the produce grown on the foundation's land, along with locally made products from other sustainable Hawai‘i businesses, and sells it to the public. Snag treats like fresh papayas and guavas, as well as Sweet Land Farms goat caramel and Lā‘ie vanilla extract.

The foundation also has the **Kōkua General Store**. This shop sells products to help reduce single-use plastic consumption. Reusable water bottles, shampoo bars and beeswax wraps are just the beginning. There's also a secondhand consignment section known as **Kōkua Vintage**.

All of the profits from these storefronts go back to the Kōkua Hawai‘i Foundation to help continue the work they do for the community and the environment.

Spot Lounging Honu

Hawaiian sea turtles await

Just 2 miles outside of the main Haleʻiwa town, **Laniākea Beach** consistently has *honu* lounging on its shores and swimming in its waters. Though you may be tempted to get an up-close look, be sure to give the turtles their space. Not only are these *honu* a threatened species, it's illegal to disturb them. Volunteers are stationed at Laniākea Beach, primarily to protect the *honu*, but also to answer any turtle-related questions.

SUP on the ʻAnahulu River

From the ocean, inland

One of the best places to SUP on Oʻahu is around the **ʻAnahulu River**. Connected to **Haleʻiwa Harbor**, it offers the best of both worlds – ocean paddleboarding and river paddleboarding. Stick around at the harbor for a bit of a wavy challenge and sunset views, or venture inland under the famous **Rainbow Bridge** for calmer waters and greenery galore. No matter which of the two options you choose, keep an eye out for *honu* heads breaching the surface!

There are quite a few SUP rental places near the mouth of the ʻAnahulu River, including **Surf N Sea** *(surfnsea.com; per hr $20)* and **Blue Planet Adventure Company** *(blueplanetadventure.com; 2hr $40)*. For something a little different, pair up with some pups on a tour with **SUPDog Hawaii** *(supdoghawaii.com; $125)*. You and your rescue dog will get to hang out and go on a guided outdoor paddleboarding adventure for a full 1½ hours. It might even be the highlight of your trip!

Stop & Smell the Plumerias

A visit to Little Plumeria Farms

Though plumerias aren't indigenous to Hawaiʻi, they have become a sort of hallmark of the islands. You can find them absolutely everywhere, from local parks to grocery store parking lots to the stunning Koko Crater Botanical Garden (p142). But to dive deep into the plumeria planting and growing process, you'll want to venture up a little dirt road to **Little Plumeria Farms** *(littleplumeriafarms.com; farm tour adult/child $50/30)*.

THE ORIGINS OF SUP

While not one of the six main types of ancient Hawaiian surf sports (p187), stand-up paddleboarding is a contemporary twist on them. There are many historical instances of people standing while paddling – gondoliers in Venice, fisherfolk in South America – but doing so *on a board* was unheard of until the 20th century.

When Waikīkī got its tourism boom in the early 1900s, visitors saw the locals surfing the waves and wanted to try. Their teachers, known as Waikīkī Beach Boys, soon started using paddles to quickly position themselves to have a view of both their students and the incoming swells. This was called 'Beach Boy Surfing' and is largely credited to John Ah Choy and his sons, Leroy and Bobby Ah Choy.

EATING IN HALEʻIWA: OUR PICKS

Haleʻiwa Bowls: Takeout acai bowl stand that offers fun, healthy add-ons, like poi (steamed, mashed taro), cordyceps and Hawaiian green spirulina. *7:30am-6pm* **$$**

Jenny's Shrimp: Rumor has it that many employees from Macky's, a defunct but locally beloved shrimp truck in Kahuku, moved to this Haleʻiwa business. *10am-6:20pm* **$$**

IL Gelato Cafe: A great spot to get a coffee and a scoop of gelato – or the creamiest acai bowl in town. *9am-9pm* **$$**

Saylor's Haleʻiwa: This cozy coffee shop has nearly every milk and syrup option under the sun. It also has a little collection of Haleʻiwa-made products. *6:30am-5pm* **$**

BEACH ESSENTIALS IN HALE'IWA

Longs Drugs: You can't go wrong with Longs. This former-local-pharmacy-turned-CVS has the basics like sunscreen, sunglasses and hats.

Pakaloha Bikinis: This Maui-owned brand is fantastic for monochromatic bikinis.

Olukai: Pick up a high-quality pair of slippers (flip-flops) that'll provide support and last for years.

Surf N Sea: In addition to surfboards and surf accessories, Surf N Sea has rentals for just about every water sport – surfboards, snorkel gear, diving tanks, kayaks and more.

North Shore Surf Shop: Just in case you're still missing a few beach must-haves, North Shore Surf Shop is sure to have them. This massive store has every beach essential you can dream up.

At this charming family farm, you can embark on an hour-long partially guided tour to take in some of the most eye-catching blooms you've ever seen. Most people are only familiar with the white plumeria, but Little Plumeria Farms is bursting with the brightest shades of pink, orange and yellow as well. Many of these varieties you won't find while just out and about, as the farm is home to a rare hybrid plumeria garden. You'll learn about the various stages of plumeria tree growth, from seedlings and cuttings to fully grown trees, with North Shore mountain and ocean views all along the way. Tours are available seasonally from April to October.

Shop in Hale'iwa Town

Locally owned brands

If you're looking for keepsakes and beach essentials, start at Hale'iwa Store Lots. Here **Mahina** has easy, breezy beach outfits and **Whalers General Store** has loads of made-in-Hawai'i must-haves. Nearby you'll find **Kahala**. This 1936 brand claims to be 'the original aloha shirt' – what visitors call a Hawaiian shirt – so it's the perfect place to pick up a sophisticated take on the island staple.

Venture out of the shopping center to follow the two-lane Kamehameha Hwy to find the **Guava Shop**, which is home to everything from locally made snorkels to North Shore–scented candles to lei-making kits. Next door, **Splash! Hawaii** has all the tees and swimwear you need to look like a local. And a couple of doors after that is **Olukai**, arguably the most high-quality Hawai'i-founded shoe store brand. Find everything from beach-ready slippers (flip-flops) to classic low-top skate shoes.

Up next is **Roger**, a North Shore–inspired boutique filled with clothing that's contemporary, minimalistic and artistic all at the same time. Many of their most popular tees look as if they've been block printed, in the best way. Last but certainly not least, stop into the **Greenroom**, an art gallery filled with beautiful Hawai'i-inspired pieces from local artists Heather Brown, Aloha de Mele, Punky Aloha (Shar Tuiasoa) and Christie Shinn.

POP-UP ROADSIDE HULI-HULI CHICKEN

Around O'ahu, there have long been food vendors that would pop up on the side of the road. And we're not talking food trucks – rather local aunties with tables stacked with fresh fruit from their backyards, fishermen with more fresh catches than they can eat, and the local favorite – *huli-huli* chicken. Sort of like Hawaiian-style rotisserie chicken, *huli-huli* chicken has always been best when eaten piping hot from a random roadside stand. And while they have become more elusive than ever in recent years, Hale'iwa has one strong and steady vendor in the Mālama Market parking lot called **Roy's Kiawe Broiled Chicken**. It's open 10am–4pm on weekends.

Beyond Hale'iwa

Once at the height of military and agricultural development, Waialua and Mokulē'ia are now quiet residential areas with beaches, coffee fields and a soap factory.

Waialua and Mokulē'ia may be the only parts of the North Shore that tourists don't usually visit. Tucked away to the west of Hale'iwa – after the Kamehameha Hwy and Kaukonahua Rd turns that return you to Waikīkī – most people don't even realize that there's even more to the North Shore!

However, once upon a time these two towns were never overlooked. Mokulē'ia became a military stronghold during WWII, after the bombing of Pearl Harbor (p112). At the same time, Waialua was home to one of O'ahu's largest sugar factories for decades, during the time when sugar was the islands' main export. While Waialua's sugar mill closed down in 1996, its buildings now house some of the coolest businesses in town.

Places

GETTING AROUND

Waialua is accessible by car or bus. Parking is rarely an issue and bus routes are surprisingly efficient, so either option works for getting around. Mokulē'ia is a bit of a different story. The last few bus stops are right on the Waialua–Mokulē'ia border and have infrequent service. If you'd like to go deeper into town (which you do), you'll want a car.

Waialua

TIME FROM HALE'IWA: **5MINS**

The Waialua Sugar Mill put this North Shore town on the map back in the 1860s. As the demand for sugar increased, so did the hustle and bustle of Waialua. And when the industry met its inevitable end in the 1990s, the once sugary sweet town settled into a quiet, laid-back swing of things that still lingers today. Find fruit stands popping up along the two-lane roads, wild chickens crossing the street and the now-repurposed sugar mill, filled with the most charming of small businesses.

Sugar and soap

The **Waialua Sugar Mill**, one of the largest sugar mills in the islands, opened its doors in 1865. At its peak, this sugar mill produced over 20,000 tons of sugar per year. In fact, sugar consumption was so high that the Waialua Sugar Mill, along with the many other Hawai'i sugar mills, hired immigrant laborers from all around the world – from Japan to Portugal to the Philippines – to help meet the demand. The Waialua Sugar Mill, in particular, continued to churn out sugar until it closed its doors in 1996. To this day, locals will still tell you about the smoky caramel scent from the factories' burnt sugarcane wafting through the air.

HAWAI'I'S NOT-SO-SWEET SUGAR HISTORY

Ironically, Hawai'i's sugar history isn't all sweet; this booming industry had a dark side with terrible consequences. While there was a whole host of economic, cultural and political factors at play, the greed in the sugar industry significantly contributed to the overthrow of Queen Lili'uokalani and the Kingdom of Hawai'i in 1893. Of the 'American businessmen' – as they're often dubbed – responsible for this coup, the main leader, Lorrin Thurston, had substantial investments in the sugar industry. Thurston's counterpart, Sanford Dole, later claimed the position of the president of the Republic of Hawai'i and found ways to loosen the sugar market restrictions. With their efforts, Hawai'i's sugar mills continued producing sugar for the next century or so.

KELLY HEADRICK/SHUTTERSTOCK

North Shore Soap Factory

While you won't get to experience that sugary smell these days, the old Waialua Sugar Mill is now filled with other aromatic delights, such as at the **North Shore Soap Factory** *(northshoresoapfactory.com; tour from $22)*. This small, family-owned business is committed to making the best natural skincare products with island-inspired scents.

If you only have time for a quick visit, pop into their shop and see the soap-makers in action. They'll be mixing, swirling, cutting and boxing loads of their island-inspired soaps. As you watch, wander through their variety of soaps, sniffing as you go, until you find your personal favorites – the classic Hawaiian plumeria or the out-of-the-box acai bowl, perhaps?

For a longer visit to the North Shore Soap Factory, go on a 30-minute guided tour to get into the nitty gritty of what it takes to make a bar of soap, along with the factory's other products like bath bombs, body butters and chapsticks. At the end, you'll be gifted a few soap samples that you can stamp with a fun island- or holiday-inspired design. Tours must be booked at least 24 hours in advance.

Mokulē'ia

TIME FROM HALE'IWA: **10MINS**

While some off-the-beaten path explorers venture to Waialua, very few drive the extra five minutes to Mokulē'ia. A few beaches and hikes dot the mountain-butted landscape, but the main draw of this North Shore town is the Dillingham Kawaihāpai Air Field, where you can take to the skies for some bird's-eye adventures, maybe even getting back to land via parachute.

A skydiving adventure

Not far from the old Waialua Sugar Mill, you'll find the **Dillingham Kawaihāpai Air Field**, the best place to go skydiving on O'ahu. Take to the skies in a little airplane with **Skydive Hawai'i** *(skydivehawaii.com; from $198)* and get ready for the thrill of a lifetime.

Since the airfield is at sea level, you can skydive a full 15,000ft – the highest height possible without the use of air masks. And more height equals more airtime, meaning you'll get to take in Mokulē'ia's bright blue waters, golden sand and thriving greenery for a few extra seconds.

Skydive Hawai'i also offers a 20,000ft tandem dive (from $1600) – a rarely available experience. Also called a HALO (high altitude, low [parachute] opening) jump, this jump is only for the most extreme thrill-seekers, as it does require supplemental oxygen and temperatures can reach up to -25°F. It also requires four days' notice and a $300 upfront deposit.

A beachfront horseback ride

There are so many ways to experience the best of O'ahu's beaches – snorkeling, suntanning, diving and surfing all come to mind. But why not enjoy the golden shorelines on horseback? With **Hawaii Polo Trail Rides** *(oahuhorsebackrides.com; from $148)*, you can do just that.

After getting matched with your horse, you'll ride along the golden shores in Mokulē'ia, taking photo stops along the way. If you book the 5pm tour, you'll get the ride and the gorgeous sunset views. The friendly horses are ideal for first-time riders and young riders (though you have to be at least eight years old to participate).

FOLLOW THE COUP CONSEQUENCES

After the coup by Lorrin Thurston, Sanford Dole and their fellow American businessmen, Queen Lili'uokalani was held under house arrest at **'Iolani Palace** (p58) in Honolulu. Dole later went on to rule (and loosen sugar industry restrictions) from **Ali'iōlani Hale** (p61), just across the street.

WHAT IS HAWAI'I PIDGIN?

As you travel around Hawai'i, you'll likely hear the locals speaking something that you can't quite understand – it's likely not Hawaiian, but Hawai'i Pidgin. Pidgin is essentially a mash-up of many of Hawai'i's immigrant languages, including Japanese, Cantonese, Portuguese, English, Korean, Tagalog, Ilocano, Samoan and Tongan, along with Hawaiian. Pidgin evolved when all of the island's immigrants arrived when the sugar plantations started gaining momentum.

There is some controversy about how to categorize Hawai'i Pidgin. Some call it a slang, others call it a creole, many call it a dialect, and a staunch but strong few go so far as to call it a language. Despite years of debate, the conversation about Pidgin's categorization is still ongoing.

Pūpūkea

SURF COMPETITIONS | BEACH DAYS | WATERFALL HIKES

GETTING AROUND

Make the sustainable choice and get around Pūpūkea by bus. During surf competitions, this may actually be easier than driving. Designated parking lots are small and rare, so there's a good chance that you'll end up parking along the side of the road (if that option is even available). While this issue is exacerbated during competitions, don't be surprised if you struggle to find parking on any day.

TOP TIP

Ocean safety is important in Pūpūkea, as it's home to the island's largest waves. Since ocean conditions vary widely by season, it's impossible to know if the water will be safe from research alone. Ideally, stick to beaches with lifeguards. Better yet, chat with them about the day's ocean conditions – no one knows the beach better than they do.

Best known for its incredible surf, the beach-lined region of Pūpūkea is home to world-renowned surf events, including the Eddie Aikau Big Wave Invitational and the Vans Pipe Masters. In summer, when the waves are nearly nonexistent, many of the same beaches that host these competitions become incredible swimming and snorkeling spots.

Once you've had your share of salty sunshine, head to Waimea Valley for a different look at nature. A tropical plant-lined walkway guides you to the beautiful 45ft cascade that is Waimea Falls.

Locals rarely use the term 'Pūpūkea' for the region. Rather, it's encompassed by 'the North Shore.' To get more specific, locals will use the beaches for reference, such as 'across the street from Sunset Beach' or 'between Waimea Bay and Three Tables.' But, for the purposes of this guidebook, Pūpūkea is between Haleʻiwa and Kahuku, or – using the beaches as reference – starting at Waimea Bay and ending just before the Turtle Bay Resort (p192) property.

Spend the Day at Waimea Bay

Beloved by locals and visitors alike

Pūpūkea is home to some of the best beaches on Oʻahu, and each one offers something a bit different. Some are great for snorkeling, others are known for surfing, and many offer both, depending on the season. Going from west to east, you'll hit **Waimea Bay Beach Park** first.

The ocean conditions at this beach change drastically from season to season. In summer its warm waters are ideal for swimming and cliff jumping (spot the famed cliff jumping rock on the left side of the beach!). However, in winter the ocean conditions can become precarious for anyone except the most professional of surfers, with waves reaching over 25ft high. No surprise, then that the Eddie Aikau Big Wave Invitational (p189) takes place here.

HIGHLIGHTS
1 'Ehukai Beach Park
2 Pūpūkea Beach Park
3 Sunset Beach Park
4 Waimea Bay Beach Park
5 Waimea Valley

SIGHTS
6 Waimea Falls

ACTIVITIES
7 'Ehukai Pillbox Trail
8 North Shore O'ahu Surf School
9 Shark's Cove
10 Three Tables

EATING
11 Jax Pizza
12 Seven Brothers
13 Sunrise Shack
14 Ted's Bakery

ENTERTAINMENT
15 Toa Luau

A BASIC BEACH PACKING LIST

Reusable beach bag: Don't forget yours and end up having to use a paper grocery bag.

Reef-safe sunscreen: Protect your skin and O'ahu's marine life.

Sunglasses and a hat: Double-up on sun protection.

Swimwear and slippers (aka flip-flops): You need beach attire to hit the beach.

Water shoes: While not a must at most beaches, Shark's Cove is rocky. Protect your feet.

Goggles & gear: There aren't many beach rental spots in Pūpūkea. Bring your own goggles and other gear (eg snorkel gear, fins, boards).

Beach towel: Use it as a mat or simply to dry off.

Beach mat: The ones that roll or fold into bag form are ideal.

Reusable water bottle: Stay hydrated (and sustainable)!

Snacks: Stay fueled. Some beaches don't have anywhere to eat within walking distance.

Cooler: Keep your bites and sips cool. (Note that it's illegal to drink alcohol on Hawai'i beaches.)

NAOMI RAHIM/GETTY IMAGES

Shark's Cove, Pūpūkea Beach Park

A Trio of Snorkeling Adventures

The best of Pūpūkea Beach Park

Pūpūkea Beach Park is more commonly known as two separate beaches – **Three Tables** and **Shark's Cove**.

Within walking distance of each other, these beaches are known for their wonderful snorkeling opportunities. Like most North Shore beaches, ocean conditions can get too dangerous for snorkeling in winter. That said, the protective rocks and reefs help to shelter the main snorkeling areas, meaning these beaches are often safe for snorkeling for a smidge longer than the surrounding ones. However, be sure to err on the side of caution, as there aren't any lifeguards at Pūpūkea Beach Park.

Before highlighting the differences between these two snorkeling spots, it's important to note that Shark's Cove has two distinct sections: the tide pools and the main cove. The tide pools are found in the area enclosed by jagged rocks, where you'll see most people venturing, and the main cove is just to the right of that. So, when we add Three Tables into the mix, there are essentially three different snorkeling experiences at Pūpūkea Beach Park.

The Shark's Cove tide pools are the best snorkeling option for kids, with water rarely reaching over 4ft deep and fish, sea urchins and sea cucumbers hidden among the rocks. The two remaining snorkeling areas, Shark's Cove's main cove and Three Tables, have surprisingly similar snorkeling experiences. Both are semi-sheltered from the open ocean – by the cove borders of the former and by the three 'tables' or flat coral reef formations that appear during lower tides of the latter – and both are home to larger marine animals than the tide pools at Shark's Cove. Keep an eye out for *honu*, lobsters, squid and loads of tropical fish.

Watch Pro Surfers at 'Ehukai Beach Park

The surfing capital of the world

About a mile from Shark's Cove lies **'Ehukai Beach Park** (also called Banzai Pipeline or just Pipeline). Most of the year, these waters are for professional surfers only. The waves are simply too large and strong to be safe for much else. After all, that's why Banzai Pipeline is one of the most esteemed surfing beaches in the entire world. But, surprisingly, 'Ehukai Beach Park can be quite calm in summer. On its most peaceful days, this beach has excellent snorkeling and swimming opportunities. If you're unsure in any way, it's best to check in with a lifeguard for more information.

HOW TO CHOOSE A BEACH

There are so many great beaches in Pūpūkea. And while it would be great to be able to hop between them all as you please, the parking situation (and bus stop and bike lane situation) doesn't exactly allow for that. Instead, simply situate yourself at one beach for the day – which, in reality, is whichever one has parking when you happen to pass by – and enjoy it to the fullest! After all, there really are no 'bad' choices when it comes to beaches in this part of the island.

Sunset Views at Sunset Beach

Plus swimming, snorkeling and surfing

Sunset Beach Park offers similar conditions to 'Ehukai Beach Park. Summers are great for snorkeling, when the waters are filled with tropical fish and *honu*. On the other hand, winters are ideal for surfing. As a matter of fact, Sunset Beach – and its three separate surf breaks – is often called one of the longest stretches of surfable area in the world. Watch the pros do what they do best at one of the many Sunset Beach surf competitions (p187). Finally, regardless of the time of year – and as its name implies – Sunset Beach is a pretty epic place to watch an O'ahu sunset.

Take a North Shore Surf Class

Surf where the pros do

After popping by all of the iconic North Shore surf spots, like Waimea Bay, 'Ehukai Beach Park and Sunset Beach, many visitors want to attempt to surf these iconic waves on their own. Though you likely won't be rocking those 20ft waves any time soon, you can still make those surf dreams come true.

First and foremost, don't attempt to figure out how to surf on the North Shore solo; for the safest, most successful attempt, do it with an experienced surf teacher. While surf lessons on the North Shore may not be possible year-round (those large winter waves are not for beginners), there are a few different surf schools in Pūpūkea for you to choose

NOT READY FOR THE BIG WAVES?

If you're not quite ready to hit the waves on the North Shore, consider Waikīkī instead. Often home to smaller swells, the **Waikīkī breaks** (p83) tend to be less intimidating for beginner surfers.

Dining here? Watch for the wild chickens!

EATING IN PŪPŪKEA: OUR PICKS

Sunrise Shack: Grab your tropical acai bowl or smoothie and enjoy it on the beach across the street, or dine at a sunshine-colored picnic table. *7am-6pm* $$

Ted's Bakery: This long-standing local bakery just after Sunset Beach Park is known for its chocolate and *haupia* (coconut) cream pie. *8am-6:30pm* $

Jax Pizza: Family-owned standout in the Pūpūkea food truck scene. Their sourdough crust, fired over *kiawe* (mesquite) wood, is absolutely delicious. *11am-8pm* $$

Seven Brothers: Also in the food truck park across from Shark's Cove, Seven Brothers serves up deliciously juicy burgers with an ocean view. *11am-8:30pm Mon-Sat* $$

BEACH SAFETY TIPS

Don't turn your back on the ocean. Ocean conditions can change at a moment's notice, and a rogue wave may surprise.

Know your own capabilities and don't try to exceed them.

Research the beach in advance to inform yourself about any potential dangers.

Swim with a buddy for extra safety.

Heed posted signs and flags. These will tell you about wave size, rip currents, jellyfish and other ocean dangers.

Chat with the lifeguards for the best and most up-to-date information about the beach.

from, including **North Shore O'ahu Surf School** *(northshoreoahusurf.com; 2hr from $100)*, a pro surfer–founded establishment.

North Shore O'ahu Surf School's experts can gauge the day's ocean conditions before (hopefully) taking you to one of the calmer North Shore beaches for a surfing lesson. Learn the basics – how to paddle out and pop up – while still on shore, and then put your newly learned skills into action as you catch your first wave. By the end of your two-hour session, there's a good chance that you'll have caught the surfing bug.

If you already know the basics of surfing, North Shore O'ahu Surf School also has intermediate and advanced classes. Improve your skills even more, and scratch surfing on O'ahu's North Shore off your bucket list.

Swim at the Base of a Waterfall

Wonderful Waimea Valley and Falls

One of the most naturally lush landscapes on O'ahu has quite a storied past. While not much is known about the **Waimea Valley** *(waimeavalley.net; adult/child $26/18)* prior to the 1700s, it is believed to have been ruled by ancient Hawaiian high priests. However, like many places in Hawai'i, the situation drastically changed once colonizers arrived on the islands. From then, the valley underwent stages as farmland and as a tourist-focused commercial ranch, before being returned to Native Hawaiian hands and turned into a botanical garden of sorts.

Without a doubt, the first thing you'll notice when you get to Waimea Valley is all of the thriving plant life. All around, you'll find towering trees, blooming flowers and brightly colored geckos – and that's before you reach the ticket booth.

After you pay the entrance fee, the flora and fauna continues with colorful hibiscus, hanging *'ulu* (breadfruit) and preening peacocks. You'll even find a bit of history and culture dotted between the plants, including **Hale O Lono**, a heiau (ancient stone temple) constructed in 1470 CE to worship Lono, the Hawaiian god of agriculture and fertility.

Eventually, the greenery opens up to a stunning 45ft cascade known as **Waimea Falls**. If the weather allows, you can swim in the pool at the base of the falls – you'll just have to wear a lifejacket at the behest of the local lifeguards. (Note that most – if not all – of Hawai'i's fresh waterways may contain leptospirosis. When infected by the bacteria through an open wound, it can cause flu-like symptoms.)

An Authentic Lū'au Experience

Welcome to Toa Luau

Taking place in the Waimea Valley, the **Toa Luau** *(toaluau.com; adult/child from $165/125)* is one of the most authentic *lū'au* on the island, particularly since it's Native Hawaiian-owned and -operated. Nearly every aspect of this lū'au has historic or cultural ties – from the conch shell *(pū)* blowing introduction and the whole *kālua* pig to the dance performances

CHRISTIAN MUELLER/SHUTTERSTOCK

Waimea Falls

from five different Polynesian islands. While all of the activities are wonderful, the fire knife show steals the spotlight. And don't miss the coconut cake for dessert!

As an added bonus, a Toa Luau ticket also grants free entry to Waimea Valley. If you book the later 5pm lūʻau, be sure to arrive early to see the valley, which closes to the public at 4pm; you'll want at least 1½ hours to explore. If you'd prefer to spread out the activities, your Toa Luau ticket will allow you to visit Waimea Valley anytime during the week of your lūʻau.

Hike to History in the Hills

The ʻEhukai Pillbox Trail

Though not a well-known fact, Pūpūkea is actually home to the northern end of the Koʻolau Range. While most people stick to the beaches, these peaks have quite a lot of history hidden within them, starting with the **ʻEhukai Pillbox**, one of many abandoned military observation towers dotted around the island. The start of the trail is hidden across the street from ʻEhukai Beach Park (p183; at the turn-in for Sunset Beach Elementary School), and the adventure begins with lush greenery, so much so that it feels like a stark contrast from the sandy beaches less than 100ft away. Instead of sunshine and salty air, it's slightly muddy pathways and a muggy, rainforest-esque atmosphere.

About midway up this mile-and-a-half (round-trip) hike, you'll come across a picnic table covered in painted handprints. Made by the students at Sunset Beach Elementary School (where the hike started), this picnic table is a good place to stop for a snack or water break if you need one.

Before you know it, you'll have reached the graffiti-covered ʻEhukai Pillbox. Take a seat on the top of the cement observation station, where you can soak up the views of ʻEhukai Beach Park for as long as you'd like. All in all, this one-hour adventure is certainly worth your while.

HOW TO CHOOSE A LŪʻAU

Ideally, a lūʻau should be Native Hawaiian-owned and operated like Toa Luau, but these options can be few and far between.

If you can't find a Native-owned one that works for you, there are a number of factors that you should consider: the food, events and activities. Does the menu include authentic Hawaiian dishes like *kālua* pig, *laulau* (leaf-wrapped bundle of pork or chicken) and *haupia*? While most (if not all) lūʻau will include a hula performance, some have bonus traditional Hawaiian activities like lei making.

There's also the price to think of. Lūʻau are one of the priciest activities in Hawaiʻi – but pricier doesn't always mean better. Pick one that fits your budget.

Vans Pipe Masters (p188)

TOP EXPERIENCE

Surf Competitions

As the North Shore temperatures start to cool down, the waves get larger in size, and with those 20ft to 30ft or higher swells come world-renowned surf competitions, such as the Vans Pipe Masters and the Eddie Aikau Big Wave Invitational, at some of Oʻahu's best surf beaches – a stretch sometimes called the 'Seven-Mile Miracle.' You'll be blown away as you watch famed surfers take to the massive waves on a series of thrills, twists and turns.

DON'T MISS

- Sunset Pro (p188)
- Vans Pipe Masters (p188)
- Da Hui Backdoor Shootout (p189)
- Eddie Aikau Big Wave Invitational (p189)
- HIC Hale'iwa Pro (p189)

History of Surfing in Hawaiʻi

The earliest evidence of surfing can be traced back to 12th-century Polynesia, thanks to a few small cave paintings illustrating the sport. That said, once surfing made it to the Hawaiian Islands, the Hawaiian people caught on quickly and began to advance the sport even more.

The earliest Hawaiian surfers called the sport *heʻe nalu*, or wave sliding. Everyone could ride the waves, regardless of gender or social standing, although there were laws in place correlating the latter with the type and quality of boards used. The earliest surfers also held their very own surf competitions, although back then it was more about speed and distance, whereas today's events are judged primarily on difficulty and maneuvers.

Things took an unfortunate turn when Captain James Cook landed in the islands in 1778, inciting Hawaiian colonization. Like many Native Hawaiian practices, including speaking ʻŌlelo Hawaiʻi (the Hawaiian language) and worshiping ancient

TROPICALPIXSINGAPORE/GETTY IMAGES

Eddie Aikau Big Wave Invitational (p189)

OTHER HAWAIIAN SURF SPORTS

While most people know about surfing, it's actually just the first of traditional Hawaiian wave-riding sports. There are six in total: board surfing (what we know as surfing today), bodysurfing, bodyboarding, skimming (also known as sand sliding or sand surfing), river surfing and canoe surfing. Each makes use of a different board type or location, and all are still practiced.

Hawaiian gods *(akua)*, surfing was looked down upon and even deemed vulgar. It's no surprise that the popularity of surfing experienced a sharp decline at this time.

It wasn't until Duke Kahanamoku came along that the associations with surfing shifted again. Born in 1890, 'the Duke' was a talented surfer and swimmer – in fact, so talented that he won the silver and gold medals at the 1912 Stockholm Olympic Games. Following his wins, he went on a world tour, showcasing his swimming and, more importantly, his surfing skills, thereby bringing the once-deprecated sport to the global stage and regaining its popularity.

The Competition Surf Breaks

Not all of the North Shore's surf breaks are used for competitions. There are dozens found along this famed coastline, and locals hold their favorite spots close to their chests. After all, a crowded surf break isn't ideal.

The North Shore's surf competitions are typically held at four main beaches, each of which has at least one surf break: 'Ehukai Beach Park, Hale'iwa Ali'i Beach Park, Sunset Beach Park and Waimea Bay. While there are great surf breaks all across the island, these four in particular boast massive winter waves and some degree of difficulty from the reef conditions.

TOP TIPS

- Surf competitions need consistently large waves. That means organizers don't know if the event will actually run until that morning. The event dates you see are 'holding periods.' Check online to stay up to date.
- Wake up early. Parking, and even bus riding, can be a hassle on competition days.
- Pack a meal – there may not be any food spots within walking distance of the beach.
- Bring binoculars (or a fancy camera lens) to catch the action in the distance.

SURFING IN THE OLYMPICS

Today surfing is more popular than ever before, in large part thanks to its introduction in the 2020/2021 Olympic Games, where Native Hawaiian surfer Carissa Moore won the women's gold medal. And with the success of surfing in the 2024 Olympics and its slated appearance in the 2028 Olympics, surfing is on track to be one of the biggest water sports around.

❶ Sunset Pro

Over the years, dozens of surf competitions have been held at Sunset Beach Park (p183). At the time of writing in 2026, the most famous of the bunch is the Sunset Pro. Part of the World Surf League (WSL) Qualifying Series, some big names in surfing ride these waves in November. And since the surfable area at Sunset Beach is so large, there are numerous possibilities for ocean conditions, meaning that no one – surfers, commentators and casual viewers alike – know exactly what's going to happen.

❷ Vans Pipe Masters

Big things have come to Banzai Pipeline at 'Ehukai Beach Park (p183) with the WSL's schedule revamp. As of 2026, the Vans Pipe Masters is no longer the season opener; it has been moved to December to serve as the final stop of the year – the last of a dozen events comprising the Championship Tour.

To keep the season-ending stakes high, the Pipe Masters now features a 1.5x points multiplier. While a win at most locations earns a surfer 10,000 points, winning at Pipeline awards 15,000 – so no one will know the winner until the event takes place.

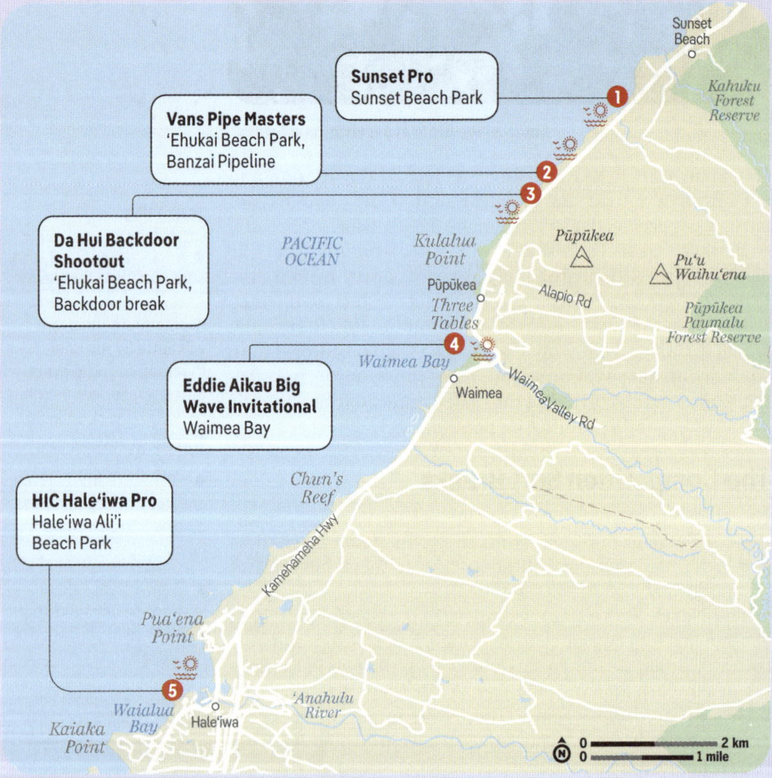

Even if you're not invested in the scoring, you'll want to watch Pipe Masters in person. These talented surfers will be riding through some of the biggest, longest barrels around – it's an exciting event to watch! In the past, surfing greats from the islands, like Carissa Moore and John John Florence, as well as others from around the globe, including Kelly Slater and Jeremy Flores, have claimed the gold at the Pipe Masters.

3 Da Hui Backdoor Shootout

Hosted by the local surfer-founded brand Da Hui at 'Ehukai Beach Park (p183), this early-January surf competition is a unique one. With its island roots, Da Hui Backdoor Shootout (in memory of Duke Kahanamoku) is one of the rare competitions without ties to the WSL, and it's one of the only surfing events where you'll hear the broadcasters speaking Hawai'i Pidgin, Hawai'i's local dialect (see p179).

On top of its strong Hawai'i ties, the conditions at 'Ehukai Beach Park's Backdoor break are especially distinct. While most surf competitions use the Pipeline surf break, this event uses the Backdoor break. (There's also a third break at 'Ehukai Beach Park called 'Off-the-Wall.') With the very shallow reef and deep tubes, the Backdoor break is challenging for even the most experienced of surfers, making the Da Hui Backdoor Shootout a thrill to watch.

4 Eddie Aikau Big Wave Invitational

The Invitational is arguably the most prestigious of all of O'ahu's surf competitions. Taking place at Waimea Bay (p180 the Eddie Aikau Big Wave Invitational – locally just called 'The Eddie' – has some stringent conditions. The waves have to consistently reach over 20ft during the holding period (usually December to March) for the competition to even occur. Since these conditions are so rare, this particular surf competition has been held less than a dozen times since its inception in 1984. Locals and visitors alike go all out for this particular event.

5 HIC Hale'iwa Pro

The HIC Hale'iwa Pro is arguably the most popular surf competition held at Hale'iwa Ali'i Beach Park. Much of the excitement around this early-December surf competition comes with the challenging conditions.

Given that waves break 300 yards from the shore, paddling out at this North Shore beach is already a feat, particularly when swells reach 25ft or more in winter. Add the strong rip current and the shallow reef into the mix, and these surfers have quite a few obstacles to maneuver in order to catch a great wave.

As if that weren't special enough, the HIC Hale'iwa Pro is a WSL Qualifying Series (QS) Event. This means you'll see hungry amateurs – who frankly, to the average viewer, look as incredible as the pros – trying to win their spots in the big-time WSL championships.

MEASURING WAVE SIZE

Measuring the size of waves can be a tricky business. Hawai'i's method measures from the wave's crest to sea level, whereas international methods measure from the wave's crest to the wave's trough. For example, if, according to Hawai'i's method, waves are 20ft, international methods record it as 40ft – and the actual surfable wave face is somewhere in between. This guidebook uses Hawai'i's measurement method.

THE STORY OF EDDIE AIKAU

Eddie Aikau was a beloved local lifeguard and surfer. As the first lifeguard at Waimea Bay, he saved over 500 people. Not a single life was lost while he was on lifeguard watch.

In 1978 Aikau joined the *Hōkūle'a*, a canoe built for the recreation of the Polynesian migration between Hawai'i and Tahiti. When the canoe capsized 12 miles south of Moloka'i, Aikau paddled for help. Although the rest of the voyagers were rescued by the Coast Guard, Aikau was sadly never found.

Lāʻie & Kahuku

POLYNESIAN CULTURE | SHRIMP TRUCKS | FARM VISITS

Lāʻie and Kahuku are often talked about as a pair – sometimes with the third little town of Hauʻula added into the mix. Though usually thought of as simple pit stops on the drive from the Windward Side (p135) to the rest of the North Shore, Lāʻie and Kahuku are both more than meets the eye.

This lovely pair of towns boasts a sleepy, laid-back energy that only manifests when you're far removed from chain restaurants and traffic noises, and find yourself less than a couple miles from the beach at any given time. They're great places to just lounge on the beach or go for a quiet walk through flourishing trees. At the same time, these two North Shore towns are home to some of the most unique attractions on the island – from TV filming locations to authentic Polynesian cultural experiences.

GETTING AROUND

It's easy enough to get around Lā'ie and Kahuku by car or bus. Parking is rarely an issue, and there's always a bus stop close by. One thing to note – there aren't always sidewalks around the bus stops, which means you could end up walking a few hundred feet along the main road to get to one. Stay safe out there!

Experience a Glimpse of Polynesia

Island culture beyond Hawaiʻi

Diving into the history and culture of not just the Hawaiian Islands but also many of the Polynesian Islands, the **Polynesian Cultural Center** *(polynesia.com)* is a living museum of sorts that simultaneously educates and entertains. There are three main parts to the center, starting with the **island 'villages'** *(adult/child $95/76)*.

Representing six different Polynesian Islands – Hawaiʻi, Tonga, Tahiti, Sāmoa, Fiji and Aotearoa (New Zealand) – the villages provide visitors with some insight into each of these island cultures. Toss a spear in Tonga, dance hula in Hawaiʻi, and watch a traditional haka (war dance) in Aotearoa. These island villages are often staffed by people who are actually from those places (typically students at the neighboring Brigham Young University), making this Polynesian Island experience that much more authentic.

TOP TIP

Due to Lā'ie's large Latter-day Saints (LDS) community, there is no alcohol for purchase in the town; not even at the grocery store. Instead, head to Kahuku to find your beverage of choice – hello, **Kahuku Beer Garden & Bottle Shop**!

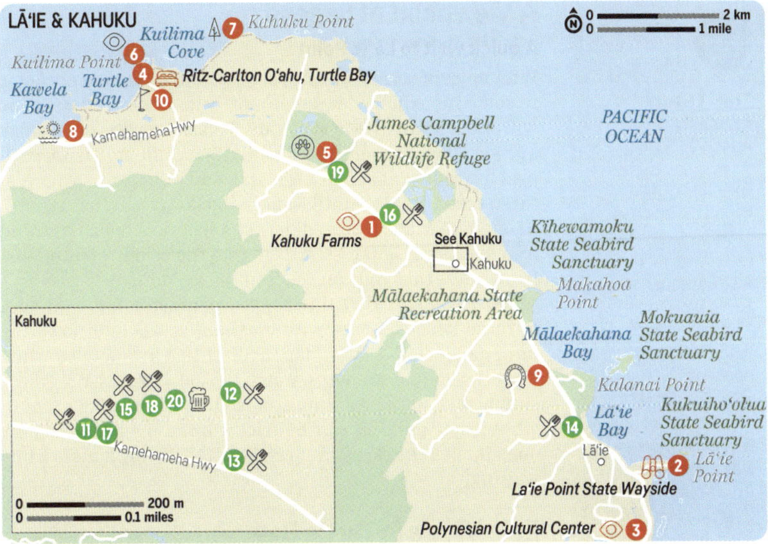

HIGHLIGHTS
1 Kahuku Farms
2 La'ie Point State Wayside
3 Polynesian Cultural Center
4 Ritz-Carlton O'ahu, Turtle Bay

SIGHTS
5 James Campbell National Wildlife Refuge
6 Kahuku Pillbox
7 Kahuku Point
8 Kawela Bay

ACTIVITIES
9 Gunstock Ranch
10 Turtle Bay Golf

EATING
see 4 Beach House by Roy Yamaguchi
11 Da Bald Guy
12 Eighty Chicken Sandwiches
13 Giovanni's Shrimp Truck
14 Ken's Fresh Fish
15 Raised by the Waves
16 Romy's Kahuku Prawns & Shrimp
17 Ry's Poke Shack
18 Seven Brothers at the Mill
19 Tanaka Kahuku Shrimp

DRINKING & NIGHTLIFE
20 Kahuku Beer Garden & Bottle Shop

A Lū'au & a Show

An evening at the Polynesian Cultural Center

Don't leave the Polynesian Cultural Center after you've seen the villages! Stick around into the evening for a lū'au and a show (adult/child from $139/111).

Officially called the **Ali'i Lū'au Buffet**, you'll dine on Hawaiian and local bites like *kālua* pig, *pipi kaula* (a traditional Hawaiian seared beef short-rib dish), fried saimin (a local noodle dish) and fresh 'ahi shōyu (soy sauce) poke. Throughout dinner you can enjoy Hawaiian *mo'olelo* and hula dancing.

Round out your night with the **HĀ: Breath of Life** evening show. This 75-minute, Broadway-esque performance has over 100 performers to bring this fictional love story to life. Bits of each Polynesian island village culture make an appearance, ending with *hā* – the Hawaiian word for 'the breath of life' – when the couple has their first child.

For the best deal, get a combo ticket with all three attractions (adult/child from $158/127).

POLYNESIAN ROOTS

Anthropologists believe that the original Native Hawaiians were likely Polynesians who traveled from the Marquesas Islands (now part of French Polynesia) sometime between 1000 and 1200 CE (though there is some debate about this). Given the 2400 nautical-mile journey, likely done via traditional double-hulled canoes, this journey was quite a feat.

TURTLE BAY RESORT: A MOVIE STAR

Over the years, countless movies and TV shows have been filmed around the Ritz-Carlton O'ahu, Turtle Bay property – from the beaches to the forests to the poolside bar. Nearly all of *Forgetting Sarah Marshall* (2008) was filmed here, as well as many scenes from *Hunger Games: Catching Fire* (2013). Much of the wedding antics from *Mike and Dave Need Wedding Dates* (2016) took place at this North Shore resort as well, along with many of the jungle shots from *Jumanji: Welcome to the Jungle* (2017). And the hit TV show *LOST* filmed on-site at a specific banyan tree so often that it received its own film-focused commemorative plaque!

A Viewpoint of Legend

A quick visit to Lā'ie Point

With miles of oceanfront property, Lā'ie and Kahuku are home to some incredible views that mostly go unnoticed, starting with **Lā'ie Point State Wayside**. This untouched peninsula's ancient Hawaiian *mo'olelo* starts with a giant *mo'o* (supernatural lizard) who lived in Lā'ie. It would kill anyone who ventured there – that is, until Kana, a legendary warrior, arrived. In one visit, Kana defeated the giant lizard, chopped his head into five pieces and tossed them into the ocean, creating the five islands that you can see from Lā'ie Point.

Today you can visit this rugged peninsula for a glimpse of these islands, along with crashing waves and flowering *naupaka* (a native Hawaiian shrub with a five-petaled white flower). Snap a few photos, watch the local fishers at work, or simply take in the calming atmosphere while at Lā'ie Point.

Note that parking can be tricky, but a spot will usually open up in a couple of minutes. Don't block any houses while waiting.

Epic Views in Turtle Bay

Golfing and hiking opportunities

Not far from Lā'ie Point is the **Ritz-Carlton O'ahu, Turtle Bay** *(Turtle Bay Resort; turtlebayresort.com)* in Kahuku, a locally beloved accommodation option that's known for its beachfront golfing opportunities at **Turtle Bay Golf** *(turtlebaygolf.com; 9 holes for visitors from $150)*. As you hit your way along one of their two 18-hole courses, ocean views will greet you around every turn, along with the occasional *mōlī* (Laysan albatross) and Muscovy duck.

Luckily, you don't have to be a golfer to experience the best views. The Ritz-Carlton O'ahu, Turtle Bay property is zigzagged with 12 miles of relatively flat hiking trails that take you to oceanfront lookouts and forest-like landscapes. Wander your way to the hidden **Kahuku Pillbox**, the quiet **Kawela Bay**, or the massive banyan tree from the TV show *LOST*. There's even an ancient *ahupua'a* marker from old Hawai'i still standing on one of these lovely paths.

Look for their other locations dotted around the North Shore!

EATING IN LĀ'IE & KAHUKU: OUR PICKS

Kahuku Farms (p194): A working farm with a to-go food stand serving locally grown acai bowls and veggie-laden paninis. *11am-4pm Thu-Mon* $

Beach House by Roy Yamaguchi: Enjoy fancy Pan-Asian food in a casual environment at this chef-owned Turtle Bay Resort restaurant. *11:30am-2:30pm & 4:30-9pm* $$$

Eighty Chicken Sandwiches: There's just one item on the menu – a buttermilk-fried chicken sandwich, and they've mastered it. *noon-3pm Sat & Sun* $

Seven Brothers at the Mill: This juicy burger joint is a convenient spot for a casual lunch or dinner. *11am-9pm Mon-Sat* $$

CHRISTIAN MUELLER/SHUTTERSTOCK

Lā'ie Point State Wayside

Volunteer at Kahuku Point

Keep the island beautiful

Kahuku Point, also known as Kalaeokauna'oa, is a small peninsula home to many endemic and endangered Hawaiian species, including *'ohai* (O'ahu riverhemp), *honu* and *'īlioholoikauaua* (Hawaiian monk seals), just to name a few. However, rising tides have slowly eroded away Kahuku Point, making a smaller habitat for these precious species.

The **North Shore Community Land Trust** *(northshoreland.org)* welcomes volunteers to help restore the peninsula to its former glory. On the second Saturday of every month, this group removes invasive species, plants native species and improves dune stabilization – and you can join them!

Kahuku's Best Shrimp Truck

Tiny treasures, big flavors

Hawai'i has a long shrimp-eating and shrimp-farming history. Today you'll find several shrimp trucks dotting the North Shore, but there are three main contenders for the title of the best shrimp truck – and all of them are in Kahuku: Giovanni's, Romy's and Tanaka Kahuku Shrimp (formerly Fumi's).

First, there's **Giovanni's** *(giovannisshrimptruck.com)*. With three locations – Kahuku, Hale'iwa and Kaka'ako – it's arguably

NORTH SHORE SHRIMP HISTORY

Shrimp, known as *'ōpae* in Hawaiian, were part of ancient Native Hawaiian diets. For a long time, catching shrimp was a long, painstaking process – usually done by women – of crouching near rivers and sweeping them up into *hīna'i 'ōpae* (braided shrimp-catching baskets). Eventually, the shrimp were moved into fishponds, making the harvesting process a bit easier.

It wasn't until hundreds of years later – the late 1900s to be specific – that commercial shrimp farming became a viable industry in Hawai'i. Shrimp farms started popping up all around Kahuku, and in 1993 Giovanni's opened as the first North Shore shrimp truck.

Try the 'firecracker' special or the Lao-style poke.

Ken's Fresh Fish: A small to-go eatery offering some of the freshest seafood on the North Shore. Try the 'ahi sandwich. *11am-3:45pm Tue, Wed, Fri & Sat* $$

Ry's Poke Shack: This tiny establishment has some of the best poke on the North Shore, using fresh fish and delicious bold flavors. *11:30am-7pm* $$

Raised by the Waves: Casual, sustainability-focused cafe serving delicious plant-based bites, acai bowls and smoothies. *7:30am-5pm* $$

Da Bald Guy: Da Bald Guy showcases Hawai'i Regional Cuisine at its finest, with dishes like *furikake*-crusted salmon and *kalbi* short ribs. *6am-2pm Mon-Sat* $$

BEST TOURS IN KAHUKU & LĀ'IE

Roxy and Matt Ortiz, the artists behind Wooden Wave *(@wooden_wave)*, share some of their favorite tours in Kahuku and Lā'ie.

Kahuku Farms Grand Tour: We always recommend the Kahuku Farms Grand Tour to restaurateurs or people interested in farm-to-table experiences. It's a great example of using the vegetables that they grow and then having a pretty simple but very tasty menu.

Gunstock Ranch Horseback Riding Tours: They have beautiful acreage in the mountains, especially in the afternoon glow – just soft lighting, the layers of mountains and the atmospheric haze. It's quintessentially pastoral.

James Campbell National Wildlife Refuge Tour: We're planning on doing the bird-watching at this National Wildlife Refuge. [You can see protected birds here like *'alae kea* (Hawaiian coot), *ae'o* (Hawaiian stilt) and *kioea* (bristle-thighed curlew).]

Shrimp from Giovanni's (p193)

the most popular of the trio, at least for visitors. Known for their garlic-marinated, garlic-topped shrimp scampi plate, this buttery dish is a delicious, if messy, eating experience. While Giovanni's tries to source as much shrimp as possible from local farms, the supply can't keep up with the demand. Most of the other iconic North Shore shrimp trucks will simply say they're sold out of shrimp for the day, but Giovanni's has chosen to supplement with wholesale frozen shrimp.

Then there's **Romy's Kahuku Prawns & Shrimp** *(instagram.com/romyskahukuprawnsandshrimp)*. While their address has changed, Romy's long-standing, beloved menu has stayed the same, complete with fried, steamed and sautéed shrimp options. For certain dishes, the shrimp heads are left on, which can be a pro or a con depending on your preferences.

Last, but certainly not least, is **Tanaka Kahuku Shrimp** *(tanakakahukushrimp.com)*. The spicy garlic shrimp is their most popular choice, which is no surprise given the mouth-watering burst of flavor of the well-cooked local shrimp. The slice of Kahuku pineapple on the side is also a welcome bonus.

It's safe to say that locals and visitors alike are split on which Kahuku shrimp truck is their favorite, so the only way to figure out which one's for you is to try all three!

Visit Kahuku Farms

Locally grown bites

Established in 1971, **Kahuku Farms** *(kahukufarms.com)* has become a special North Shore spot over the years. Situated on old sugarcane lands, Kahuku Farms was originally known for growing the best watermelons around. In the years since, they have continued to expand and innovate, including with the addition of a delicious farm cafe. You can now enjoy farm-fresh delights – grown using sustainable, regenerative practices – right where the produce has been grown and harvested.

Given the popularity of the farm cafe, most visitors come to Kahuku Farms for a bite to eat – whether it be as a stopping point on the drive up the Windward Coast or an intentional destination for North Shore explorers. Since it is still a working farm, it's also a casual eatery – think compostable containers, grassy lawns and picnic tables. It's all of the best farm-to-table goodness without any of the pretentiousness that's often associated with the cuisine. Feel free to lay out your picnic blanket and play a pick-up game of volleyball as you wait for your food to be prepared.

As for what to order, the farm pizza and side salad (a large veggie-topped bruschetta-esque plate), the *haupia* (coconut cream) pineapple smoothie, and the grilled banana bread with vanilla *haupia* syrup are all crowd favorites. The seasonal acai bowl topped with *liliko'i* (passion fruit) butter, apple bananas and graham-mac-nut crumble is also a special treat since it may be the only acai bowl on the island made with locally grown acai berries!

Take a Tour of Kahuku Farms

Learn where your food comes from

After you enjoy your meal, take a self-guided tour of sorts around a portion of the Kahuku Farms property. (Don't worry, you won't accidentally go where you aren't supposed to go; there are tall trees fencing in the area that's open to the public.) Before you head out, snap a picture of the map by the acai bowl pick-up booth, which identifies the different plants around the walkable area. With that photo in hand, you'll be able to identify all sorts of tropical fruit plants, including *liliko'i*, acai, dragonfruit and starfruit (most of the plants already have signage posted next to them as well).

If you'd like something a little more structured – and that offers the guidance of someone with more farm knowledge – take the 1½-hour **Grand Wagon Tour** *(adult/child $75/50)*. Hitch a ride on a tractor-pulled wagon for a closer look at how a local family has kept this farm surviving and thriving for over a century. Along the way, you'll get to taste tropical fruits straight off the tree, and maybe even try a little nibble of an unprocessed cocoa pod if it's ripe enough.

At the end of it all, you'll be inspired in one way or another – whether that's to start a garden of your own, implement more sustainable practices or enjoy more locally grown fruit – the latter of which is very easy to do as Kahuku Farms also sells some of its produce at its farm stand. Grab some *'ulu*, noni, papaya, guava or starfruit before you head out.

WHY I LOVE KAHUKU FARMS

Sarah Etinas, O'ahu local and Lonely Planet writer

I find myself visiting Kahuku Farms every couple of weeks because it's a great place to get fresh, tasty food while also enjoying nature. I visit so frequently that I have a go-to order – either a farm pizza or an acai bowl, along with a box of *liliko'i* butter mochi.

Once I've eaten, I'll wander around the property, checking in on the *liliko'i*, dragonfruit and whatnot. Then, I'll pop back over to the farm stand, where I'll buy fresh fruit to take home – anything from avocados and oranges to guavas and starfruit. I'll have treated myself to a tasty meal, a nature walk and farm-fresh grocery shopping, all in one stop!

WANT TO STAY ON THE NORTH SHORE?

Despite its popularity, the North Shore only has a few accommodations. Refer to the Places We Love to Stay guide (p119) for recommendations.

Hiking trail, Nuʻuanu Pali State Wayside (p160)

JOHNER IMAGES/GETTY IMAGES

TOOLKIT

The chapters in this section cover the most important topics you'll need to know about in Honolulu, Waikīkī & O'ahu. They're full of nuts-and-bolts information and valuable insights to help you understand and navigate Honolulu, Waikīkī & O'ahu and get the most out of your trip.

Arriving

Most visitors will arrive on Oʻahu via the Daniel K Inouye International Airport, also known as the Honolulu Airport. The only other mode of transportation to reach the islands is via cruise, though most routes focus on inter-island journeys, rather than sailing from the US mainland or an international destination.

Airport

There's only one commercial airport on Oʻahu, the Daniel K Inouye International Airport, commonly referred to as Honolulu Airport. It's very walkable, though you also have the option to take the Wiki Wiki Shuttle.

Visas

If you're a US citizen, a visa is not required. For those from Visa Waiver Program (VWP) countries, a visa isn't required for stays under 90 days, but you do need to apply via the Electronic System for Travel Authorization (ESTA).

Money

While you likely won't need cash immediately upon arriving, the Daniel K Inouye International Airport is filled with convenient ATMs, along with a few currency exchange booths in the International Terminal.

Customs

For those arriving from an international destination, you'll have to go through your standard customs inspection. Have your passport out and ready!

Transport from Airport to City Center

	Waikīkī	Haleʻiwa	Ko Olina
BUS	1hr **$3**	1½hr **$3**	N/A
RENTAL CAR	20min **$75 per day**	45min **$75 per day**	30min **$75 per day**
RIDE-SHARE	20min **$40**	45min **$100**	30min **$60**

AGRICULTURE INSPECTION

The State of Hawaiʻi has strict agricultural restrictions regarding taking produce, plants and other agricultural materials to and from the islands. On or a few days before your flight into Honolulu, you'll be asked to fill out an online Agricultural Declaration Form, stating whether or not you have any of the prohibited items in your possession. If you do, you'll be asked to discard those items in designated bins. Similarly, pets (assuming they are allowed in the islands at all, unlike hamsters, snakes and ferrets) are required to undergo a two-week animal quarantine upon arrival.

When you leave the islands, your bags will also undergo an agricultural inspection to make sure you don't possess any produce or plants.

Getting Around

Nothing beats having your own car on O'ahu, especially if hikes and botanical gardens are on your itinerary. But O'ahu's public bus system, TheBus, is a close second and a much more sustainable choice.

TRAVEL COSTS

Car rental
per day $75

Gas
per gallon $4

Bus pass
per single fare ride $3

Skyline rail pass
per single fare ride $3

Traffic Considerations

Time and time again, O'ahu ranks as having some of the worst traffic in the US – sometimes beating out big metro areas like Chicago and Los Angeles. Try to time your activities to avoid rush hour – essentially, don't head into Honolulu before 9am and don't try to leave between 4pm and 7pm.

Road Conditions

O'ahu's road conditions aren't the best. There are almost always potholes, and the lanes can be tight. This is especially true in Downtown Honolulu neighborhoods, like Mānoa and Chinatown. In recent years, the state has also added quite a few speed bump crosswalks on many major non-highway roads.

TIP

Costco and Sam's Club (you'll need a membership) are by far the cheapest places to buy gas. Luckily, there are many locations on the island.

O'AHU'S CONTRAFLOW SYSTEM

To combat O'ahu's terrible traffic, the Department of Transportation uses a system called 'contraflow.' This temporary traffic flow reversal essentially takes a lane from the opposite side of the road and uses it for traffic in the 'wrong' direction. Usually, this takes place in the mornings, and it's used on major roadways headed in the direction of Honolulu.

DRIVING ESSENTIALS

Drive on the right.

55

The speed limit is between 55mph and 65mph on highways, and 25mph elsewhere.

.08

The blood alcohol limit is 0.08%.

Parking

In the tourist hubs of Waikīkī, Honolulu and Ko Olina, you'll likely have to pay for parking. If you park in a metered spot, some take cards, while others require coins and a few require an app. Outside of those regions, you rarely have to pay for parking, but be prepared to park on the side of the road.

Transportation Passes

O'ahu's public transportation system now includes TheBus (public bus system) and the Skyline (public light rail). Get a reloadable HOLO card at a Skyline Rail station (via vending machines) or select stores, like ABC Stores (day passes) or 7-Eleven (week passes).

Electric Vehicles

O'ahu may be one of the best places to have an electric car, thanks to the abundance of charging stations and the limited land area (the entire island is just 597 sq miles). Occasionally, car rental companies will even run deals on electric vehicles.

Money

CURRENCY: US DOLLAR ($)

Credit Cards

Credit (and debit) cards are the most popular form of payment on O'ahu. They'll work for all of the essentials, including accommodations, car rentals and attractions. The exception may be the small, long-standing food vendors, who are sometimes cash-only. On occasion, there are businesses that are card-only as well.

Cash

In addition to having a credit (or debit) card in your wallet at all times, it's a good idea to have cash too. Some of the most beloved little food vendors – think shave ice stands – are cash-only businesses. On a similar note, you'll want coins for the occasional parking meter that hasn't been updated yet.

Digital Payments

While many businesses accept digital payment methods, such as Apple Pay, it's not necessarily the norm. To make sure you always have a means of paying, make sure you have a physical credit or debit card on you at all times.

HOW MUCH FOR...

a (paid) nature hike
$5

snorkel gear rental
per week $50

a surf lesson
$120

a lūʻau (traditional Hawaiian feast)
$170

HOW TO... Save Money

Accommodations Splurging on beachfront luxury hotels can be great, but there are also more affordable accommodations, like campsites, hostels and even just hotels a little further from the beach.

Dining Happy hour is your best friend. Several O'ahu restaurants offer dishes for a discounted price if you eat a little earlier or later than usual.

Activities Many of O'ahu's best nature activities, including most botanical gardens, beaches and hikes, are free to visit.

LOCAL TIP

Since some businesses are cash-only and others are card-only, it's best to have both forms of payment on you at all times.

HIGH COST OF LIVING

O'ahu is without a doubt a pricey travel destination. A lot of this cost accrues from importing goods to its remote location. It's estimated that up to 90% of Hawai'i's food (by weight) is imported! These added shipping costs then roll over into consumer costs and an overall high cost of living. Consequently, locals often have three (if not four) generations of family members in one house – and when that doesn't work, many locals (including Native Hawaiians) are forced to leave their home in the islands and move to the US mainland.

Accommodations

Beachfront Hotels & Resorts

Most visitors to Oʻahu want to spend as much time as possible at the beach – and that includes sleeping hours. Luckily, there are countless beachfront hotels and resorts to choose from. Most are clustered in Waikīkī, but you can find a few in Ko Olina and on the North Shore.

Vacation Rentals

Given the lack of hotels and resorts outside of the downtown area, vacation rentals are a popular alternative for off-the-beaten-path travelers. But ensure your vacation rental is licensed! To combat the limited housing caused by vacation rentals and Airbnbs, the local government issues a limited number of vacation rental licenses, so many properties operate illegally. Note that most properly licensed vacation rentals are still in popular tourism hubs like Waikīkī and Ko Olina.

Camping

Many Oʻahu state parks, botanical gardens and beaches have designated tent campgrounds, but arranging a campsite can be complicated. All reservations must begin on a Friday and must be for three or five days. (State campsites are closed Wednesdays and Thursdays.) Reservations open 14 days before the first date of your stay and come with the required permit.

Hostels

There are just a half a dozen or so hostels on the island, but they're all great if you're traveling on a budget. From Pūpūkea to Waikīkī, you can find hostels with a small, comfy bed and kind staff. And who knows? With the communal environments, you might even become friends with your fellow hostel-stayers!

HOW MUCH FOR A NIGHT IN...

a B&B
$350

a luxury hotel
from $600

a public tent campsite
$10–30

B&Bs

Surprisingly, there aren't all that many B&Bs on Oʻahu, but there are a few dotted throughout Honolulu and Kailua. These accommodations are great if you're looking for that homey feel but with an island twist.

ACCOMMODATION PRICE RANGES

$ less than $200

$$ $200–500

$$$ more than $500

HEFTY ACCOMMODATIONS TAXES

There are a few Oʻahu accommodation-specific taxes that you'll want to make room for in your budget, because they're pretty significant. First, there's the Hawaiʻi Transient Accommodations Tax, which is 10.25%. On top of that, Oʻahu has its own Transient Accommodations Tax for another 3%. Once you add Hawaiʻi's standard 4.712% General Excise Tax (the state's replacement of sorts for sales tax) to the mix, that's a combined tax rate of 17.962%. It's quite a doozy, especially if you're not expecting it. This means that your $500 per night accommodations will end up costing nearly $600 per night, simply because of these additional taxes. Do note that these taxes do not include other additional fees that often come with hotels, like resort fees and overnight parking fees. Mandatory resort fees are also subject to the full 17.962% tax rate, while parking fees are subject to the 4.712% General Excise Tax.

Family Travel

O'ahu is a dream for families with kids. Babies have a blast splashing around at the calmest beaches, young kids like diving underwater on Atlantis Adventures submarine rides, and teens love ATV-riding through the mountain-framed Kualoa Ranch. Not to mention, both Waikīkī and Ko Olina are filled with family-friendly accommodations, ready to serve as your home base.

Car-Seat Laws

Car-seat rules vary a bit state to state. In Hawai'i, children under two years old must use a rear-facing car seat with a harness, children under four years old must use a rear- or forward-facing car seat with a harness and children under 10 must use a booster seat.

Refer to the state of Hawai'i website for more information: hidot.hawaii.gov/highways

Sights

Nearly all O'ahu sights offer discounted rates for children, though the cut-off age is typically around 12 years old. If your child is eligible, you could be looking at 20% (or more) off some of the island's best activities, including the Polynesian Cultural Center *lū'au* (p191).

Kids Portions

If you're looking for an after-dinner treat but you don't want your little ones to get a sugar high, you'll be happy to note that many dessert spots – shave-ice and ice-cream shops, in particular – have kids (or *keiki*) sizes.

Kids Menus

Surprisingly, many of the fanciest restaurants on O'ahu offer well-thought-out *keiki* menus. Some standouts include **Roy's** in Waikīkī (p84), Ko Olina (p125), and Hawai'i Kai (p140), and **Merriman's** (p80).

KID-FRIENDLY PICKS

Hanauma Bay Nature Preserve (p138)
Snorkel through calm waters, getting a glimpse of *honu* (green sea turtles), and *he'e* (octopus).

Dole Plantation (p168)
Ride on a train, race through a maze, and devour pineapple treats at this Wahiawā attraction.

Kualoa Ranch (p162)
Try a ride on an All Terrain Vehicle ride at this nature-filled, movie-filming location.

Honolulu Zoo (p87)
Make some new animal friends, including the endemic nēnē (Hawaiian goose) and *'io* (Hawaiian hawk).

A DASH OF PIXIE DUST

O'ahu is home to one of the only 'stand-alone' Disney hotels in existence – the **Aulani, A Disney Resort & Spa** (p126) – and this sprinkle of 'the Happiest Place on Earth' is practically guaranteed to be kid friendly. Even without a room, you can enjoy character dining, trade pins and say hello to some of your favorite classic and island-inspired Disney characters. If you do book a room at the Aulani, the number of kid-friendly activities soars – race down waterslides, hang out in the *keiki* splash zones and learn how to make a lei at the kids-only **Auntie's Beach House**.

Health & Safe Travel

HURRICANES & TSUNAMIS

As one of the middle islands in the Hawaiian archipelago, O'ahu manages to get by mostly unscathed when it comes to hurricanes and tsunamis. The last major hurricane was way back in 1992. That said, the state still has a tsunami warning siren system in place, which tests on the first business day each month.

Wildfires

The destructive Maui fires of August 2023 showed that wildfires are becoming a major issue on all the Hawaiian Islands, including O'ahu. Though 90% of local fires are caused by humans, they're exacerbated by droughts, climate change and flammable non-native plants. These blazes put lives at risk and take Hawai'i's endangered plant and animal species closer to extinction.

Petty Theft

While crime overall is very low on O'ahu, petty theft is a problem. It's not uncommon for cars to be broken into. When possible, leave your valuables at home or in your accommodations. If that's not feasible, store the items in your car's center console or glove compartment, or below the seats, airplane-style.

LEPTOSPIROSIS

Hawai'i's freshwater sources harbor leptospirosis bacteria. Entering via wounds or ingestion, it can cause flu-like symptoms. Find out more at cdc.gov/leptospirosis

Flash Flooding

Flash flooding is the most likely natural disaster you'll face on O'ahu. Avoid any waterways (even if they're dry). If necessary, take shelter and/or move to higher ground. Do not attempt to cross flooded roads.

Bites & Stings

On land, there's the occasional stinging centipede or scorpion, but you're unlikely to encounter either. The water is where more of Hawai'i's dangerous creatures like to hang. Jellyfish and Portuguese man o' war are the most common, and signs will inform you when they're present. There are also eels and cone snails (in cone shells). The latter seems innocuous but is the most venomous of the bunch.

UNHOUSED POPULATION IN HAWAI'I

Hawai'i has one of the highest rates of unhoused people per capita in the US and much of the state's nearly 12,000 unhoused residents live on O'ahu.

While some are quick to dismiss it with 'at least they're homeless in paradise,' that mindset undermines the issue. High housing costs, lack of housing, low-paying jobs and lack of career progression opportunities all contribute to the high homelessness rate in the islands.

FROM LEFT: NEW AFRICA/SHUTTERSTOCK, FOOTMADE0525/SHUTTERSTOCK

Food, Drink & Nightlife

When to Eat

Breakfast (6–10am) Breakfast on O'ahu is set up for those looking to get an early-morning start, perfect for catching some waves or tackling a hike.

Lunch (11am–2pm) Casual take-out spots for poke, bentos and plate lunches are often particularly popular at noon.

Dinner (5–8:30pm) Sit down for a proper meal at the end of the day. Time it with sunset for a magical view.

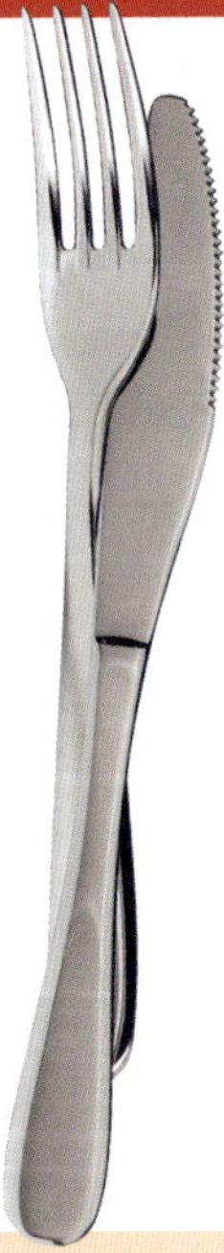

Where to Eat

Cafes Start your day at a cafe. Do note that it can be hard to find ones serving 100% Hawaiian coffee.

Farm-to-table spots Hawai'i's agricultural movement is on the rise – and its adorable and casual farm-to-table eateries along with it.

Walk-up counters Walk up, order your poke or shave ice of choice, and then go.

Sit-down restaurants Take a seat for just about any kind of meal, from casual bites to anniversary-worthy establishments.

Grocery stores These are often the go-to eateries in smaller neighborhoods. Think poke counters, grab-n-go bentos and warm Spam *musubis*.

EATING PRICE RANGES

$ less than $20
$$ $20–40
$$$ more than $40

HAWAIIAN FOOD VERSUS LOCAL FOOD

Here in the islands, there's a distinction between Hawaiian food and local food. Hawaiian food consists of the traditional dishes that Native Hawaiians ate. They're often, but not always, the foods that are associated with a lū'au. Some of the most well-known Hawaiian dishes include *kālua* pig (traditional Hawaiian shredded pork), poi (purple paste made by pounding taro), *laulau* (*ti* [native plant] and taro leaf-wrapped meat) and *haupia* (coconut pudding).

Local food, on the other hand, refers to dishes that are unique to the islands in some way or another. They're foods that came to be through the melting pot of immigrant cultures. For example, poke started off as a traditional Hawaiian dish of raw, cubed fish seasoned with salt, nori (seaweed) and *'inamona* (*kukui* nuts).

However, when the sugar plantation boom happened and immigrants from around the world arrived in the islands, poke started to change. Soon shōyu (soy sauce) from Japan and green onions from China became staples in this now-local dish. Other quintessential local foods include *manapuas* (meat-filled buns), *musubis* (a local snack made of a rectangle of rice, a slice of shōyu-seasoned Spam and nori), *malasadas* (Portuguese-style doughnuts) and even shave ice.

When in doubt, it's always best to call something a local food (or even a Hawai'i food) rather than a Hawaiian food.

CONFUSED ABOUT THE MENU?

Reference the helpful Menu Decoder on p206.

CLOCKWISE FROM LEFT: NINELL/SHUTTERSTOCK, BONCHAN/SHUTTERSTOCK, CHAINFOTO24/SHUTTERSTOCK

HOW MUCH FOR...

a cup of Hawaiian coffee **$7**

shave ice **$7**

a poke bowl **$16–22**

an acai bowl **$15**

a casual farm-to-table meal **$25**

a fancy dinner **$100**

a cocktail **$16–22**

HOW TO... Order Shave Ice

First thing's first, it's *shave* ice, not *shaved* ice. If you see a sign that says shaved ice, know that it's likely inauthentic; skip it in favor of somewhere that says shave ice.

Once you're in a shave ice shop, ordering your treat can seem complicated. Most shave ice places will have a sign with clear steps to guide you. On the off chance that they don't, here's what you'll do.

Step 1 Pick the size of your shave ice.

Step 2 Pick any fillings, such as azuki beans or ice cream.

Step 3 Pick your shave ice flavors. This is where you'll find the most options and where your shave ice will get its bright colors. You'll often find fun tropical flavors like *li hing mui* (salty dried plums) and *liliko'i* (passion fruit), alongside more familiar flavors like strawberry and cotton candy.

Step 4 Pick your toppings. These go on top of the shave ice and often include mochi (Japanese rice cake) balls and snow caps (condensed milk).

If that all seems a little overwhelming, keep in mind that you only really need to do steps 1 and 3 – the size and the flavors. The fillings and toppings are optional and often come with an additional cost.

The Original Way to 'Shave' Ice

The concept of shave ice can be traced back to a similar Japanese dessert known as *kakigori*. Since *kakigori* has been around for a millennium, the fancy shave ice machines of today didn't exist back then. Instead, they used a sword to shave the ice!

100% HAWAIIAN COFFEE...OR NOT

Some visitors to O'ahu think that most – if not all – of the coffee that they'll find on the island will be 100% Hawaiian coffee. And given that Hawai'i grows nearly 30 million pounds of coffee per year, that's not a totally unreasonable assumption – it's just not the case.

Most coffee shops will have a dedicated 100% Hawaiian coffee drink or two, but even that's not guaranteed. That said, both **Kona Coffee Purveyors** *(konacoffeepurveyors.com)* in Waikīkī and **Morning Glass Coffee** (p109) in Mānoa make it easy for you to select or upgrade to 100% Hawaiian coffee. That way, you can be sure.

Menu Decoder

Since Hawai'i's food scene has been influenced by so many cultures, it's common to find words from a bunch of different languages – as well as the local dialect, Hawai'i Pidgin – on local menus. To help make things a *little* less confusing, here's a menu decoder of sorts.

Acai South American berry
Adobo Filipino stew with meat, vinegar, shōyu and garlic
'Ahi Yellowfin tuna
Aku Skipjack tuna
Apple banana Small, sweet banana variety
A'u Marlin
Azuki bean Asian sweet bean in local desserts
Bao Chinese steamed bun
Bento Japanese-style packed lunch with a compartment for each component
Chantilly Spin-off of the synonymous French cream, using butter and evaporated milk
Char siu Cantonese barbecue pork
Chicken long rice Local chicken and cellophane noodle dish
Daikon Japanese white radish
Dim sum Chinese meal consisting of dumplings and other bites
Edamame Soybeans
Furikake Seasoning mix with nori flakes and sesame seeds
Gau gee Fried wonton-like *pūpū* with Asian-flavored pork filling
Hamachi Amberjack (or *kāhala* in Hawaiian)
Hapa rice Half white rice, half brown rice
Haupia Coconut-cream dessert
'Inamona Roasted *kukui* nut mix used for poke
Ikura Salmon roe
Kalbi Grilled Korean short ribs
Kālua pig Traditional Hawaiian shredded pork
Katsu Japanese cooking preparation of breading and frying
Kiawe Species of mesquite wood, often used for fire roasting
Kimchi Korean spicy fermented vegetables, usually cabbage or radishes
Laulau *Ti* and taro-leaf-wrapped meat
Lechon Filipino spit-roasted pork
Li hing mui Sweet, tangy dried plum powder
Liliko'i Passion fruit
Limu/ogo Seaweed used in poke
Loco moco Local dish composed of rice, a hamburger patty, gravy and a fried egg on top
Lomi lomi salmon Raw salmon and tomato salad
Lū'au Hawaiian dish made with meat (usually chicken or squid), coconut milk and *kalo* (taro) leaves
Lumpia Sweet or savory Filipino spring roll
Malasada Portuguese-style doughnut
Manapua Meat-filled bun
Matcha Pulverized green tea
Meat jun Egg-battered, deep-fried beef
Miso Fermented soybean paste
Misoyaki When a meat is seasoned with miso and grilled
Mochi Japanese rice cake
Mochiko chicken Local fried chicken using rice flour
Musubi Local snack made of a rectangle of rice, a slice of shōyu-seasoned Spam and nori
'Nalo greens Leafy greens grown in Waimānalo
Nori Seaweed sheet
Onaga Snapper
Ono Mackerel (similarly, the Hawaiian word for 'delicious' is *'ono)*
Opah Moon fish
Pancit Filipino noodle dish
Plate lunch Term for a standard local lunch, typically including white rice, macaroni salad and a local main dish
POG Passion fruit, orange and guava juice mix
Poi Purple paste made by pounding taro
Poke Seasoned, cubed raw fish
Pūpū Appetizer
Ramen Japanese noodle soup
Saimin Local dish derived from a variety of Asian noodle dishes
Sashimi Sliced, high-quality, raw fish
Shave ice Dessert made with ice flakes and fruity syrup
Shōyu Soy sauce
Snow cap Condensed-milk drizzle on shave ice
Spam Canned pork
Tako Octopus
Taro Root vegetable widely used in Native Hawaiian cuisine; also called *kalo*
Teriyaki Sweet shōyu-based sauce
Ube Japanese purple potato
Unagi sauce Eel sauce
Uni Sea urchin (occasionally called by its Hawaiian name, *wana)*
Wasabi Japanese horseradish
Wonton Chinese dumpling
Yuzu Asian citrus

MATT MUNRO/LONELY PLANET

Responsible Travel

Climate Change & Travel

It's impossible to ignore the impact we have when traveling; Lonely Planet urges all travelers to engage with their travel carbon footprint, which will mainly come from air travel. While there often isn't an alternative, travelers can look to minimize the number of flights they take, opt for newer aircrafts and use cleaner ground transport, such as trains. One proposed solution – purchasing carbon offsets – unfortunately does not cancel out the impact of individual flights. While most destinations will depend on air travel for the foreseeable future, for now, pursuing ground-based travel where possible is the best course of action.

The **UN Carbon Offset Calculator** shows how flying impacts a household's emissions.

The **ICAO's carbon emissions calculator** allows visitors to analyze the CO2 generated by point-to-point journeys.

In Honolulu and Waikīkī, there are Biki bike stations galore. Peddle around to help the planet and get an unintentional workout in.

With its limited land and ubiquitous charging stations, O'ahu may be one of the best places to drive an electric car.

LEARN NATIVE HAWAIIAN HISTORY & CULTURE

Unfortunately, Native Hawaiian history is filled with erasure. Since Western discovery, many parts of Native culture have been forbidden or looked down upon, including *he'e nalu* (surfing), Native Hawaiian *akua* (deities) and 'Ōlelo Hawai'i (Hawaiian language) – not to mention that the islands were forcibly taken from the Kingdom of Hawai'i and never returned. Travelers can help preserve what's left by visiting some of O'ahu's most informative Native Hawaiian historic sites like **'Iolani Palace** (p58) and **Waimea Valley** (p184), and experiencing the current Hawaiian culture revival through the **Prince Lot Hula Festival** and the Native-owned **Toa Luau** (p184).

SUPPORT NATIVE-OWNED BUSINESSES

When you shop at Native Hawaiian-owned businesses, you'll find incredible products and services while supporting the Native Hawaiian community. The trickiest part is finding the businesses, but Kapolei's Ka Makana Ali'i shopping mall and kanakaeconomy.com are good starting points.

Made-in-Hawai'i Movement

In recent years, there's been a push to buy local – and given that there are thousands of local businesses, it's often easy to do. And you can find everything from locally grown fruit to beauty products to baby gear. To see hundreds of incredible Hawai'i makers at once, visit the **Made in Hawai'i Festival**, held each August at the **Hawai'i Convention Center**. Vendors from across the Hawaiian Islands showcase their wares.

Give Back Through Voluntourism

Invest in the local O'ahu community through voluntourism. Beach clean-ups tend to be the easiest option – simply show up at a designated beach and pick up trash using the provided supplies. But there are also opportunities to help plant *kalo* in *lo'i* (wetland taro fields) in **Kane'ohe** (p157), clean up the USS *Missouri* at **Pearl Harbor** (p112) and work on sand-dune restoration in **Kahuku** (p193).

Get Down & Dirty with Agritourism

While agritourism is often tied to voluntourism on O'ahu, some agrarian experiences are just for fun. Enjoy farm-fresh flavors at **Kahumana Farms** (p130) in Wai'anae, or take a farm tour at **Kahuku Farms** (p194) on the North Shore.

In 2021 Hawai'i outlawed the sale of chemical sunscreens to protect the islands' marine habitats. Instead, use reef-safe sunscreen, ideally from local brands like Little Hands Hawai'i and Mama Kuleana.

Locally owned vintage shops have been popping up in the islands – from Honolulu to Kailua – encouraging shoppers to purchase secondhand instead of contributing to fast-fashion waste.

Green Hawai'i

According to the US Sustainable Development Report 2021, Hawai'i ranks number 8 out of 50 states, thanks to its push for clean water, clean energy and responsible consumption, among other factors.

RESOURCES

planning.hawaii.gov/sustainability
A dedicated state government branch focused on sustainability.

sustainablecoastlineshawaii.org
A local nonprofit dedicated to cleaning beaches and oceans.

gohawaii.com/malama
This tourism authority's website features a dedicated Mālama – or voluntourism – page.

TOP LEFT: BIKI; BOTTOM LEFT: BIRD VISUAL/GETTY IMAGES

LGBTIQ+ Travelers

Hawai'i as a whole is very welcoming to the LGBTIQ+ community. As a matter of fact, in ancient Hawai'i, LGBTIQ+ people were not only recognized, they were often given positions of religious power. Much of that positivity continues on the islands today, where you'll find gay bars, beaches, clubs and cruises.

Māhū in Ancient Hawai'i & Today

In ancient Hawai'i, while there were *kane* (men) and *wahine* (women), there were also *māhū*, those who preferred a third non-binary identity. (The term sometimes referred to intersex people as well.) *Māhū* were highly respected people who were often given religious positions of power or became healers.

It is important to note that, unlike in ancient Hawai'i, when the term *māhū* is used today, it can have either negative or positive connotations. Use the tone or facial expressions of the speaker to get an indication of the implication.

EVENTS

The **Honolulu Rainbow Film Festival** is one of the longest-running LGBTIQ+ festivals in the US. Every September this event features half a dozen films centered on local stories.

The **Honolulu Pride Festival** takes place each October, and the entire month is filled with burlesque performances, cruises and cabarets. It all culminates with the official festival, which features local LGBTIQ+ icons, cultural performances and epic concerts.

Resources

Hawai'i LGBT Legacy Foundation *(hawaiilgbtlegacyfoundation.com)* highlights local programs and services in place for the LGBTIQ+ community.

Gay Island Guide *(gayislandguide.net)* is a great resource for LGBTIQ+ events in Hawai'i, in particular, though it also includes recommendations for accommodations, transportation, activities and more.

LGBTIQ+ BUSINESSES

Salvage Public *(salvagepublic.com)* Contemporary men's fashion company.

Pipeline Bakeshop & Creamery *(pipelinebakeshop.com)* Kaimukī dessert shop.

The Curb *(thecurbkaimuki.com)* Top-notch coffee shop.

The Gay Agenda Collective *(thegayagenda.co)* Native Hawaiian–owned wedding planning service.

GAY BARS & CLUBS

Since nearly all of O'ahu's nightlife is concentrated in Honolulu and Waikīkī, all of the gay bars and clubs are located there, too. Mingle at **In Between**, show off your vocal chops at **Wang Chung's** (p92) karaoke bar, or catch a drag show at **Hula's Bar & Lei Stand** (p92). The latter even has an in-demand gay catamaran cruise every Saturday afternoon.

Queen's Surf Beach

Located across the street from Waikīkī's Kapi'olani Regional Park, **Queen's Surf Beach** (p82) is widely regarded as the most popular gay beach on O'ahu. While at first it was really only frequented by members of the LGBTIQ+ community, allies now enjoy the sand and surf as well.

 NITO/SHUTTERSTOCK

Accessible Travel

O'ahu's accessibility accommodations are both good and bad. While organizers sometimes have things like free-to-rent all-terrain wheelchairs for beaches, there is often room for a lot of improvement.

Public Transportation

Both TheBus and the Skyline, O'ahu's public transportation, are wheelchair accessible. They offer discounted fares for passengers with disabilities who have a filled-out Disability Reduced Fare Application and government-issued ID.

Airport

The Daniel K Inouye International Airport (Honolulu International Airport) offers terminal-to-curbside assistance for travelers with disabilities. Since this service is offered by the airline, contact your airline for more information.

Accommodations

Most large hotels and resorts on O'ahu have accessible accommodations for travelers with disabilities. Some standouts include the **Hilton Hawaiian Village** (p84) and the **Ritz-Carlton O'ahu, Turtle Bay** (p192) on the North Shore.

DISABILITY PLACARDS

Hawai'i honors disability placards issued by the authorities of any other state or country, so bring yours from home.

Rental cars For travelers with disabilities, most O'ahu rental-car companies gladly install hand controls, provide accessible transportation from the airport to the car pickup location, or deliver the car to the airport terminal, if you let them know beforehand.

All-terrain wheelchairs Hanauma Bay Nature Preserve, Ala Moana Beach Park, Sans Souci Kaimana Beach Park, Kailua Beach and Kualoa Regional Park have all-terrain wheelchairs free to use for those with disabilities. There's a two-hour limit.

RESOURCES

Hawaii Disability & Communication Access Board
The most comprehensive information on traveling with disabilities in Hawai'i. It primarily outlines the government-funded initiatives.

Hawai'i Interpreting Services
Interpreting services in both American Sign Language (ASL) and Hawai'i Sign Language (HSL).

TRAVEL WITH GUIDE DOGS OR SERVICE DOGS

If you have a guide dog or service dog, you must enter through Honolulu's Daniel K Inouye Airport, rather than connecting via another island. Ensure your dog has a current rabies vaccine and documentation; a microchip; a passing OIE-FAVN test, done within three years of arrival; and a health certificate issued within 30 days of arrival, showing tick treatment with Fipronil or similar within 14 days prior.

Guide Dogs

For more information about getting your guide dog or service dog to Hawai'i (and the contact information for the Hawai'i Department of Agriculture) visit hdoa.hawaii.gov.

O'ahu Hiking Safety

O'ahu is filled with gorgeous hiking trails – from beachfront paths to jungle-esque treks. However, there are a few tips you'll want to keep in mind to stay safe.

Hike with a Buddy

The first rule of hiking – on O'ahu or anywhere else – is to always hike with a buddy. If something goes wrong, whether it's suffering an injury or getting lost, it's always better to have another person there to help.

Research the Trails

Before tackling a hike, it's important to know about the terrain, distance, turns and even parking. Screenshot or download the most important information you find online. Many of O'ahu's trails don't have cell service, so you won't be able to look up anything when you're on the go.

Check the Weather

During O'ahu's rainy season (October to March), some of the hikes on the island can become dangerous. Not only do the paths become muddy and slippery, but they can also be prone to deadly flash floods. (This is especially true of waterfall hikes.) Before you head out, check the weather forecast to make sure that it won't rain that day.

Lace Up Your Shoes

Some visitors don't think to bring hiking shoes on their O'ahu vacations and instead try to tackle the trails in slippahs (flip-flops). That's not the best idea. If you've forgotten hike-appropriate shoes, pick up a pair – general athletic shoes will work on most trails – and head out.

Stay on the Trails

Though you might be tempted to wander off and explore off-the-beaten paths, don't do that. The plant life on O'ahu is often very dense, making it difficult to find your way back. Though there aren't many dangerous wild animals on the island, wild boar are the exception – and you don't want to run into any of them. Since they have learned to stay away from trails well trodden by humans, they likely won't bother you if you simply stick to the designated paths.

Don't Drink from the Waterways

O'ahu's fresh waterways contain a bacteria known as leptospirosis (p203) that enters the body through ingestion or open wounds. Though some people are asymptomatic, others end up with flu-like symptoms – not a great way to spend your trip to the island.

Know Your Own Capabilities

Don't try to tackle a trail you know that you won't be able to handle. It's OK to start with the easy hikes and work your way up. Besides, many of O'ahu's easier hikes have stunning views!

WHAT TO DO IN A HIKE EMERGENCY ON O'AHU

Call 911. Ask for fire and rescue and inform them of the situation and your location. Stay calm, stay put and stay warm. Try to attract the attention of rescuers or other hikers.

O'ahu Ocean Safety

Spending time in the ocean or on the beach is a must during your O'ahu visit. However, there are a few safety tips that you should keep in mind before diving in.

Never Turn Your Back on the Ocean

This is the number one rule of hanging out at the beach. Ocean conditions can change in an instant, and if you're not looking at the ocean, you won't know it. A wave could surprise you and sweep you off your feet (which isn't nearly as romantic as it sounds).

Swim with a Buddy

If something goes wrong while you're swimming around, it's always better to have another person there to help. They can call out to the lifeguard, keep you calm or even find a solution to whatever problem is at hand.

Stay Away from Cliff Faces

Many visitors like to get a closer look at, well, everything. But, at the beach, a closer look isn't always the best move.

Sometimes getting a closer look ends up putting people in precarious positions. At **Lā'ie Point State Wayside** (p192), for example, visitors often want to get a closer look at the waves crashing against the peninsula. They'll edge closer and closer to the cliff faces, and all it takes is one slightly larger wave to sweep them off the jagged rocks. It's not unheard of to see news headlines like 'tourist swept off to sea,' so don't be one of them.

Obey Posted Signs

There are lots of signs posted on O'ahu beaches, and they're always there for your safety. They might let you know about large waves, rip currents, jellyfish or Portuguese man o' war, just to start. Be sure to always follow them.

Know Your Own Capabilities

Don't try to jump into the ocean in conditions you won't be able to handle. If the waves are too large, enjoy the shoreline instead – or head to another beach where the water is peaceful. Kailua Beach and Lanikai Beach (p146) in Kailua tend to be calm all year-round.

CHAT WITH THE LIFEGUARD

No one knows a beach better than the local lifeguard. They'll be able to tell you about jagged reefs and rocks that are always around, as well as the day-to-day factors that often change like waves, rip currents and jellyfish. Who knows? They might even give you the inside scoop on where to see some of the coolest underwater creatures.

FROM LEFT: JOSHUA RAINEY PHOTOGRAPHY/SHUTTERSTOCK, NICHOLAS FLOYD/SHUTTERSTOCK

'Native Hawaiian' Versus 'Local'

Though many people outside of the islands tend to use the terms 'Hawaiian' and 'local' interchangeably, the distinction between the two is important.

The Difference Between 'Hawaiian' & 'Local'

The term 'Hawaiian' only applies to people who are Native Hawaiian – meaning indigenous to Hawai'i – along with their culture, language and history. In Hawaiian, the term is Kanaka Maoli (plural: Kānaka Maoli).

'Local,' on the other hand, is used to indicate someone who is from Hawai'i and not necessarily Native Hawaiian. There is still a Hawaiian language term for locals – *kama'āina*, or 'people of the land' – although this word is now mostly used within the phrase *kama'āina* discount, the discount that locals can get with a Hawai'i state ID.

What's the Big Deal?

Native Hawaiian history is filled with erasure. Over the centuries since Western discovery in 1778, many parts of Native culture have been forbidden or looked down upon, including *he'e nalu* (surfing), Native Hawaiian *akua* (deities) and 'Ōlelo Hawai'i (Hawaiian language).

All of that cultural erasure doesn't even touch on the fact that American businessmen, led by Lorrin Thurston and Sanford B Dole, forcibly took the islands from Queen Lili'uokalani and the Kingdom of Hawai'i. When the US government had the chance to return the islands to their rightful owners, it chose not to.

While US Congress did issue the Apology Resolution in 1993 – a full century after Queen Lili'uokalani was overthrown – it doesn't actually undo the damage that was done; the Hawaiian Islands are still under US control and Native Hawaiian culture is still struggling to recover from its early suppression.

When people call everyone from Hawai'i 'Hawaiian,' it continues the erasure that has plagued this Indigenous group for hundreds of years. If this practice of making 'Hawaiian' and 'local' synonymous were to become widespread, not only would Hawaiians have a stifled language and culture, they wouldn't even have a distinguishing group name, essentially making them unidentifiable.

Simply put, while people from California call themselves 'Californian,' people from Hawai'i will never call themselves 'Hawaiian' unless they are Native Hawaiian.

SO, WHO IS 'LOCAL'?

This terminology situation gets a little trickier when you realize that 'local' may not apply to *everyone* who lives in Hawai'i. For example, no one would consider someone who moves to the island for six months to be a local, but then the question is, how long does it take for someone to be considered a local? Does someone have to be an active participant in the local community? Do they need to befriend locals or speak the local dialect known as Hawai'i Pidgin? Ultimately, the answers to those questions are all pretty subjective, as is determining who is a 'local.'

LANGUAGE

Kama'āina Hawai'i locals; literally means 'people of the land'

Kapu Forbidden. While it once meant things that were 'taboo' or against the law in ancient Hawaiian society, today it is typically used to mean 'no trespassing,' typically when there are sacred Hawaiian spots nearby.

Keiki Children

Lānai Porch, veranda or balcony

Makai Ocean (typically used for directional purposes, as in toward the ocean)

Mauka Mountains (typically used for directional purposes, as in toward the mountains)

'Ōpala Trash

Nuts & Bolts

OPENING HOURS

Despite being the busiest and most bustling of all of the Hawaiian Islands, O'ahu still does follow laid-back island time sometimes.

Banks 9am–4pm Monday–Thursday, 9am–6pm Friday, some to 1pm on Saturday

Bars 11am–midnight Sunday–Thursday, 11am–2am Friday and Saturday

Cafes 6am–4pm

Clubs 10pm–2am, with a few exceptions closing at 4am

Parks 6am–7pm (often sunrise to sunset)

Pharmacies 9am–7pm Monday–Friday, 10am–5pm Saturday and Sunday (Longs Drugs often has longer hours)

Restaurants 11am–9pm

Shops 10am–8pm Monday–Saturday, 10am–6pm Sunday

Supermarkets 6am–10pm, some locations 24 hours

Tap Water

Hawai'i consistently ranks as having some of the best tap-water quality in the US.

Internet Access

Most hotels, malls, restaurants and the Daniel K Inouye International Airport offer free wi-fi.

GOOD TO KNOW

Time Zone
GMT-10

County Code
+1

Emergency Number
911

Population
1 million

Electricity

120V/60Hz

PUBLIC HOLIDAYS

O'ahu participates in both US holidays and Hawai'i state holidays. Most businesses only close for the most popular ones like Thanksgiving and Christmas Day.

New Year's Day January 1

Martin Luther King Jr Day Third Monday in January

Presidents' Day Third Monday in February

Prince Jonah Kūhiō Kalaniana'ole Day March 26

Good Friday March/April

Memorial Day Last Monday in May

King Kamehameha I Day June 11

Independence Day July 4

Statehood Day Third Friday in August

Labor Day First Monday in September

Veterans Day November 11

Thanksgiving Day Fourth Thursday in November

Christmas Day December 25

THE HONOLULU, WAIKĪKĪ & OʻAHU

STORYBOOK

Our writers delve deep into different aspects of Honolulu, Waikīkī & Oʻahu life.

Kamehameha the Great Statue (p63) on King Kamehameha Day (p33)

ANTHONY QUINTANO VIA WIKIMEDIA COMMONS

A HISTORY OF O'AHU IN 15 PLACES

Likely originally settled by Polynesian voyagers around 1200 CE, O'ahu – and the rest of the Hawaiian Islands – started with a rather quiet existence. But Western discovery brought a whole new set of economic and political challenges to these isolated islands.

O'AHU HAS A storied past. It all starts with voyagers from the Marquesas Islands, who settled in Hawai'i sometime between 1000 and 1200 CE. For a few hundred years, they were able to exist relatively peacefully, living off the land and sea.

Then, in the late 1700s, two major historic events happened: Captain James Cook became the first Westerner to visit the islands and King Kamehameha I unified all of the Hawaiian Islands. The former introduced Hawai'i to global influences, economies and politics, while the latter kept the interisland skirmishes to a minimum and created a sense of united Hawaiian identity.

With the presence of Hawai'i known to the rest of the world, the islands – and O'ahu, in particular – became forever changed. Missionaries flocked to preach Christianity, dismissing ancient Hawaiian *akua* (deities). Sugar and pineapple plantations popped up, bringing immigrant workers from across the globe. And the Hawaiian monarchy was ultimately overthrown, unjustly putting Hawaiian lands in non-Native hands.

Today, O'ahu is more than just a popular tourist destination and surfing hot spot – though both of those facts are true; it also continues to be a home to Native Hawaiians, locals and residents alike.

1. Moli'i Fishpond

A PEEK INTO ANCIENT HAWAI'I

Hawai'i's first settlers traveled 2400 nautical miles via double-hull canoe, bringing their social structures, beliefs and culture with them. When these trans-Pacific journeys stopped around 1300 CE, Hawaiian society was left to develop on its own.

In ancient Hawai'i, *ali'i* (chiefs) were believed to be descendants of the *akua* (gods) and ruled the different *ahupua'a* (land divisions). The people built heiau (temples) to worship *akua*, like Hale O Lono (p184) in the Waimea Valley. The people respected the *'āina* (land) and believed in reciprocity – if they took care of the land, the land would take care of them. So they picked just the produce they needed and sustainably harvested seafood from fishponds, like the ancient Moli'i Fishpond at Kualoa Ranch.

For more on Moli'i Fishpond, see p162.

2. Nu'uanu Pali State Wayside

THE UNIFICATION OF THE HAWAIIAN ISLANDS

It wasn't until 1795 – nearly two decades after Captain James Cook landed in the islands – that all the Hawaiian Islands were unified. Already holding control of both Maui and Hawai'i Island (the Big Island), King Kamehameha I led the conquest of O'ahu, with the fight coming to a head during the Battle of Nu'uanu (or Kaleleka'anae). During this bloody battle, over 800 warriors fell to their deaths off the 1000ft cliffs at what is known today as the Nu'uanu Pali State Wayside. Soon after, the island of Kaua'i surrendered, and King Kamehameha I became the first ruler of the Kingdom of Hawai'i.

For more on Nu'uanu Pali State Wayside, see p160.

3. Kawaiaha'o Church

THE MISSIONARIES ARRIVE

By 1820 the first missionaries sailed to the islands. That same year the Kawaiaha'o mission was started, with the goal of converting Native Hawaiians to Christianity. The missionaries documented many parts of Hawaiian culture, but also deemed some to be vulgar, including *he'e nalu* (surfing) and 'Ōlelo Hawai'i (the Hawaiian language), sometimes actively working to suppress these activities and beliefs.

Kawaiaha'o Church opened in 1842 after five years of laborious construction, making it the first Christian church built on O'ahu. Frequented by Hawaiian monarchs, it was officially made the chapel of the royal family and the national church of the Kingdom of Hawai'i.

For more on the Kawaiaha'o Church, see p62.

4. Waialua Sugar Mill

A SWEET ECONOMIC BOOM

Around the same time that the missionaries arrived, people started experimenting with growing sugarcane *(kō)* in the islands. The first few attempts weren't successful, but by the middle of the century, the industry was booming. In 1865 Waialua Sugar Mill, one of the largest sugar mills on O'ahu, opened for business.

With the high demand for sugar, more laborers were needed. Immigrants from all around the world – from Japan to the Philippines to Portugal – moved to the islands in search of sugar-plantation work. To communicate with each other, these immigrant workers developed Hawai'i Pidgin (p179), a local blended dialect that is still used in Hawai'i today.

For more on Waialua Sugar Mill, see p177.

'Iolani Palace (p58)

CO LEONG/SHUTTERSTOCK

5. Wo Fat Building

IMMIGRANT LIFE

The immigrants who moved to O'ahu for work on the sugar plantations started to build communities of their own. Honolulu's Chinatown really started growing in the 1840s and '50s. By 1882 the Chinese community grew so large that it made up half of the sugar-plantation workforce.

Unfortunately, many of the buildings of early Chinatown were burned in a pair of destructive fires. But one, the Wo Fat Restaurant, was rebuilt in the same spot both times. In fact, before its closure in 2009, it was believed to be the oldest operating restaurant in Hawai'i.

For more on the Wo Fat Building, see p73.

6. 'Iolani Palace

PALACE TURNED PRISON

'Iolani Palace was built in Honolulu between 1879 and 1882 to serve as the official residence of the monarchs of the Kingdom of Hawai'i. For about a decade, this gorgeous palace did exactly that, even getting electricity in 1886 (five years before the White House).

Unfortunately, things took a turn for the worse in 1893. Lorrin Thurston, Sanford B Dole and their fellow 'American businessmen,' as they're often dubbed, launched a violent coup to overthrow Queen Lili'uokalani. To avoid bloodshed, Queen Lili'uokalani surrendered, though she technically didn't abdicate. Rather, in a carefully worded document, she temporarily yielded to the US (rather than this new provisional government) with the expectation that they would return the Kingdom of Hawai'i to her.

For more on 'Iolani Palace, see p58.

7. Ali'iōlani Hale

POST-COUP HAWAI'I

Following the overthrow of the Kingdom of Hawai'i, Sanford B Dole took the reins as the President of the Republic of Hawai'i for five years. He made Ali'iōlani Hale – across the street from 'Iolani Palace – his home base. Dole and his comrades hoped the US government would annex Hawai'i, removing sugar tariffs and increasing profits.

Queen Lili'uokalani and her supporters pressed the US government to return the islands to their rightful rule (even when Queen Lili'uokalani was held under house arrest at 'Iolani Palace for eight months). President Grover Cleveland seemed inclined to restore the monarchy, but nothing ever came to fruition. When pro-annexation William McKinley became president, hope was lost. On July 7, 1898, Hawai'i was officially annexed as a US territory.

For more on Ali'iōlani Hale, see p61.

8. Dole Plantation

PLENTY OF PINEAPPLES

Amid all the political upheaval, the Dole Plantation was planting its earliest roots. Originally named the Hawaiian Pineapple Company, this tropical fruit corporation was started by James Dole – the cousin of Sanford B Dole – in 1901. Starting with a few flourishing pineapple fields in Wahiawā, the Hawaiian Pineapple Company was already off to a great start. Add a series of national advertisements and a speedy new canning system to the mix, and Hawai'i quickly became synonymous with pineapples and the Dole brand stamped onto the cans (although technically it wasn't renamed to the Dole Company until 1961).

For more on the Dole Plantation, see p168.

9. Moana Surfrider

THE START OF O'AHU TOURISM

O'ahu started to establish itself as a tourist destination. The San Souci Hotel opened in 1884 – on the banks of the beach of the same name. But the San Souci's life was short lived, and it closed in 1900. Then, with the turn of the century, came the Moana Hotel. Opened in 1901, the Moana Hotel (now the Moana Surfrider) featured 75 guest rooms equipped with the latest technology, including telephones and electric elevators. The first guests of the Moana Hotel paid just $1.50 per night. Despite the San Souci Hotel's short stint, the Moana Surfrider is often referenced as Waikīkī's first hotel.

For more on the Moana Surfrider, see p84.

10. Duke Kahanamoku Statue

A SURFING REVIVAL

Hawai'i made a splash in the sports world when Duke Kahanamoku, a Native Hawaiian surfer and swimmer, won not one, but two medals in swimming at the 1912 Olympic Games in Stockholm. Following his Olympic wins, Kahanamoku set out on a victory world tour. Though he intended to showcase his swimming skills, this tour gave Kahanamoku a global platform to share the sport of surfing. With every wave he rode, more and more people wanted to try it themselves. And with this global demand, the negative connotations of surfing – brought by the early settlers and missionaries – began to fade.

For more on the Duke Kahanamoku Statue, see p87.

11. Aloha Tower

A FRIENDLY FIRST SIGHT

Around 25 years after the opening of the Moana Surfrider, the 10-story Aloha Tower welcomed its first visitors. Serving as the disembarkation point for ocean liners, this Honolulu waterfront landmark – and its 'Aloha'-inscribed clockface – greeted every tourist that arrived to O'ahu's shores. (The first commercial flight to Hawai'i didn't take place until 1935.) For 40 years, this 184ft-tall structure stood as the tallest building in the islands.

For more on the Aloha Tower, see p61.

12. Pearl Harbor

WWII HITS O'AHU

On December 7, 1941 – two years into WWII – the Japanese military bombed Pearl Harbor, killing 2403 people and injuring another 1178. Though the US hadn't planned on joining the war, this surprise attack prompted their participation.

During the war, the US government built internment camps for Japanese immigrants all over the country. Since Japanese people made up a large portion of Hawai'i's population, many were spared from this atrocity.

SHANEWAZHERE/SHUTTERSTOCK

Dole Plantation (p168)

That said, approximately 400 Hawai'i residents of Japanese descent were held at the Honouliuli Internment Camp in Wahiawā from 1943 to 1945.

Four years after the initial bombing, Japan surrendered while aboard the USS *Missouri*, which is now docked at Pearl Harbor.

For more on Pearl Harbor, see p112.

13. Hawai'i State Capitol

THE 50TH STATE

By the mid-1900s, Hawai'i had been under US rule for half a century and played a vital role in US war efforts. Hawai'i had welcomed thousands of US tourists to its shores, but somehow the push for Hawai'i's statehood kept getting held up in Congress or the House of Representatives. It wasn't until August 21, 1959, that Hawai'i officially became the 50th US state. Construction on Hawai'i's Capitol building started six years later, in 1965, and was completed a few years after that. In the interim, 'Iolani Palace served as the Capitol building. Over a decade later, a Queen Lili'uokalani statue was placed nearby to pay tribute to her taken sovereignty and the Kingdom of Hawai'i.

For more on the Hawai'i State Capitol, see p60.

14. Waimea Bay

HOME TO HAWAI'I'S MOST ICONIC LIFEGUARD

In the 1970s there was a resurgence of Native Hawaiian pride and some locals decided to follow the migration route from Polynesia to Hawai'i in a traditional double-hull canoe. Beloved local lifeguard and surfer Eddie Aikau (p189) joined the 1978 *Hōkūle'a* crew for the second journey. Aikau was Waimea Bay's first lifeguard and saved over 500 people – not a single life was lost on his watch. When the canoe capsized 12 miles south of Moloka'i, Aikau paddled for help. The Coast Guard rescued the rest of the voyagers, but sadly, Aikau was never found. Today, a plaque at Waimea Bay commemorates him. Scattered around the island are signs, tees and stickers that say 'Eddie would go,' in reference to his sacrifice.

For more on Waimea Bay, see p180.

15. Banzai Pipeline

THE SURF CAPITAL OF THE WORLD

Modern-day O'ahu is known for surfing. O'ahu's North Shore is home to some of the greatest surfing conditions in the world – from Hale'iwa Ali'i Beach Park to Sunset Beach. But the most famous surf beach of all is Banzai Pipeline. Officially known as 'Ehukai Beach Park, this sunny shoreline is home to three distinct surf breaks and many prestigious surf competitions (p186), including the Vans Pipe Masters and the Da Hui Backdoor Shootout. Some of the greatest names in surfing today, including Carissa Moore, John John Florence and Kelly Slater, have competed in and won these beloved events.

For more on Banzai Pipeline, see p183.

MEET THE O'AHU LOCALS

'Āina (land) appreciators, talk story experts and internationally inspired potluck participants. SARAH ETINAS introduces her people.

THERE'S ALWAYS A reason to have a feast on O'ahu – a baby's first birthday, the end of the kids soccer season, or just a long weekend with good weather. In fruit tree–filled backyards, grassy parks or sunny beaches, locals come together to celebrate, arms laden with both international and local dishes. Juicy chicken katsu, sweet *pandesal* (fluffy, slightly sweet Filipino bread rolls) and a big ol' plastic container of Zippy's chili, just to start. If you're extra lucky, an uncle or auntie – in the islands, these terms reference nearly anyone older than you in a casual setting – might bring a batch of their homemade fresh poke (cubed, raw fish with island- and Asian-inspired seasoning).

Once your plates are heavy with scoops and samples, it's time to talk story – a Hawai'i Pidgin phrase that loosely translates to 'chit-chatting.' It's a casual sort of chat, the kind that you have when you're with people that make you feel at ease. Older aunties and uncles might reminisce on their *hanabata* days (loosely translates to 'younger days'), and high school kids might share the times when they tried to surf waves that were a little too big.

While international cultures – both from sugar plantation–era immigrants and from modern-day immigrants (in 2024, 19% of Hawai'i's population was foreign-born) – have an impact on the islands, the islands have an impact on them as well. Some of my classmates while growing up were Jordans and Johns, Sams and Sarahs, but people of all backgrounds also had Hawaiian names like Keoni, Kainoa, Malia and Anuhea. Many common Hawaiian names have 'kai,' meaning sea, incorporated in them, emphasizing the locals' love of the ocean.

Speaking of the ocean, it should come as no surprise to find out that we O'ahu locals love hanging out in nature. Based on absolutely no data besides my personal experience, it seems as though there might be a slight preference of the type of nature activity, depending on where you grew up. North Shore and Leeward Coast kids seem to lean toward beach days – preferably ones where surfing is involved. Those who spend more time on the Windward Coast tend to like hiking more, which makes sense considering there are greenery-filled hikes around every Ko'olau Range corner. And it's the townies – the people from Honolulu and Waikīkī – who are the wildcards. However, no matter what part of the island you're from, there's an almost instinctual need to treat the *'āina* with care.

Part of the reason why O'ahu is so incredible is because of the influence of the immigrant cultures here. But, at the heart of it all, what really makes Hawai'i so special are the Native Hawaiian people and their culture. The desire – the need, even – to care for the *'āina*, to talk story, to put good out into the world in the hopes that it comes back to you, all ties back to core Native Hawaiian beliefs.

Today's Native Hawaiian Population

Of the approximately one million people living on O'ahu, about 25.6% (or nearly 260,000 people) identify as having some Native Hawaiian heritage, as of the 2020 Census.

CLOCKWISE FROM TOP LEFT: VALERIA VENEZIA/SHUTTERSTOCK, NOEL HENDRICKSONS/GETTY IMAGES, ROSANNA U/GETTY IMAGES, MATT MUNRO/LONELY PLANET

I'M AN O'AHU LOCAL, BUT I'M NOT NATIVE HAWAIIAN

I was born and raised on O'ahu in the Leeward-side city of Kapolei. Growing up, I spent my days – *hanabata* days, as the locals call them – swimming at the beach, searching for *'opihi* (limpet) shells and munching on *musubis* – a handheld snack food made of rice, Spam and nori (seaweed).

Even though 'Hawai'i local' is the closest I come to personally identifying with a place, I'm not Kanaka Maoli (Native Hawaiian). And I'm not part of one of the many families with generations upon generations of history in the islands, most of whom can trace their ancestry back to the immigrants from the sugar plantation days. Rather, my parents moved to the island just five years before I was born. My roots are small and still growing, but they're rooted on O'ahu, nonetheless.

Ka'ena Point (p131)
FERRANTRAITE/GETTY IMAGES

MĀLAMA 'ĀINA

How to take care of the islands – from *mauka* (mountains) to *makai* (ocean). By Sarah Etinas

ONE DAY WHEN I was in preschool, my best friend Lauren and I were playing in the sandbox when we found a beautiful, tiny pink shell hidden among the golden grains. It immediately became our little treasure and the two of us spent the rest of recess admiring the shell, carefully passing it back and forth between our little three-year-old hands.

Soon enough, the bell signaling that recess was ending rang out, and Lauren and I rushed to figure out what to do with our rosy find. We decided to dig a little hole for it – just an inch or two deep – in a corner of the sandbox with plans to return the next day to unearth it. But when we eventually returned, our small, pink shell was nowhere to be found, likely buffeted by island trade winds and toddler feet.

Many years went by and I ended up telling this same story during one of my college classes in California. All of my fellow classmates – none of whom were from Hawai'i – were baffled by our actions. If we loved the shell so much, why did we rebury it? Why didn't we just take it with us? I had to take a moment to consider the questions because, to me, of course we left the shell where it was. And I realized that's because it's something that most of us, if not all of us, born and raised in Hawai'i, picked up on at an early age – to leave nature (or anything from the *'āina* [land]) as it is, or make it better. Of course, our little toddler brains didn't process the fact that the sand from the sandbox had already been removed from its natural habitat, but the point remains.

The Roots of Mālama 'Āina

The concept of leaving nature as it is or making it better is referred to in the islands as *mālama 'āina*, meaning 'to care for the land' in Hawaiian. (While *'āina* literally means 'land' or 'earth,' it doesn't necessarily equate to just the land; waterways and animals are included under this umbrella term as well.) This ideology has roots deep in ancient Hawaiian culture. As a matter of fact, the Hawaiian word for locals, *kama'āina*, means 'people of the land.'

The earliest Native Hawaiians believed that if they took care of the land, the land would take care of them by providing them with what they needed to survive in the isolated archipelago. They took this responsibility very seriously and found multiple ways to ensure the *'āina* was used as sustainably as possible. Starting from the ground up (literally and figuratively), the land in ancient Hawai'i was divided to promote ideal land management. Known

as *ahupuaʻa*, each of these land divisions ran from the mountains to the ocean, ensuring that every community had access to freshwater mountain streams, fish-filled oceans and agricultural land in between. From there, the ancient Native Hawaiians sustainably harvested only the produce, meat and seafood they needed. According to ancient Hawaiian law, people could even be put to death if they tried to overfish!

Why Mālama ʻĀina

To this day, Native Hawaiians still take this concept to heart. As Annie Daly and Kainoa Daines nicely sum it up in the book *Island Wisdom:* 'Hawaiians will often tell you that it is your responsibility and privilege to *mālama* the land so that it will *mālama* you back, which is also true for their ancestors.' It's not just Native Hawaiians anymore either – long-time Hawaiʻi locals tend to adopt this mindset as well. And seeing the beauty of the mountains and the oceans, the birds and the fish day-to-day just reinforces the why of it all.

Within its stunning landscapes, Hawaiʻi is home to 578 endangered or threatened species. Put another way, the islands house over 40% of the endangered and threatened species in the entire US! No wonder it's often nicknamed the 'endangered species capital of the world.' With those sorts of statistics, preserving the local *ʻāina* and the habitats of these plants and animals becomes even more vital. The well-known *ʻīlioholoikauaua* (monk seals), *honu* (Hawaiian green sea turtles) and red *ʻōhiʻa lehua* blossoms are just the beginning.

Mālama ʻĀina Movements

To visitors, caring for the many different parts of the *ʻāina* may sound like a big undertaking, one in which large-scale actions need to be taken. And, yes, sometimes that's true. Today these larger *mālama ʻāina* acts are often framed as eco-friendly, sustainability or animal welfare movements – and these heavily backed causes can lead to monumental changes.

Take the nēnē (Hawaiian goose) population, for example. In 1952 there were just 30 nēnē left in the wild. Over a 60-year period, the US Fish & Wildlife Service, the Hawaiʻi Department of Land & Natural Resources and the Honolulu Zoo, among

Nēnē (Hawaiian goose)

others, worked together to restore the population through predator control, breeding and habitat restoration. The nēnē was even named the official bird of Hawai'i in 1957 to bring even more awareness to the cause. Those efforts paid off, and the nēnē population has rebounded to nearly 4000 strong today.

Similarly, there's the current problem of Rapid *'Ōhi'a* Death. This fungal outbreak causes once-healthy *'ōhi'a lehua* trees to die within a few days or weeks of infection. While scientists at research institutions like the University of Hawai'i are searching for a solution, other organizations are doing what they can as well. The Sustainable Tourism Association of Hawai'i and Go Hawai'i (the official Hawai'i tourism authority website) are both working to spread the word about the outbreak and how to contain it. Community leaders and local writers are also finding ways to share the cultural significance of the tree.

There are also little things that locals and visitors alike can do to help mitigate Rapid *'Ōhi'a* Death and keep this endangered species alive. Stay on designated hiking paths, wash your shoes with rubbing alcohol before entering a Hawai'i forest, don't touch any dead branches along the way, and thoroughly wash your clothes and shoes post-hike. While all of these actions don't take much effort, they can immensely help *'ōhi'a lehua* trees and the greater *'āina*.

'Ōhi'a lehua

FROM LEFT: BILL PERRY/SHUTTERSTOCK, DAVID EICKHOFF/FLICKR/CC BY 2.0

How You Can Mālama 'Āina

In reality, the average Hawai'i local isn't leading big, bold *mālama 'āina* movements or conducting sustainability research. Rather, we take care of the islands through how we live our day-to-day lives. When we see a monk seal or *honu* lying on the sand, we'll give it space. When we head to the grocery store or farmers market, we'll bring our reusable bags to hold the locally grown produce that we purchase. When we go to the beach, we'll pick up the random pieces of trash littered around. And, yes, we'll clean our hiking shoes to prevent Rapid *'Ōhi'a* Death and participate in the occasional nature-focused volunteer opportunity, too.

Visitors to the islands can do their part to care for the land in many of the same ways that locals do. Toss reef-safe sunscreen and a reusable bag in your suitcase, and you're already off to a great start. Or, find more hands-on ways to *mālama 'āina* with voluntourism opportunities. While some volunteer opportunities require long-term participation and are only suitable for locals, many are also open to one-time or short-term volunteers. Remove invasive seaweed species in Maunalua Bay in Hawai'i Kai (p142), plant *kalo* (taro) in Kāne'ohe (p157), or help with sandbar restoration in Kahuku (p193), just to start. (Just remember to go into it with a mindset of a 'learner' rather than a 'rescuer.') In the end, these small, sustainable actions – multiplied over O'ahu's millions of annual visitors – can make all the difference.

Kamehameha the Great Statue (p63) on King Kamehameha Day (p33)

ANTHONY QUINTANO VIA WIKIMEDIA COMMONS

HAWAIIAN ROYALTY

After conquering and uniting the islands, Hawai'i's royalty ruled for barely 100 years. By Ryan Ver Berkmoes

HAWAI'I WAS ONCE a sovereign nation, with its own royalty. Polynesians in canoes arrived in this tropical archipelago more than a millennium before Westerners landed here in the 1800s. They found an island kingdom created by Kamehameha the Great. Less than 100 years later, his royal dynasty – and the kingdom – were no more.

Early Hawai'i

After trans-Pacific voyaging stopped completely around 1300 (for reasons unknown today), Hawaiian culture evolved in isolation. Nevertheless, it retained a family resemblance to other Polynesian cultures. Ancient Hawai'i's highly stratified society was run by *ali'i* (chiefs) whose right to rule was based on their hereditary lineage from the gods. Several layers of *ali'i* ruled each island, and life was marked by warring battles as they jockeyed for power and status.

Kamehameha the Great

Initially welcomed in 1778, British explorer Captain James Cook ended up dead on a Big Island beach after a minor conflict escalated, but his ship's visit ended centuries of Hawaiian isolation. In the years following Cook's death, a small, steady number of trading ships sought out Hawai'i as a mid-Pacific supply point, and increasingly the thing that Hawaiian chiefs traded for most was firearms. Bolstered with muskets and cannons, Kamehameha, one of the chiefs on the Big Island, began a tremendous military campaign in 1790 to conquer all the Hawaiian Islands.

Within five bloody years, Kamehameha had conquered all the main islands but Kaua'i (which eventually joined peacefully). The campaign on O'ahu started with a fleet of war canoes landing on the shores of Waikīkī in 1795. Kamehameha then led his warriors up the Nu'uanu Valley to meet the entrenched O'ahuan defenders, who made a doomed last stand.

Kamehameha's victory set the stage for the center of Hawaiian power to shift to O'ahu. In 1809 Kamehameha the Great (as he was now known), who had been living in his royal court in Waikīkī, decided to move to the Honolulu Harbor area. The king wanted to maintain control over the growing foreign presence and make sure Hawaiians got a fair deal in any trade.

By the time of Kamehameha the Great's death in 1819, nearly 3500 people lived in Honolulu and it continued to boom as more foreigners arrived. Ships brought

ROYAL TIMELINE

1790 Kamehameha, a chief in Hawai'i, launches a military campaign to gain control over all the Hawaiian Islands.

1795 Kamehameha the Great conquers O'ahu, nearly completing the unification of the Kingdom of Hawai'i.

1810 Kamehameha the Great moves his seat of power to O'ahu.

1819 Kamehameha the Great dies, leaving his kingdom to son Liholiho, with his favorite wife, Queen Ka'ahumanu, as regent. The *kapu* (taboo) system is abolished, and many heiau (ancient temples) are destroyed.

1823 After allowing the first Christian missionaries to land on O'ahu in 1820, Kamehameha II (Liholiho) becomes the first Hawaiian king to travel abroad and dies of measles in London in 1824.

1854 Kamehameha IV ascends the throne. He passes a law mandating that all children be given a Christian name along with their Hawaiian name.

1874 King Kalākaua gains the throne and begins a reign that promotes Hawaiian culture and features lavish spending.

1893 Having only assumed power in 1891, Queen Lili'uokalani is overthrown by pro-US business interests.

1917 Queen Lili'uokalani dies, having waged a years-long and unsuccessful campaign for compensation for the annexation of Hawai'i by the US.

BILL PERRY/SHUTTERSTOCK

Queen Lili'uokalani Statue (p63)

sailors and whalers, who turned Honolulu into a rollicking port of vices.

Missionaries also arrived, and in time they gained enough influence with Hawaiian royalty to have laws enacted against drunkenness and prostitution. Meanwhile, plantations were established for sugar and later pineapples, which brought great wealth to outsiders.

As the sugar industry boomed, Hawai'i's native population declined, largely as a result of diseases introduced by foreigners. In 1845 Kamehameha III, the last son of Kamehameha the Great, established Hawai'i's first national legislature, provided for a supreme court and passed the Great Mahele land act, which established religious freedom and gave all (male) citizens the right to vote.

Fall of the Monarchy

King David Kalākaua, who reigned from 1874 to 1891, worked to restore Hawaiian culture and native pride. He resurrected hula and its attendant arts from near extinction, much to the dismay of the missionaries. Wanting Hawai'i's monarchy to be equal to any in the world, he built Honolulu's 'Iolani Palace, holding an extravagant coronation ceremony in 1883.

Meanwhile, a secret, anti-monarchy group of mostly non-Native Hawaiian residents was formed, calling itself the Hawaiian League. In 1887 it forced Kalākaua to sign a new 'bayonet' constitution that stripped the monarchy of most of its powers, and changed the voting laws to include only those who met certain income and property requirements – effectively disenfranchising all but wealthy, mostly Caucasian, mostly O'ahu-based business owners.

When King Kalākaua died in 1891, his sister and heir, Princess Lili'uokalani, ascended the throne. The queen fought against foreign intervention and control as she secretly drafted a new constitution to restore Native Hawaiian voting rights and the monarchy's powers. In 1893, before Lili'uokalani could present this constitution to Hawai'i's people, a hastily formed 'Committee of Safety' put into violent motion the Hawaiian League's long-brewing plans to overthrow the Hawaiian government. Without an army to defend her, and opting to avoid bloodshed, the queen stepped down on January 17.

TODAY, THE HAWAIIAN ROYALTY ARE RECALLED BY PEOPLE WHO ADVOCATE FOR GREATER, OR EVEN COMPLETE, INDEPENDENCE FOR HAWAI'I AND REDRESS FOR THE COUP.

King Kamehameha Day (p33) parade

GORDON FAHEY/SHUTTERSTOCK

After the coup, the new provisional government immediately requested annexation by the US. However, much to its surprise, President Grover Cleveland refused: he condemned the coup as illegal and he requested that Lili'uokalani be reinstated. Unbowed, the Committee of Safety instead established its own government, the Republic of Hawai'i.

For five years, Queen Lili'uokalani pressed her case (for a time while under house arrest at 'Iolani Palace) – even collecting an anti-annexation petition signed by the vast majority of Native Hawaiians – to no avail. In 1898 the US annexed the Republic of Hawai'i as a US territory.

Today, the Hawaiian royalty are recalled by people who advocate for greater, or even complete, independence for Hawai'i and redress for the coup.

Public displays asserting pride in all things Hawaiian are becoming more common. Every January 17, thousands march in Honolulu to assert native pride in what's unofficially known as 'Downfall of the Monarchy Day.' Similar marches are held throughout the islands.

More mainstream is King Kamehameha Day on June 11. An official state holiday, there is a large ceremony at the king's statue in Honolulu, followed by additional festivities that are taking on an increasingly political nature each year. Statues of Hawaiian royalty, which are found across the state, seem to attract ever more traditional decorations, including lei and symbols, each year.

INDEX

Map Pages **000**

'Walking in Honolulu always delivers delights. Whether it's Chinatown (p66; pictured), Kaka'ako (p74) or Kaimukī (p94), strolling the streets of the city's neighborhoods always brings a surprise, a treasure or a feast.'

RYAN VER BERKMOES

'Anytime I need to destress, I go to the Ko Olina lagoons (p124) for some salt, sand and seawater.'

SARAH ETINAS

'I made it my mission to find the best *malasadas* on the island and narrowed it down to two: Leonard's (p95) and Pipeline Bakeshop & Creamery (p97).'

SARAH ETINAS

FROM LEFT: WARREN LEMAY/FLICKR/CC BY-SA 2.0, HARRY BEUGELINK/SHUTTERSTOCK

Mapping data sources:
© Lonely Planet
© OpenStreetMap http://openstreetmap.org/copyright

THIS BOOK

The 8th edition of Lonely Planet's *Honolulu, Waikīkī & O'ahu* guidebook was written and researched by Ryan Ver Berkmoes and Sarah Etinas. The previous edition was also written by Ryan and Sarah. This guidebook was produced by the following:

Destination Editor
Melissa Yeager

Coordinating Editor
Gabrielle Innes

Production Editor
Hannah Cartmel

Image Researcher
Dominic Allen

Cartographer
Daniela Machová

Assisting Cartographers
Vojtěch Bartoš, Alison Lyall

Assisting Editor
Janet Austin

Cover Researcher
Matthew Dekneef

Thanks
Ronan Abayawickrema, Melanie Dankel, Jenna Myers, Darren O'Connell

MIX
Paper | Supporting responsible forestry
FSC™ C021741
FSC www.fsc.org

Paper in this book is certified against the Forest Stewardship Council™ standards. FSC™ promotes environmentally responsible, socially beneficial and economically viable management of the world's forests.

Published by Lonely Planet Global Limited
CRN 554153
8th edition – Nov 2026
ISBN 978 1 83869 798 3

10 9 8 7 6 5 4 3 2 1
Printed in Malaysia